Possible Side Effects

6

Also by Augusten Burroughs

Magical Thinking

Dry

Running with Scissors

Sellevision

Possible Side Effects

✦ ✦ ✦

AUGUSTEN
BURROUGHS

St. Martin's Press   New York

Author's Note

Some of the events described happened as related; others were expanded and changed. Some of the individuals portrayed are composites of more than one person, and many names and identifying characteristics have been changed as well.

Design by Phil Mazzone

ISBN-13: 978-0-7394-7496-9

For Bob and Relda Robison

Acknowledgments

I am deeply indebted and wish to express my gratitude to my publisher, St. Martin's Press and Picador. I would also like to thank and extend my love to my friends and family, both personal and professional. My partner, Dennis Pilsits, makes it all possible and meaningful.

Possible Side Effects

Pest Control

The first time I was star-struck, the object of my affection was a glamorous Eastern Airlines stewardess. She had towering blond hair, frosted blue eyelids, and was well into her twenties. I was eight. We were thrown together when my parents put me on a flight by myself to Lawrenceville, Georgia, to visit my wealthy grandparents.

"I call them by their first names, Jack and Carolyn," I told her with pride. "They're my father's parents. And my grandmother wears lots of jewelry, just like you."

"Aren't you *precious*?" the flight attendant said.

I smiled because I loved the name, *precious*. It reminded me of precious stones like rubies and emeralds and diamonds. And even *semiprecious* stones, like onyx, which was the black stone men wore, and the ugliest one of all.

The flight attendant returned to the kitchen, and I looked out the window, happy to see the mundane "North" pass by, far below me.

As the only member of my family for generations born above the Mason-Dixon line, I was fascinated by the impossibly exotic South.

Like, instead of dirty, gray squirrels, my grandparents had Technicolor peacocks on their lawn. And while we got hateful blizzards in the winter, my grandparents got yet more sunshine. I found it impossible to believe that snow did not cover the world but here was proof.

Though this became an annual trip for me, my grandfather traveled a lot, so I never spent much time with him. And he was gruff, so when he was around I was frightened and avoided him.

But my grandmother spent every minute with me. And I adored her.

Carolyn was blond and wore minks. She had gigantic jade and diamond rings on nearly every finger. And a gold charm bracelet that made a soft tinkle sound when she waved her hands in the air. At night, she slipped into a nightgown with fur trim along the neck and at the hem. And even her slippers had high heels. I thought she was beautiful, like a movie star.

Only when she leaned in very close to me and I saw through her thick pancake makeup to the deep lines beneath did I become slightly alarmed. Old people had always scared me a little. And while my grandmother certainly wasn't old from a distance, she seemed brittle when you looked at her very closely. Sometimes when she kissed me on the forehead at night, I flinched, worried a piece of her might chip off and stick to me.

The summer I turned seven the tooth on my upper left side became loose. And I spent the afternoon worrying it with my finger.

"Honey, just let that tooth come out all on its own accord. Don't force it before it's ready," my grandmother said.

"But Carolyn, it's almost ready. It's just about to come out."

"Well, sweetie. Just let it be. It'll come out. And then do you know what to do?" she asked.

We were sitting on iron garden chairs in her glass sunroom. I was watching television and Carolyn was paging through a mail-order catalogue, licking her fingers and then dog-earring the corners of certain pages.

"Do when?" I said.

"Do you know what to do when your tooth falls out?" she asked, smiling at me.

I didn't understand what she was asking me. Was there something I had to *do*?

"Call the police?" I guessed.

She laughed in her gentle, though somewhat mischievous way. "No, you don't call the *police,* silly. Don't you know about the Tooth Fairy?"

"The what?"

"*Honey,*" she said, now concerned. She placed her catalogue on her lap and leaned forward. "The Tooth Fairy? You know about the Tooth Fairy. How could you not? You're seven years old. Surely, you know about the Tooth Fairy."

I felt bad, like I'd done something wrong. "No," I said in a small voice.

My grandmother explained. "Goodness gracious. I knew your mother was an odd bird, but I had no idea she was raising you in a cave in that godforsaken *New England.*"

I wondered if my mother knew about a cave someplace. And if we could go there when I went back home.

"The Tooth Fairy is a fairy, like Tinkerbell? You know Tinkerbell, don't you?"

I did know Tinkerbell. The irritating cartoon insect. "Yes," I said. "I know that thing." I frowned.

"Well, the Tooth Fairy is like Tinkerbell. And whenever you lose a tooth, you place it under your pillow at night before you go to bed. And then the Tooth Fairy slips into your room and takes your tooth away. And leaves some money in its place, right there under your pillow. Real money, sweetheart. That you can spend on whatever you like."

I was horrified.

I imagined that creepy bug woman with her devil wand, sneaking into my bedroom at night while I was sleeping, and taking my teeth and leaving things under the pillow that shouldn't be there. Cash, which my father said was *very limited*. And something I knew I shouldn't have.

"Carolyn, is this real?" I asked, because I just couldn't believe it.

She smiled, then laughed as she set the catalogue on the floor next to her feet. "Baby, yes of course it's real. The Tooth Fairy is real for every child."

And I thought, why hadn't somebody warned me about this? Why hadn't any of my friends ever talked about this horrible bug that comes into your bedroom and takes your teeth?

I immediately stopped fiddling with my tooth. I tried to press it back in place.

That night, Carolyn tucked me into bed. "Open your mouth," she said.

I did.

She leaned forward. "Oh, you've still got your tooth! That means the Tooth Fairy won't come tonight. But"—and her eyes became wide—"maybe tomorrow!" The skin around her mouth was cracked and her lipstick was bleeding into the lines around her lips. Suddenly, she seemed extremely scary.

After she left, I got out of bed and checked the windows again. They were locked. But could it enter the room any other way?

I went to the bathroom that was attached to the bedroom and I grabbed all the towels, rolling them into tubes and then placing them in front of the crack under the door. I didn't know how strong the Tooth Fairy was, but I knew an ordinary insect wouldn't be able to move those towels.

Then I climbed back into bed and prayed to Jesus.

At this point, I wasn't sure where I stood, Jesus-wise.

Although my parents never attended church or mentioned Jesus except when they screamed at each other—and then they used his full name, "Jesus Fucking Christ"—they did explain that he was a man who lived in the sky and granted wishes to certain people. People he liked.

So I prayed. "Dear Jesus. Please keep It out of my room. I promise, promise, *promise* that I will be honest and very nice to everybody and I love my mother and my father and brother and all my relatives here and over in Cairo, Georgia, and I love everybody that I know and even people I don't know now but will know someday. And I promise everything. But please keep It out of my room and away from me. Thank you, Jesus Fucking Christ."

Somewhat relieved, but not altogether certain I was safe, I eventually drifted to sleep.

Only to awaken that next morning seeing a smear of blood on the cream satin pillowcase. And there, right under my shoulder near the pillow, my tooth, bloody and with a horrible dark root-thing attached.

I began to cry. I got out of the bed as fast as I could and looked closer at the pillowcase. It was blood all right. And a lot of it. And that was my tooth. And it didn't look smooth and pretty. But weird and awful and out of my mouth.

I ran into the bathroom to look at my face and there, in the corner of my mouth, more blood.

I cried harder.

I ran back to the bedroom and lifted up the pillow, to see where
the money was. But there was nothing, just the tooth and another
streak of blood.

I didn't even put my pants on. I just ran downstairs in my underwear, sobbing, looking for Carolyn.

"Baby, baby, what is the matter?" she said. She was in the
kitchen, standing at the sink, draping a paper towel over the length
of dental floss she had strung between the two cabinets. My grandmother always rinsed her paper towels and used them again. Even
though my grandparents lived in a mansion that my mother called
"half the damn size of Georgia."

She turned the water off and dried her hands hastily on her
apron. She bent down. "Sweetness, what is the matter? You stop
that crying right now. What happened?"

For lack of words, I opened my mouth, showed her the black
hole. The pit, that ached and tasted metallic, like blood.

She inhaled. "Oh! Look at you! Big boy!"

I said, "It came and It knocked my tooth out and then It left and
there's blood everywhere and I don't know how It got in and I
prayed to Jesus but It came anyway."

And then I cried some more.

My grandmother stroked my head. "There, there, baby. It's okay,
it's okay. What are you fussing about? What came? What *it*?"

"That Tooth Fairy. It came and took my teeth and I looked but
there wasn't anything under the pillow, like you said. It didn't give
me money. It just took."

My grandmother sighed. "Well, baby. Sometimes, the Tooth
Fairy, she gets the date wrong. You know what I mean? You know
how sometimes you get mixed up and you have to do something at
school? Only you forget which day? And so you don't do it?"

I had no idea what she was talking about. I just knew I wanted to
get on the first Eastern Airlines jet home.

"Listen, it's okay," she said, leading me by the arm out of the kitchen and into her bedroom.

"You sit yourself right down here," she said, tapping the soft, thick comforter on the bed.

Then she walked across her room and got her purse. She pulled out her wallet, showing me. "See? See, baby? I think the Tooth Fairy must have put your money in here. By mistake." Then she pulled out a fifty. "See! Look at this!" she cried, lifting the crisp bill out of her wallet and placing it in my hand. "This was meant for you, sugar. For you! The Tooth Fairy, she made a little error. It can happen to anyone, even a fairy. She made a little mistake and she put *your* money into *my* wallet. Imagine that!"

I took the money and looked at it. It looked just like regular money except something was different.

"It's a fifty, sweetie. Do you know what that means?"

I did know what that meant. I knew exactly what that meant. I got an allowance and that was a one. This was the same size as the one, but you could buy fifty times more things with it.

"Are you sure I'm supposed to have this?"

"I am absolutely sure," she said. "The Tooth Fairy just had the wrong tooth. And I think I know what confused her so much," my grandmother said.

Then she reached into her mouth and pulled out all of her teeth, all at once, even her gums.

And I couldn't breathe.

She smiled and gummed the words, "I lothed my eeth, ooo!"

Bloody Sunday

According to the map on my personal video screen, the British Airways 747 was halfway over the Atlantic. If the plane were to lose an engine, I reasoned, we had a good chance of *just* making the tip of Greenland. I don't like to fly, especially over large bodies of roiling black water. But this was the red-eye from New York. All the shades were down and the lights had been dimmed. So I didn't feel I was flying in a plane so much as sitting in a particularly comfortable doctor's office, waiting for a minor surgical procedure. I was filled with dread, but only a little more dread than normal. After all, in just a few hours I would be in London, a place I consider to be perfect.

Something was bothering me and I was unable to concentrate on the book I was trying to read. My nose, specifically, was giving me trouble. Not to be uncouth, but there was just something stuck in there.

I removed a tissue from the pocket of my blazer. This was a new experience for me because I never wear jackets. And here I was, in a fine jacket, with a pressed dress shirt. Slacks. Black Gucci loafers. Not only this, but I had thought ahead to bring a small pack of tissues.

Last time I came to London, I dressed like I do every day: jeans with a T-shirt and a baseball cap. I was mortified when each restaurant I went to required I wear their outdated loaner jacket, kept on hand expressly for losers like me.

I was determined not to make this mistake again, in the more formal United Kingdom. So I'd packed nothing but business attire.

I blew my nose, trying to make as little noise as possible.

And then I looked down and saw blood on my shirt. Three slug-shaped stains and a constellation of splatter. Dark red, purple-black almost, against the sky blue of my shirt.

Stupidly, I pulled the tissue away from my nose to inspect it and more blood dripped onto my shirt. I was horrified, but more than this I was fascinated. Because there was absolutely no pain and quite a lot of blood. Quickly, I brought the tissue back up to my nose and reached for the napkin next to my water bottle.

I pressed this against my nose, as well, but almost immediately it was soaking red.

I am one of those people who tend to get bloody noses easily. My brother is the same way. We spent much of our childhoods hemorrhaging and it's a wonder, really, both of us made it to maturity without transfusions.

Normally, my nose stops bleeding after just a couple of minutes. But as I sat there on the plane, pressing the blood-soaked tissue against my face, I sensed that this was no ordinary nosebleed. Something about the cabin pressure had made it much worse than usual.

I needed more tissues. I needed them immediately. Or else, I needed a blowtorch to cauterize the wound myself.

I unbuckled my seat belt with my free hand and stood, trying not to draw attention to myself. I was relieved that the cabin lights were low and many people were sleeping.

As I turned to walk back to the lavatory, I saw a passenger seated on the opposite aisle, reading a book.

The cover was orange and featured a young boy with a box on his head. I couldn't read the title but I didn't need to because it was burned into my brain. I'd written the book.

She glanced up at me just as I began walking, and then she looked back down at her book. But right away, she looked back up, eyes wide.

The front of my shirt was now quite stained with blood. I must have looked like somebody who had been unfortunately involved with a knife.

I saw her hesitate. Should she press the button to alert the flight attendant? Had I just shot the pilot? All of these thoughts were plainly visible in her eyes. And then the look of recognition, of disbelief.

I smiled at her and motioned with my free hand. As if to say, "It's okay. I won't be directing the aircraft to fly into Harrods. I just have a bloody nose."

Her lips parted and she turned my book over in her hands, examining the author photograph.

Then she looked back at me.

I looked away and resumed walking toward the tiny bathroom.

Once inside, I locked the door and began pulling the irritating runt-sized paper towels from the dispenser. I crammed them up my nostril and leaned back against the wall, looking at my sorry self in the mirror. Blood had stained my mustache and the sides of my mouth, and even drizzled down my chin. I looked like somebody who had caught a small rodent in the aisle and bitten its head off.

At that moment, it seemed to me that something in my genetic code acts as a sort of metal, magnetically attracting disasters, both major and minor. Like Carrie at the prom.

Standing in the miniscule lavatory and doing nothing except waiting for my nose to stop bleeding, I realized how long I'd been in there. How bad would *that* look? The bloody guy locked in the bathroom, probably cooking up a shoe bomb. To partially remedy this, I wet a paper towel and cleaned my face.

After ten minutes, the bleeding had stopped. I wet paper towels with cold water and began to press them against the bloodstains on my shirt.

I'd bought six "no wrinkle" shirts from Brooks Brothers in Manhattan and was astonished to watch as the blood was sucked away from the shirt, into the towels. The fabric of the shirt had held the blood, but released it when asked. My friend, the Asshole Lawyer, had told me about the shirts. If anybody knew of shirts that were blood-proof, it would be an Asshole Lawyer. Of course, it's only a matter of time before these shirts catch on among the serial killer community, I suppose.

I removed all the blood. There wasn't even a pink shadow remaining. But I now had a soaking wet shirt. Which, compared to a bloodstained shirt, was dandy. I'd merely look like a drunk who spilled a martini on himself. Instead of a freak, bleeding out of one of his holes.

I glanced down and saw that the entire lavatory area was bloody with my fingerprints. This would not do. I could not leave bloody fingerprints for the next person. Maybe I could have done this on September 10, but not now. This would surely cause the plane to be redirected to the nearest airport, where camera crews would be waiting. I would be questioned by CNN, held responsible for the delay of the flight, the imposition of three hundred passengers.

I cleaned up the toilet and left, walking back to my seat.

The woman turned herself around in her seat, to watch me walk back to mine. I knew that when she got off the plane she would call friends back home. "You'll never believe who was on the flight," she'll tell them. "What a freak."

I was in London and I had the day off. I was here to promote my book but today was a "free day" so I was on my own.

Originally—that is, while I was on the plane coming over—I thought I'd spend my free day exploring the city and then finding the bakery that Dennis fell in love with last time we were here. Before I left, he admitted that he'd had a craving for pastries from this bakery for the past year. So I thought I'd find it, buy a few things that wouldn't go stale overnight, then FedEx them to the apartment. I'd also go to some of the antique bookshops and look for old leather-bound copies of children's books—*Alice in Wonderland*, *Tom Swift*, and maybe some volumes of poetry. I'd place these in the guest bedroom back home. Because what a perfect thing to read, if you're a guest. A hundred-year-old copy of *Robinson Crusoe*.

Instead, I did none of these things. It was now five in the afternoon and I was still in my underwear. I'd been up since six A.M., watching British television and chewing nicotine gum. The pressure was building inside of me to go out. Do something. But I found it impossible to leave the television. Right then on BBC 1, for example, somebody was painting a live turtle. And I didn't know why because their Irish accent was so thick I couldn't understand a word. But I couldn't think of any reason why somebody would paint a daisy on the shell of a turtle. What's more, it seemed to be a news program. So it was somehow topical and urgent. And I had to watch it.

Earlier in the day, I watched *While You Were Out*, but it had a different title here. Something along the lines of *Misbehaving House*, but was the same show. Only with a lovely snaggle-toothed British "model" as the host. I also watched *Trading Spaces*. Although it might be *Places*. I watched these two shows and didn't see one chin between them.

Back in New York, I spend all of my available free time watching either home decorating shows or medical procedure documentaries. And chewing nicotine gum.

Which doesn't explain why, in London for a very short time, with one day off, I was doing exactly the same thing.

When I first got here and saw the hotel, the last thing I expected was that I'd be unable to leave it. I saw the date on the front, "Built in 1718," and thought, *Oh, great.* It might as well say, "No television, no Internet access, no, no, no."

The rooms here were named after literary figures, none of whom I'd heard of. My room was on the top floor, always a good sign. Except the stairs were so narrow and crooked, I tripped over my ungainly feet all the way up. I have size thirteen feet squeezed into a twelve because thirteen is simply too large.

When I reached my door and unlocked it, I found myself standing in a tiny foyer with a small oil painting on the wall. The painting was old, a landscape. I wanted to take it. Slip it into my bag and hang it up in my office at home. There's nothing I love more than old oil paintings. But the picture light attached to the wall above the painting would have given me away, as it would have then illuminated just a discolored square patch of naked wall and a picture hook.

I walked into the room and saw an enormous chestnut four-poster bed, complete with a deep red silk canopy, embroidered with gold thread. Huge, overstuffed pillows in a matching fabric were propped against the headboard. There was plush wall-to-wall carpeting throughout the room, layered with silk Persian Carpets of various sizes. All too large to roll up and slip into my carry-on.

An antique slant-top desk sat against the wall and was flanked on either side by tall walnut armoires. A scalloped-edge table near the far wall held a tall lamp. Next to this, a chair with a needlepoint seat. It was depressingly beautiful. As it always is to walk into a hotel room and discover that it is much nicer and more tasteful than your own home will ever be.

I stepped into the bathroom and saw just a claw foot tub in the center of the room. Very narrow and very deep. A brass tub filler sat on the far end of the tub and was so old, the metal appeared to be melting.

I thought it was quite possible that the plumbing in the building was original.

A small white and rectangular porcelain sink was attached to the wall, beneath the single window in the bathroom. The window had two wood shutters, which you could pull together for privacy. At either end of the sink, a faucet. One for hot, one for cold.

I walked back into the main room and noticed the fireplace. Above the mantle, another oil painting, this one much larger and lit from above with a weathered brass lamp. It would never fit in my suitcase, so I ignored it.

I tested the bed and it was soft, but unusual. It wasn't a Sealy Perfect Sleeper but I didn't know what it was. Horsehair? It was thick in a dense, padded sort of way. The sheets were such fine, thin cotton that they were nearly silk.

I instantly understood that I would be in this room for many hours. That the room was the point of the country. That no matter what London had to offer me, nothing could surpass my small hotel room.

But still. I hadn't expected to spend *all* my time here. Surely, I could enjoy the room for the evening and then go out. After all, London is one of the world's most dazzling cities. Steeped in history and pedigree. A world power that shrunk in the dryer. There was much to see. Even if all I did was go to a nearby café and sit outside, have a coffee. I could watch the people. Even watching the man collect the trash would be interesting because he would be, after all, a Brit.

None of this was to be. Instead, I sat mutely on the edge of the bed watching a show about people who find themselves at the hospital. It was *live* and only eight in the morning. I was stunned by the number of people who needed emergency surgery so early in the day. One woman, and she was very nice, said that somebody drove over her leg and then put the car in park. This was extra fascinating because the interviewer didn't ask how the driver managed to do this. Was the woman sleeping on the sidewalk? She didn't appear homeless and she talked about her two children at home. So how did it happen? Nobody asked.

And this made me like London even more. That you could go to hospital and be treated as a patient, instead of a suspect, like in America.

After this, I watched a little CNN. CNN is very different in the United Kingdom than it is in America. For one thing, there's more global coverage. They even gave the weather forecast for New Delhi. That would never play in America because people would e-mail CNN headquarters and say, "Who the fuck cares about fucking India? Give us more missing coed stories."

I glanced at the fireplace and saw that the wall-to-wall carpeting extended into the fireplace itself, right under the log holder. Obviously, the fireplace no longer worked. But also obvious was the fact that no American had ever stayed in this room before. Because an American most certainly would have attempted to build a fire. As a rule, Americans will take everything that is offered to them. "There's a fireplace in this room, and by golly, I'm gonna use it."

We're just that way. If we see it, it belongs to us. If it burns, even better.

✧   ✧   ✧

It was just after six. And I had returned to my room from my single pilgrimage outdoors to the corner market. It took hours for me to build up the motivation, but I finally left my room. I walked three blocks to the store, selected my items and paid, then walked the same three blocks back to the hotel, although on the opposite side of the street. Now, I had seen London.

At the store I bought two boxes of cookies. One flaky and plain, with just sugar on top. The other a "Chocolate Coconut Biscuit." And two Twix bars. Later, I would return to the store for more supplies.

This was the room service menu:

1. Freshly Baked Baguette filled with Parma Ham, Olives, and Chutney.
2. Freshly Baked Baguette filled with Scottish Oak-Smoked Salmon.
3. Freshly Baked Baguette filled with Chewton Cheddar with Pickles and Chutney.
4. Homemade pasta filled with either Pumpkin and Ricotta or Spinach and Ricotta.
5. Bacon Sandwich on Fresh White Bread.

So obviously, I would order the bacon sandwich. As an appetizer. And then the parma ham sandwich for the main course. And the cheddar sandwich for dessert.

After dinner, which had to be early because they stopped room service at ten-thirty, I would eat all the cookies and the candy bars.

What I loved about being here was noting how the United Kingdom is at once familiar, and totally foreign. It's almost as though it's a parallel-universe version of the United States. Allowing us to see how things *might* have turned out. Or what *could* have happened. Many of the same, familiar items exist here. But they look different. It's almost like waking up with the same person you went to bed with, only they now speak Latin and find different things funny. *Fascinating*.

Like, there was this show on earlier. It was a show where a team enters the messy home of a woman and cleans it up. In America it's called *Clean Sweep*. On this show, the woman was cleaning the bathtub with Borax. She was saying, "Borax is mined naturally. And if you sprinkle it in the tub, and then spray it with vinegar, it will clean away all the stains and your tub will look brilliant."

Nobody would ever talk about using Borax in America, specifically because it's mined naturally. We want things that are created in laboratories, tested on animals and women, and then packaged in plastic and co-branded with the latest Disney project.

On *London Tonight,* on television right now, a reporter is standing in front of a building that is under construction. It's windy, and the wind has pressed the fabric of his slacks against his body, outlining his penis. You can see everything—the length and width and the fact that he's uncut and hangs to the right.

But I bet none of the viewers even noticed.

In America, there would be letters to the station. There would be a lawsuit because a child was watching. The headlines would dub the reporter "Anchor of Shame" and he'd be fired.

When our own Greta Van Susteren got her eyes done, it was front-page news for a week. So you can be sure, if Anderson Cooper's penis were to be visible in outline beneath his trousers, he'd be on the cover of *People*, *Vanity Fair*, and *The New York Times*. We are obsessed with sex in an unnatural way.

Or maybe it was just me.

I then noticed: news anchors in London read from the papers in their hand. In America, they use teleprompters and hold papers as a prop, a nod to the past. A tradition, harking back to the days of Walter Cronkite.

But here, they still read from the papers.

And this made me want to move.

Eight P.M.

I went out for more candy bars, forgetting all about the traffic being reversed here, so I was nearly hit by a Royal Mail truck as I crossed the street. What a Royal Mail truck was doing careering through the narrow streets of Soho at eight o'clock at night is a mystery. Shouldn't their mail-truck drivers be home by five in the evening, drunk, depressed, and homicidal, like ours?

Shaken by the near miss, I walked into the twenty-four-hour store and saw something I'd missed before. Something that instantly made both of my ears become hot with need. This happens sometimes. Not only do my ears actually burn but people tell me they also glow red. So not five seconds after walking into this store, I stood there with throbbing, satanic ears looking at a package.

Slow Roasted Lamb and Mint Potato Crisps.

It can't be, I thought.

But then, it was. And there were other flavors, too. Char-Grilled Steak and Peppercorn Sauce, Oven Roasted Chicken and Thyme.

My God, why aren't these in America? Why did we ever split with Britain in the first place?

I began to suffer. I could buy a bag, but I knew what would happen. I would take them back to the room and within the space of four chips, I would become addicted. And then in four days, I would be three thousand miles away from more.

We have BBQ and Sour Cream and Onion and, wildly, Salt and Vinegar. We have "No Salt," as though that's an acceptable flavor.

And these loopy, gin-soaked Brits are whooping it up with chips in a Noah's Ark of animal flavors.

It made me sick with envy is what it did.

I am prone to envy. It is one of my three default emotions, the others being greed and rage. I have also experienced compassion and generosity, but only fleetingly and usually while drunk, so I have little memory.

Right then on the telly, live open-heart surgery. Again, why? Why don't we have this? We have similar shows on various cable stations. But they're heavily packaged. With graphics and music and a plotline, edited together to create tension and suspense. But this is relaxed surgery. It's live and it's real and a little boring. But the pay-off: the person might die. They never die on U.S. television. But here in the United Kingdom, they just might. And I will be right here, watching.

Crisps. They call them crisps, not chips. We have potato chips. They have potato crisps. Which would you rather have? Chips are things you find in a pasture filled with cows. Crisps are things flavored with the cows.

The next day.

I bought a box of Kleenex brand facial tissues at the corner store and took them back to the room, like a small animal storing food. I pulled a tissue from the box and was instantly stuck by how soft and thick it was. I checked the box to see if it was printed with special text. "New, softer, thicker tissues!" or "Special Tri-Ply Edition!" but there was no such thing. These are just the plain, old, ordinary Kleenex.

Why aren't our plain, old, ordinary Kleenex tissues in America this soft and thick? They're our fucking tissues, after all.

What happened? When did America slide off the rails?

It's just like with tomatoes. I remember when I was a kid, toma-toes were things you sometimes craved. They were almost candy-bar-wrapper red and juicy like a peach and you could eat them all by themselves, with just some salt.

Now? They are firm. They have become visual stand-ins for the original. If a slice of tomato arrives on your burger, you slide it off with the limp lettuce leaf. It's moved from actual food to garnish.

It makes me sad. Because that's not evolution. It's devolution. It's going backward and paying more for the luxury of reverse.

Here in the United Kingdom, there remains an appreciation of quality. The candy bars, for example, are richer, thicker, and more luscious. Like, the British Kit Kat is the same as the American Kit Kat except it's very thick. You get more Kit for your Kat.

I ordered a Coke from room service and it came in a tall glass bottle. I didn't even know Coke still made this bottle. The only glass bottles of Coke that I ever come across are the small bottles. If you want a large Coke, you get a plastic Coke. But here, it comes in glass.

Again, sad.

I e-mailed my friend Emily in New York and told her about the tissues. As always, she said something very wise. "The English need thicker tissues because they are all filled with so much more SNOT because of the gray skies that grow mold, and the fatty nature of their diet (which causes mucous secretion)."

So maybe it's a need thing.

I caught a glimpse of myself in the ancient mirror, which had silver showing through behind the glass, and even through the strain of the antique patina, I could see I looked hideous. I looked, unfortunately, like exactly what I was: a weirdo who'd been locked up in the same room for twenty-four hours. I hadn't shaved in three days, so I decided to at least do that much.

Then I put on a suit. So I could go for a walk. I would force myself to go outside, go for a long walk.

I put on my dark gray suit and a clean white shirt that wasn't wrinkled from the trip, and even a tie. Then I pocketed the hotel key, my wallet, and two sheets of Nicorette gum.

As I was tripping down the steps, I again saw myself in a mirror, only this time, my reflection shocked me. I had blood running down my neck, leaching into the collar of my shirt. I quickly zoomed in for a closer look and saw what I hadn't felt: I'd cut my face, shaving. Just below the ear. Blood was streaming down.

So I went back upstairs to the room, stripped off the suit, the shirt. Went into the bathroom and stuck a piece of tissue paper against the wound.

Screw it, I decided. I would stay in my room and rot and fester. There was no sense in even *trying* to be a normal American in a foreign country, having a nice time.

Wherever I went in the world, *Augusten* followed. Sure, I could go to Europe like anybody else. But I'd leave behind a debris field— empty wrappers, stained pillows, a trail of blood.

The Sacred Cow

Bentley is our French bulldog and his favorite toy is a ratty stuffed cow that emits a sickly, warbling "moooooo" noise when it's tipped upside down, or in his mouth while he shakes his head violently from side to side. The name we've given the toy is Cowcow and Bentley knows it. If you tell him to "get Cowcow" he will run to his toy basket and select the cow. Not the crackle cat or the chicken head or the bone wheel or any of the other toys. Although he will get these, too, if you ask him.

And while Bentley is a very jolly, small animal, I couldn't help but feel his life would be better if he had a real, live Cowcow to play with. Another small animal that he could push around. In the same way that porn addicts need to be weaned off video images, I felt our Bentley needed a companion that was made from more than just stuffing, fabric, and a musical tube insert.

"One is more than enough" was Dennis's opinion on the subject. But I was persistent. "How much harder can it be?" I said. "After all, if we have to walk one dog, what difference does it make if we have to carry an extra poo bag?"

"But Bentley is perfect. There will never be another Bentley."

I couldn't argue this point. So I would have to change strategies. Instead of positioning this as more of a good thing, I would position a potential second dog as a support dog. Not an addition for us. But support for Bentley. An accessory, something to make his life easier. Like parents who have a second baby to supply bone marrow to the first, favorite baby.

But still the answer was "no." And Dennis seemed unlikely to change his mind, as he is a person who could be described as "set in his ways." Or "rigid as a damn steel girder."

But even steel has a breaking point.

Fifteen months later, we happened to walk past a pet store on the way to the optometrist, and sitting in the window looking out at the street was a perfect cow, in miniature. He was black and white, spotted like a Holstein. And so tiny, he would easily have fit in the palm of my hand. He was also a French bulldog, just like Bentley. Except he was so young, his ear muscles were undeveloped. So instead of standing erect, his long ears stuck out from his head. Like a cow's.

"Dennis," I said, in a tone of voice that suggested complete submission and desperation.

"No," he said firmly.

"No, wait. Seriously. Look."

"Augusten, we're not getting another dog."

"Holy shit, look at him," I said, stunned.

Dennis looked at me. "I don't need to look at him. Come on, let's go. I have to pick up my prescription sunglasses."

"No, I mean it. *Look* at him. He's staring at us. He's, like, concentrating."

Dennis looked at the puppy in the window. We both did. It was the oddest thing. Normally, puppies in pet store windows sleep or pee or roll around on top of the other dogs. This one ignored its window-mates and was instead sitting with its nose pressed against the glass, looking at us with an extremely serious little expression on its face. An expression that seemed to me to be saying, "I am a sacred cow. Get out your wallet."

"That is a little weird," Dennis said. "The way he's just watching us. Let's move over here and see if he follows us. Or if he's just stuck in that position for some reason."

We moved to the other side of the window and the cow followed us by turning his head, not moving his body. He was a lazy thing, but he was not uninterested.

Dennis agreed that we would go into the pet store and look at the puppy. But we were not going to acquire the puppy.

We asked the pet store guy if we could see him and he said sure. "He just came in today, as a matter of fact."

I liked hearing this. He hadn't been handled. He was fresh.

Dennis and I walked to the back of the store and sat on the floor. The clerk brought the dog over and placed him on the floor between us. As soon as the dog was safely enclosed within the area of our legs, it became happy and licky. He ran to one then the other. Then he sat on the floor and watched us watching him. He appeared to be waiting for something.

"How much is he?" I asked the pet store guy. He said the store was new and he'd have to check in the back, where the papers were.

He left us alone with the little cow, who was very different from Bentley, when Bentley was that age. While Bentley was terrified, this little dog was perky and activated. Confident, if so tiny as to only have a miniscule brain. And then there was that constant eye contact.

The clerk returned and told us the price. Dennis said, "Ouch!" because it was too much to pay for any dog. At least to the average person who values paying their mortgage on time. But to me, it was a bargain. A pair of socks, plucked from a sale bin at Target. "Infertile couples pay fifty times this much to get their babies on the black market," I told Dennis.

"This isn't a human baby. It's a dog."

I said, "What do you mean?"

He looked at me. I said, "No, I'm serious. They do."

"I believe you," he said. "But this is a lot of money to pay for a dog."

I would have paid ten times the amount for the dog. But it would have been a lot to pay for a black-market baby.

"We could name him Cowcow," I said, smiling just a little and turning sideways to glance at Dennis.

And Dennis tried not to smile but he did anyway. And he admitted, "Yeah, we could name him Cowcow."

Seventeen hours later, Dennis and I were in a hotel room in Boston, trapped with what was clearly the worst impulse purchase of my life. We'd come to Boston because I had a reading. Bentley was staying with our friend Christopher, in the city. The Cow and Bentley had not even met yet. We'd taken The Cow from the pet store with us to Boston. And when he wasn't barking, he was peeing.

"I thought you said dogs won't wet their beds," Dennis said as we stripped the sheets for the fifth time.

"They aren't supposed to. This one is broken."

Normally, you'd have a young puppy like this sleep in his little kennel, next to the bed. But The Cow would have none of that. The only way we could stop him from making a terrible, constant, infuriating yapping sound was to stick him in the bed with us. But when we did this, he peed. He also peed in his kennel. In fact, the only place he wouldn't pee was on the newspapers we'd set on the floor for just that purpose.

The instant I put him in his little kennel, to go pee myself, I'd return to find the kennel floor filled with a half-inch of hot pee. The Cow would be splashing in the urine, his coat drenched. Already, I'd given him seven baths.

"He'll get better," I told Dennis. Although in my bones I knew something was wrong. I'd housebroken many puppies in my life and there was something about this dog that was different. At best, he was going to be difficult to housebreak. At worst, he would never be housebroken and we would never love him.

And that was another thing, love. Wasn't I supposed to feel at least a little love for him by now? With Bentley, I did. I felt it immediately. Powerful, a bond. Like mother and child. With The Cow, though, it wasn't engaging. All I felt was rage, regret, exhaustion, and buyer's remorse.

"We have to love him," I told Dennis as he balled the sheets up and placed them in a mound next to the door.

"Yeah, right," he said. "I'll love him when he stops pissing."

Bentley had been easy to housebreak. He went on the newspapers the instant I introduced him to the Weddings page. Bentley had never cried in the night. Never howled as though we were stretching his limbs. Unlike this little Cow, Bentley had never sat at the foot of the bed staring us down and then making a peculiar, eerily human "hmpf" sound as he let go of a gallon of fluid, while stamping his little feet.

Seventy-two hours and for the first time in years, I found myself counting time again, just like I had when I'd stopped drinking and was in early recovery counting days. I could not wait for months to pass. A year. I wanted the dog to grow a brain, fast. And gain bladder control.

On the plus side, The Cow wasn't finicky the way Bentley is. He happily consumed the food we gave him. And then he walked along the floor with his squashed face pressed to the carpet eating fingernails, dust, lint—anything he could inhale from the filthy hotel carpet.

We slept in shifts. One of us watched The Cow and steeped in regret while the other one remained unconscious and had bad dreams.

Time did not fly by. Time was constipated.

Cow was not.

We introduced the dogs to each other at our weekend house in Massachusetts. It was a small white shack of a house on a ramshackle street—not much to look at or live in. But it had a backyard. And it had a lot of floor space.

We knew that Bentley—with his bulldozer body and outgoing disposition—would like The Cow, but also kick his cow-ass into shape.

But this is not what happened.

While Bentley tried to control The Cow, dominate him, push him around the way nature intended, The Cow would have none of it. The Cow—all eight pounds of him—fought vigorously. When Bentley snapped at The Cow, The Cow snapped back at him with his gummy little mouth.

When we petted Bentley, The Cow wrestled forward and inserted his body under our hands.

When we picked up Bentley and held him, The Cow sat at our feet and looked at us and peed on the floor. Then he barked, nonstop.

The barking is what started to get to me. It was without end.

Whenever we put him into his little kennel and closed the door, The Cow would begin his ceaseless tirade to be immediately freed.

In my arms, he was a sweet little imp with tapeworm breath. At all other times he was a French bulldog meatloaf, in preparation. I was constantly eyeing the roasting pan. It would be a perfect fit.

We bought books on problem dogs. We read articles online. We tried rattling coins in a can, making sharp, sudden noises when he barked. We tried ignoring him.

Nothing worked.

The days had collected until there were thirty-two of them behind us now. We had a month's worth of love for The Cow. It was not enough.

One article suggested a squirt gun. But only as a last resort. And because I was ready for a last resort, I drove to the supermarket and bought one of those squirt guns that looks like a machine gun. With a huge trigger that you pulled out a foot and then pushed back in. I took it home and showed Dennis.

"That's insane. No, no way. We can't use that on him. That's cruel."

Five minutes later, and over a deafening tirade of barks from the little cocksucker, I was crouching in front of the cage with Dennis egging me on from behind my shoulder. "Make sure you get him in the head, right between the ears."

The gun worked. The sudden blast of water soaked The Cow and the force was such that it propelled him against the rear wall of his kennel.

From that moment on, I would never have to squirt The Cow again. Whenever he barked, I merely had to pick up the gun and say, "Don't make me."

Bentley began to shake and tremble on a regular basis.

The Cow had turned out to be not a fun companion, but punishment for all of us.

✧   ✧   ✧

Back in New York, we developed a routine. The Cow learned to relieve himself on the newspapers, but also on the floor and carpet. I reminded myself of the AA slogan, "Progress . . . not perfection." I adjusted to the constant smell of urine on my clothes. My only pleasure came when the vet gave him injections. I became drunk, giddy with joy. The horrible truth is that he was only quiet when he was suffering. "Shouldn't he also have a rabies booster?" I'd ask.

I worried I would never love him. I e-mailed everybody I knew who had children and asked if the love was immediate or if they ever felt it was all just a terrible mistake.

My friends wrote back and told me *there were moments*. There were certainly moments in the beginning.

This gave me hope.

An outside observer privileged with an objective view into my life might remark that somehow a poor little puppy had found its way into the apartment of a guy who was so inept he probably couldn't operate a vending machine.

By the third month, The Cow had grown larger. Possibly because I was feeding him four meals a day, with the hope that he would grow faster. I did not want to risk any nutritional deficit. Nothing that would delay adulthood. I would pour his food into the bowl, add plenty of canned food, and say, "Here, Cow. Grow a brain."

Bentley, too, began eating four meals a day.

We learned quickly: what one gets, the other wants.

Pre-Cow, Bentley would eat once a day or once every other day. We offered him food constantly. But he was disinterested. He preferred to smack the floor with his front paws or play flashlight games or chew on bones. Food was not his top priority in life.

But for The Cow, food was everything.

And this helped, when it came to training. I soon began carrying scraps of things in my pocket. Dog treats, bits of chicken left over from lunch, whole slices of bread. The Cow quickly grew tired of the same treat day after day, and would stop performing his only trick, which was to pee outside. So in order to keep him interested—and urinating—I had to constantly indulge his palate.

We'd tried to do everything right and it hadn't worked. Now we were forced to do everything wrong and it was working. Soon enough, The Cow would be housebroken. But he would be spoiled beyond reason. He would be a brat. In other words, he would be like many of the children in our Upper West Side Manhattan apartment building.

The Cow is six months old. He is housebroken. Except sometimes, when he is not housebroken. But this is okay. He will eventually decide to be completely housebroken.

He is smarter than Bentley. But Bentley needs us more. Cow is dominant. But Bentley is bigger and still retains power.

If I had to choose, I could not. Cow is my left arm, Bentley is my right. They both sit on my lap in the morning while I read e-mail. Dennis cooks them hamburgers sometimes. We feed them ice cubes, and after they melt on the floor, both dogs bark at the wetness that remains. They slap at the spots with their front paws as if to say, "Get up! Be ice again!"

Bentley is graceful, like a seal. Cow is low-slung and close to the ground. When he walks, he shifts from side to side like a bouncer at a nightclub whose shoulder muscles are too huge.

I do not recall a specific day when I began loving The Cow. Dennis doesn't, either. It's interesting because we were so aware of our original lack of affection for him, that it seems remarkable to have come from there to here. From a place where we wanted to return him like a pair of defective shoes. To a place where we crave him, like water. The Cow has come to mean everything to me. It is impossible to believe I was happy before him. I may have *thought* I was happy. I was mistaken.

They follow us everywhere. But if Bentley is sleeping on the chair and I go into the kitchen for a bottle of ginger ale, Cow will follow me, too. He never, ever lets me out of his sight.

At night after his walk, I say, "Straight to bed," and he walks directly from the front door, under the dining room table, between the legs of the chair, and into his bag. He waits for my face, which appears within seconds. He waits for my hands, which grab the scruff of his impossibly soft neck and then stroke his face. My giant head zooms in close to his and I kiss him softly. He snores, instantly.

Sometimes, I sit here and watch The Cow. I watch Bentley. Dennis is in the other room or he is at the store or in the yard. And I sit alone with my sleeping small animals and I think, I couldn't have kids because it would kill me. These two, they nearly kill me. More precious to me than anything. Children would be worse. Intolerable, that love would be. Already is. Nearly.

My sacred Cow, who still fits in a roasting pan.

Team Player

I collect college T-shirts. Every time I visit a town with a university, I make a point of going to the college bookstore and picking up a shirt with the school logo on it. And then I wear the T-shirts when I get home.

People occasionally stop me and greet me with great enthusiasm, and I will get the terrible feeling that I slept with them in a drunken blackout and have forgotten them entirely. But then they point to my shirt, "What year? I was 'eighty-six."

My favorite is my Harvard T-shirt because I am delusional enough to imagine myself a Harvard grad. And that's what they're called, Harvard Grads. Never graduates.

"Did you go to Harvard?" some bitch I'd never seen before in the elevator in my building asked. Something in her tone almost made it sound like, "You didn't go to Harvard." That tiniest note of accusation put me on the defensive. But I also loathed the idea of speaking to her just because of her smug haircut.

"Uh, no," I admitted. "I just . . ." And let the sentence die in my mouth, hoping I wouldn't have to explain why.

"Just what?" she said, now crossing her arms across her chest. She was smiling but it was clearly a hostile smile.

"Well, I just like college T-shirts," I said. And I smiled, too. But I did so in a way that I hoped made me look friendly and not terribly intelligent. Thus, harmless.

The elevator landed at the lobby and the door opened. I stood aside to let her go first. Maybe I have a mean brain, but I have manners, compliments of my Lawrenceville, Georgia, grandmother, Carolyn. Even though it's quaint and possibly sexist, I always open doors for women, let them through first. If I'm on the sidewalk with a woman, I walk near the curb in case a car splashes through a puddle. I do this on the driest summer days, as well.

But she didn't leave the compartment of the elevator. Instead she crinkled up her nose and tipped her head to the side just a little bit and she said, "You wear T-shirts from colleges you didn't attend?"

I was surprised that the conversation was still continuing, after twenty-eight floors. "Yeah," I said in a clipped tone. "I just like college T-shirts."

"Don't you think that's a little deceptive?" she asked.

"Deceptive?" I said.

"Almost like telling somebody you're a doctor or a police officer when you're nothing of the kind."

Like many people in New York City, she was bossy and had a raging sense of entitlement. "Well," I said, darker now. "I don't think it's any more deceptive than wearing four-inch come-fuck-me pumps when one has no intention of ever fucking anybody." I smirked and looked down at her pumps, then at her pinched, tight little spinster mouth.

That shut her up, and she walked out of the elevator. I could feel the heat of resentment wafting off her flesh.

And I felt guilty. Because the truth is, not only did I not go to Harvard, I didn't even go to high school.

I have an elementary school education. I shouldn't be wearing Ivy League merchandise. I should be wearing a Scooby Doo T-shirt.

And somehow, the mind-reading New York shrew had known this and called me on it.

I remained in the elevator where I pressed the button for my floor. Then I went back inside my apartment, removed my T-shirt, and put on something I bought at The Black Dog bakery on Martha's Vineyard.

I'd spilled scalding coffee on Dennis at this place on vacation a few years before. So I was entitled to wear the shirt.

Though a good deal of my job as a writer involves sitting in front of a computer in filthy sweatpants and a baseball cap, another element is traveling around the country giving talks. Awhile back, a lecture agent contacted me and asked if I was interested in speaking at colleges and universities. "Speaking about what?" I asked, laughing into the phone.

"About you," she said, her voice wavering like she might have had the wrong number.

I found it impossible to believe that colleges would want me to come to their campuses and talk about myself. What if somebody asked me a Proust question?

She assured me that there would be no such questions. What's more, I would be paid.

"In credits?" I asked. I have always wanted a college degree but am unwilling to do the actual work, so I simply entertain the fantasy that some struggling college will one day award me an honorary degree. A BSN, perhaps. Or a degree in pharmacology. Something I could fall back on.

"They'll pay you in cash," she told me. "And they'll pay for your hotel room and your gas if you have to drive. And your airfare."

"So let me see if I understand this," I said. "Yale is going to pay for me to come speak in their auditorium? And speak about nothing except myself?"

"Right," she said. "That's pretty much it. Talk about yourself, your childhood, your books. Maybe some places will want you to talk about advertising or publishing in general. You know, just be your regular funny and charming self."

Many people assume I have a "funny and charming self." Many people are wrong. In person, I am not especially funny. I am serious and exhausted. I am tired from having lived seventeen different lives, compressed into the space of one. My back hurts, my hair is gone, I have bad skin. I try to be funny but come off instead as sloppy and a little pathetic. I dress like a nineteen-year-old and use seventy-five-dollar wrinkle cream around my eyes.

Still, I accepted this speaking agent's offer. Who am I to turn away free money? And a free night in a glamorous hotel?

So I said, "Great!" and within a month, I had my first gig. This one involved no travel. It was downtown at New York University.

I was to speak for an hour and a half. Before going on, I imagined this time would fly by. As it happened, I was able to stand on stage and explain everything about myself that's not in a book, and still have an hour and fifteen minutes left.

I was in awe of time's elasticity. Sometimes it compresses. Sometimes it stretches. And yet it always does one when you need the other.

An hour and fifteen minutes is a long time to stand on a stage when you have absolutely nothing left to say.

But imagine being in the audience. Imagine watching the author unscrew the top of the Evian bottle and take a long, slow drink.

And then wipe his mouth on his sleeve. And then smile out at you. And shrug.

"Next time, I'll be more prepared," I told my agent. "It won't happen like that again."

And to my credit, it didn't. After this, I gave more thought to what I would say. And I discovered that things really became interesting when the audience became involved. So I extended the Q&A from fifteen minutes to an hour.

Now, not only would the school pay me, they would do all the work. All I had to do was stand on display like a zoo animal. One that can answer questions.

I also enlarged my college T-shirt collection. And I did so without guilt. Because who could blame me for wearing a Rutgers T-shirt when I had, in fact, "given a talk" at the university? Surely, this was at least as prestigious as being a graduate?

But where was my coveted Harvard shirt?

Since the incident in the elevator I'd been unable to wear it. And when I went looking for it, finally feeling justified because of my new para-career, it was nowhere to be found.

I'd returned to the apartment in haste that morning, angry and guilty and hurrying to remove it from my body. But where did I put it?

It wasn't in any of the usual places.

Like socks in a drier, it had vanished into the ether.

So I waited. I waited for my agent to call me and say, "Can you do Harvard next week?"

But instead, my agent called and asked, "Can you do Skidmore in two months?"

I'd heard of Skidmore. And it sounded glamorous. *Skidmore.* I could work *that* into a conversation. "Oh, sorry, I can't that night. *I'm lecturing at Skidmore,*" I could tell somebody. Of course, I would need to be invited somewhere, which almost never happens. But if it did happen, this is what I would say.

Skidmore is north of New York City, about three hours by train, in the town of Saratoga Springs.

When I arrived, exhausted from merely sitting, a genuine Skidmore student met me at the station. He was adorable and rumpled and had intelligent eyes. He called me "Mr. Burroughs," which made me realize I could be his father. If not in age, certainly in experience. I am one of those people other people describe as having "wise eyes." Which is a nice way of saying "craggy, old eyes in need of cosmetic surgery."

He said, "I'll take you to your hotel so you can relax. And then I'll come back and pick you up at seven and we'll head over to the venue."

I slid into the tiny front seat of his Kia and we took off.

The streets of Saratoga Springs are broad and elegant. These streets were designed for cruising in huge American cars. Cadillac Fleetwoods, Packards. Cars as large as Manhattan studio apartments.

"This town is just dripping with money, isn't it?" I commented.

Alex said, "Yeah, pretty much. And it's old money."

The phrase "old money" has always made me sad. Reminding me of the bald fact that I come from generations-deep dysfunction and have all the pedigree of an electric chair. Though distantly related to Scottish royalty, there is nothing majestic in my past. So even if I were to have money, it would be "new" money, and thus still not valuable in the most important ways.

As we continued to cruise down the boulevard, the houses became spaced further and further apart, the trees in the front yards expanding in girth. The money was getting older with every block.

Finally, we came upon an enormous field. And in the center of the field, a mansion. To my surprise, Alex pulled in the driveway. "This is it," he said.

I looked at the stone façade, the huge solid chestnut door, the gravel driveway, and I thought, No way is this place going to have wireless access in the rooms.

Inside the Inn, I was slapped in the face with the smell and thick air that surrounds age. It seemed a thin veil of dust clung to everything. The ancient oriental carpets were well worn and had almost merged with the wood of the floor. The building was grand, but it was not maintained to my unreasonable standards. It was like an aging industrial heiress who sunbathes daily and absolutely refuses to have any work done on her face.

Alex escorted me to my room, which was on the second floor. He opened the door and I stepped inside.

The room was wallpapered in a pattern of tiny pink roses and green leaves. There was a simple twin bed with a white cotton bedspread. Lace curtains in the windows. A nightstand with a reading lamp. A rocking chair. It was incredibly charming. And I don't do well with charming. Charming makes me itch. "If you need anything, just give me a call," he said. He smiled and I smiled and he left me alone.

I heaved my bag onto the bed, which bounced the bag right up and onto the floor.

First, I looked around the room for the minibar. Was it hidden inside this tall armoire? I opened the door and saw nothing but shelves. I scanned the room again but it was hopeless. There was no minibar crowded with soda.

There was a tiny color television on a small wood table, directly across from the bed and next to the fireplace, which I'm sure was clogged with squirrels. There was a desk against the wall opposite the windows. But there wasn't even a phone.

And there was a faint smell that was difficult to identify at first. I continued to stand in place, sniffing the air like a farm animal, and then recognition hit me: Gillette Speed Stick deodorant.

It was strangely comforting to have this small bit of the last person here in the room with me. As though they'd departed only moments before and could still be caught in the hallway: "Wait! Take me with you? Do you have a rental car?"

As charming as the room was, I knew it wouldn't work for me. I do not need charming. I need to be online, at all times. I need surge protection. I need a blow-dryer mounted on the bathroom wall in case my hair decides to grow back in the night.

In order to think, I needed a Coke. I could not think of a proper course of action without one. So I stepped outside my room and went back downstairs to the front desk.

However, there was no front desk. I hadn't paid attention when we first walked in. I had been so mesmerized by the place, I'd failed to notice this one missing detail.

I walked to the area where the front desk should have been and encountered instead a short passageway leading to a kitchen.

A woman of indeterminable age was standing in the center of the kitchen, holding a rag. Her simple dress, more of a smock, and her posture made me think she'd been standing in that very position since the beginning of time. "Can I help you?" she asked. She had kind eyes and less than a full mouth of teeth.

"Hi," I said, as sweetly as possible. "Could you tell me where the vending machine is?"

She looked at me for a moment and then answered, "There ain't no vending machine. I can get you some water, though."

"That's okay," I said. "But thank you." I said this effusively, to make up for every bad thought I have ever had about another person. The way I thanked her, you'd think she just handed me a sack of cash. It was a guilty thank you. I felt terrible for having so much calcium in my mouth.

I went back upstairs to my room and looked out the window. There was nothing but field there. And this Norma Desmond Inn was right in the middle of it. I was miles from the nearest 7-Eleven. In the car, Alex had told me, "An award-winning poet is staying at the Inn tonight. Maybe you two will get together for tea." Clearly, this was a young writer's fantasy about two other writers. The pretentious poet and the trashy memoirist would be having their tea separately, thanks.

I used my cell phone to go online. Thanking God for cell phone service, I pulled up Google and did a search for local hotels. I found the number of a Holiday Inn and called them.

"Yes, we have rooms," she said.

"Can you do me a favor?" I asked. "Can you reserve a room for me, but also, can you call me a taxi? I'm in town right now, but stuck in the middle of nowhere and my cell phone is dying and there's no plug for it."

She said, "Of course." And the way she said this made me think it had happened before. There was no surprise in her voice, none at all. In fact, she even guessed where I was staying. "You're up at the Inn, right?"

"Yes! How'd you know?"

"Oh, I've had this exact same call before," she said.

Fifteen minutes later, I was stepping into a cab, the key to my charming room left behind on the charming bed.

After a brief trip to the center of town, I found myself at the front desk of a Holiday Inn. When I am exhausted and stressed out, nothing in the world gives me more pleasure than the sight of a popcorn ceiling and a woman with a brass nameplate on her chest that reads, "Kelli—Front Desk."

"I just need to swipe your credit card," she told me. And I handed it over to her. If she'd asked me to hand over my entire wallet and my watch, I probably would have. I was in a sudden, extremely good mood. I was flooded with relief, thrilled to be away from the *charming* inn, and now just moments away from my own charmless box of a room. I could almost smell the foam pillow.

After much clacking of the keyboard and a signing of a paper, she handed me my key. "Your room number is three-oh-five and you're on the third floor. The elevators are just down this hallway, take your first right, then a left."

Already I was lost. Her directions had simply passed through my head, utterly unprocessed. No matter. I smiled and took the key. "Thanks," I said. Then I began to walk away but turned back. "Is there a vending machine?" I asked.

"On every floor." She smiled.

I did get lost trying to find the elevator. I ended up in a banquet room. But eventually I found the elevators and stepped inside. The ceiling was low, which made me feel hugely tall. A short person would be extremely happy in this elevator, I thought, because they're always looking for ways to feel better about their deformity.

I stepped off on my floor and began walking down the longest hallway in the universe. All through the journey I imagined how it would feel to hear the words "You've got mail!" blast from my laptop's speakers.

When I finally reached Room 305, I slid my flat plastic credit-card key thing into the door and the green light illuminated. The lock disengaged. I opened the door.

Something was off, but I wasn't sure what. Then I got it: the room was very dark. Odd, I thought. And right away, I saw the bathroom light was on, a towel on the floor.

"Oh, fuck," I said out loud.

She'd given me the key to the wrong room. Now I would have to turn around and walk all the way back down the *2001: A Space Odyssey* hallway, find the elevator, go through the maze downstairs, crawl back to the front desk, and get another key.

As I turned to leave I noticed a suitcase on the bed, and a gray T-shirt spilling out. Something about the shirt was familiar. The color of the logo on the front. Deep, rich red. "Hello?" I said.

Nothing.

I looked down the hallway, saw nobody.

I had to check. Just to see.

I propped the door open with my suitcase and stepped inside, carefully. "Hello?" I said again. But the room felt empty. And as my eyes adjusted to the dark, I saw that it was.

I smiled because, with my luck, there'd have been a dead body on the bed. And now my fingerprints on the door.

I thought, I can't do this. This is absolutely insane. But still, I carefully picked up the T-shirt and read the name embossed across the front. Harvard.

Extra large.

My size. My shirt.

I couldn't *take* it, of course. The guy who owned it—and this was a guy's room, because I could smell his cologne—would notice. And the front desk would immediately know that I had taken it because I would be going back downstairs any moment to get a new room. But if I could put another T-shirt in place of this one, the guy might not notice until the next day, when he checked out.

So, very carefully, I lifted up the pile of clothing in his suitcase and I saw a similar shirt. It was also gray, but had no logo. This would do.

I took the Harvard shirt and draped the other gray T-shirt in its place.

I made sure it looked like it did when I first walked in, the arm of the shirt hanging over the suitcase handle.

I turned around and walked to the door.

The hallway was empty.

I quickly unzipped my bag and stuffed the Harvard T-shirt inside.

As I walked down the hallway, I began to feel guilty. The reality of what I'd just done settled on me. I have just stolen something from another person, I told myself. I have just engaged in a criminal activity.

But then when I reached the elevator door, I smiled. Because it was true that I had stolen, but it was also true that the Kelli at the front desk had given me this key. And if I were a highly religious person, which many people are, it could be argued that I was meant to have this T-shirt.

After all, how many people own a Harvard T-shirt, love it dearly, then lose it mysteriously? And then, of these people, how many are given the key to a room containing one, lying out, begging to be taken?

No. It was clear, I was meant to have this T-shirt. And the guy I stole it from? More than likely he was a true Harvard graduate, so he didn't need to be showing off with a pretentious Harvard T-shirt.

Killing John Updike

Tonight, my lunatic friend Suzanne worked me into a frenzy. "Baby," she said, "Do you realize John Updike is like eighty! He's got to be at least eighty! He could even be ninety. He has been a legend forever. And I just right now read the life expectancy of the average male is seventy-seven-point-six years. And that means he could die at any moment. Buy his first editions, NOW!!!" She was calling from California—land of the vineyards—and her voice contained a slight chardonnay edge. Suzanne and I met in California, when we worked at the same ad agency, but at different times. First me, then her. They loved her much more. Because Suzanne can sell anything.

"I don't know," I said. First editions are expensive. Did I really want to spend a couple of hundred dollars on a book I couldn't even read, because it had to remain perfect?

"I'm telling you, this man is gonna drop dead any minute," she said. "And he's the most famous writer in the world. My God.

Whatever you buy will double, triple in value. Possibly overnight.
He may be DEAD BY MORNING. BUY NOW!"

Now that was an interesting point. If Updike died tonight, my
two hundred dollars could be worth four hundred dollars tomorrow. I could stick his book on eBay, and with the profit, I could buy
a slew of novels at Barnes and Noble. I would preorder whatever
Elizabeth Berg had coming out. I would buy every Joyce Carol
Oates, because it's time to read her. Or maybe only every fifth book
of hers. I would buy multiple copies of Kathryn Harrison's *The Kiss*
in paperback and give them as gifts.

Maybe Suzanne was right.

So I went online and found a bunch of Updikes. But they were
horrifyingly expensive. One of them was two thousand dollars. And
he wasn't even dead yet. Some of them were signed, which made
them much more valuable. But the fucker could still sign. If you
forced him to sign, put a pen in his hand and a gun to his head, he
could still sign his name. So imagine how much these would be
worth when he could no longer sign at all, even at gunpoint, due to
death.

If I was going to spend two thousand dollars on a book about a
rabbit, that old man better well be dead by morning, or I was going
to be furious.

I selected a signed first edition from the list. A moderate first, in
the five hundred dollar price range. Then I e-mailed Suzanne.
"Okay, baby. DONE. Bought Updike. Now what?"

She wrote back immediately. "FANTASTIC. XOXOXOXOX. BUY
MORE NOW. I JUST HAVE A FEELING. I KNOW THESE THINGS."

She was crazy, and tonight she was crazed. We allowed that since
she and I had both been published through sheer desperation and
willpower, surely we could land this one little . . . coup. Using our
minds. Suzanne has been collecting Updike first editions since she
was fourteen. When she published her first novel with Updike's

publisher, she immediately sent a box of his first editions to her editor and all but demanded that the old man sign them. Mr. Updike did this, and returned them. "It's ironic," she wrote, "because his innate generosity and kindness in the past now make him doubly worth killing."

It was uncanny. She seemed certain of the great novelist's impending death. Was there even a remote possibility that she would have something to do with it? If so, was it wrong of me to then buy these first editions? The last thing I wanted was to get myself involved in some sort of "insider trading" nightmare.

Then she sent another e-mail. "The thing is, I worship John Updike. I'd crumple from awe if I saw him alive and in person. I think he is the greatest male writer of the twentieth century. I would drink his bath water and shine his little Yankee shoes. But I still hoard those first editions as though they were a very life insurance policy on the man, and I am his nineteen-year-old wife. It's just awful. I blame money and the fact of its usefulness in every single situation except death."

And I was the same way, just as hateful and greedy. So couldn't I buy more? It wasn't like I was throwing money away on particle-board nightstands at Wal-Mart. These were enduring classics. In Extra, Extra Fine condition, no rips, stains, or price clips.

So I went back online and bought two more books. Now, I had purchased three books, which cost me more money than some people spend on their first cars.

I e-mailed Suzanne. "Okay, now I'm broke. I bought two more, so I have three. He'd better die."

She said, "Okay, let's do it. Let's kill him."

I said, "Sure. How?"

She said, "Let's constantly think of him as dying. Let's concentrate very hard. And in the morning, we'll watch CNN. I bet you anything they'll announce that he died in his sleep. And nobody will be able to trace it to us. Because who even knows where he lives, and we're all the way over here, where we live."

Suzanne was a diabolical genius, which is why I adored her. She then said, "BUY SIGNED FIRST EDITIONS OR NOT AT ALL. Check out Alibris.com and Powell's."

So for the remainder of the night, we exchanged e-mails. I bought *Couples*. $495. Signed by the author, with light wear to dust jacket.

She wrote, "HE'LL BE DEAD BY MORNING."

"How do you think he'll die?" I wrote. "Do you think he might choke? I could see that. I was just looking at a picture of him and he has a slender, graceful neck. The perfect neck to trap the jagged edge of a corn chip. I bet he chokes."

She wrote back, "Maybe. But I think stroke. Flip a switch, nothing. He's gone. Clean and simple. In his sleep. He is the greatest living American writer so we can't have him suffer. At least not very much."

She was right. Whatever killed him, had to kill him fast.

And then I realized: someday, this will be me. Some horrible, selfish, greedy bald writer will buy my early books online and then pray for my immediate demise. In fact, it was probably happening right this very minute.

I decided to check. I'd never looked up my own name on a used-book Web site before. It never occurred to me that I could be collectable, like a cup from Burger King. So I went back to the Web site where I bought the Updike books and typed in my own name.

Running with Scissors. First edition. © 2002 Augusten Burroughs. St. Martin's Press, New York, New York. Memoir about author's unusual childhood. Unread. As new. In dust wrappers. Signed on title page. $200.

I was shocked. It was already happening. People were selling my books online, collecting them, waiting for me to relapse with multiple drugs and then die. I'd make Page Six, "*Scissors* Author Dead, Apparent Alcohol Overdose."

Then that two-hundred-dollar book would be worth four hundred, five hundred dollars. About the same price as a damaged Updike, nondead.

What else were people selling? I wondered.

I decided to log onto eBay.

There, I typed my name into the little box and hit "search."

A moment later, listings appeared. Books, books, books, and then MY WATCH.

I looked at my computer screen in utter disbelief. I clicked on the link next to the picture of the watch and was taken to a page.

"Rolex GMT Master. Stainless steel, black face. Watch worn for publicity during promotion of # 1 bestselling book, RUNNING WITH SCISSORS. Watch appears on author's wrist in many magazine photographs, including ENTERTAINMENT WEEKLY, PEOPLE."

The ad gave the name of the seller. My brother.

I called him immediately. "What the fuck are you doing, you Ass Burger?"

As usual, he was unmoved. "Huh? What are you talking about?"

"I just saw my watch on eBay. What are you doing?"

My brother said, "What do you mean, what am I doing? I'm selling the watch. You said you wanted me to sell it and you gave it to me to sell. So I'm selling it."

He was correct, of course. I had given him the Rolex to sell. I'd bought it with my dirty advertising money, so every time I looked at my wrist to check the time, I thought, *Storyboards, focus groups, asshole boss with a backward baseball cap.* I'd reached a point where I would prefer to drag a sundial in a wagon behind me than wear that watch for one more minute. So I'd given it to my brother, assuming he'd sell it to his friend, who owns a jewelry store. I never expected him to sell it on eBay. With all those . . . words.

"Well, it's weird," I said.

"What's weird about it?" he asked. "We already have three bids."

The whole thing reeked of Billy Beer II.

In the 1970s when Jimmy Carter was elected president, his trailer trash brother launched a line of beer. Billy Beer. Mortifying the president.

Another thing came to mind: Demi Moore's mother posing nude in front of a potter's wheel for a porn magazine.

But my brother thought there was nothing strange about selling my watch on eBay. "Look, you gave me the watch to sell. I'm selling it. You want me to take the ad down, I can take the ad down."

"No," I said. "Keep it up. Sell it. Get rid of it." My greed was far more powerful than my pride.

And then I had an idea. "Do you think people would buy other things?" I asked him.

He didn't have to think about this for very long. "Oh, sure. People will buy all sorts of things. What else do you want to sell?"

Well, hmm. I could sell my silver keychain. I hated it. It was worth maybe twenty-five cents. But would somebody pay fifty bucks for it? "Sure," my brother said. "I bet somebody'd pay a hundred for it."

Shit. Maybe people would buy my empty Blenheim Ginger Ale bottles. If I packaged them in a tasteful brown cloth sack and said, "Blenheim Ginger Ale bottles, empty. Consumed by Augusten Burroughs while writing first essay collection. $1,000."

Maybe I could e-mail my writer friend, Haven. We e-mail every single day, all day, constantly. Perhaps I could gather together a dozen of our e-mails and sell these as a package. Say for three hundred dollars. Then I could send her half. And we could each go out to Red Lobster.

I thought of John Updike. Surely when he dies, somebody will be riffling through his home, looking for things to sell. It was unlikely that his own children, if he had any, would sell his nail clippers, underwear, or ChapStick. But certainly cousins would do this. Nieces and nephews would absolutely offer his pens, unused pads of paper, bookends for sale. Probably other things.

John Updike, legendary American author. For auction: Chair cushion, blue toile fabric. Cushion from desk chair, used daily by celebrated author. Distinctive impressions in pillow, from correlating anatomical features of author. Condition is described as "well enjoyed." Cushion manufactured circa 1940. Believed to be from Sears Roebuck & Co. This is an authentic piece of Americana, from the personal estate of one of the country's most famous and widely read authors. Truly a unique collectable. One of a kind. Minimum bid: $3,500.

But that's what happens when you die. The vultures come. Sometimes, even before you die.

Long before my grandmother passed away, the vultures around her carted Persian carpets, Ming vases, expensive Italian fruitwood tables out of her house. They used vans. And they did this *years* before the woman was in a wheelchair and on a breathing machine, let alone dead. She had simply slowed down, is all. And there they were, greedy little hands outstretched, gimme, gimme, gimme.

If one were to watch us from a great distance, with the sound off and in fast-motion, one would see an individual begin to limp, and then dozens of other individuals invade the territory of the infirm individual, carting away belongings, clinging near the deathbed, waiting.

We are animals, true. But we are also like insects.

And here I was, with my three new John Updike novels, checking the CNN home page every five minutes for BREAKING NEWS.

John Updike—American legend dead. Story to follow.

Well, I decided, if he was dead by morning, there would be nobody to blame but me. If John Updike was dead when I woke up, then I had killed him with my hateful greed. Suzanne, too, would be guilty. But somehow, I was the most guilty because I got the most excited.

After all, she had merely suggested I buy his books. I'm the one who actually spent the money. That shows true pathology.

If anybody deserved to die in his sleep tonight, or choke on a tortilla chip, it was me.

I turned off my computer and climbed into bed. Dennis would be home in an hour. And he would find me in bed, as though sick.

I tucked into Ira Levin's *Rosemary's Baby*, which was swiftly proving to be the finest, most elegant book ever written.

And then I thought, hey. Wait a fucking minute.

And I got out of bed and went back online. Where I found a first edition, though not signed.

I clicked, ADD TO CART.

And then I said out loud, "Okay, Ira. Your number's up."

Attacked by Heart

Plumbly's restaurant was *the* place to be seen in downtown Amherst, Massachusetts, in 1979. Amidst hanging spider plants and macramé wall art, you sat with your best woman friend and discussed Israeli Prime Minister Menachem Begin or the possibility of exploring a lesbian relationship. The tables were repurposed wine barrels, solid oak. You could throw on your favorite pair of clogs, order a cheese fondue, and know that you were living entirely in the thrilling moment. Plumbly's was not just the local hot spot, it was also the place where my life changed when I overheard a snippet of conversation between two women having lunch.

She: Like an actual beating sensation? In your chest?

Her: Yes. Like a flutter.

She: I don't think that's normal. I don't think you're supposed to be aware of your heartbeat.

And with these words—*I don't think you're supposed to be aware of your heartbeat*—this unknown woman in a burnt orange poncho doomed me to a life of pathological overawareness of my own cardiac activity.

It was as if somebody simply reached over and flipped a switch on my body that I hadn't known existed. I'd gone from being blissfully unaware of my inner workings to constantly thinking about its every contraction, picturing my rambunctious heart suddenly freezing still inside my chest.

By the end of that fateful afternoon, I had convinced myself that I had been born with a clunker of a ticker. Both wrists were red from my frantic grabbing at my own limbs, searching for a pulse and counting the beats, not knowing what was normal and what was not, but sensing something just wasn't right.

And then I felt a sudden jerk in the deep interior of my body, a region that until now had never tried to communicate with me. I halted in place, waiting. I cocked my head, as though listening. And it happened again. An ominous contraction. As though I'd been startled, but I hadn't. And then just as suddenly, it resumed its normal, defective ways.

I went to bed knowing it was quite possible, if not likely, that I would not wake up in the morning. I'd heard adults say, "Kids think they're invincible. They never think they'll get old or die." If this was true, maybe the reason I was in bed thinking about dying was because I somehow knew I would. I thought about what I'd miss, and instead of a wildly colorful rush of images, very little came to mind.

But I did wake up and the next day was far less nervous about my heart. I recognized my hysteria as yet another of my endless list of tics and obsessions. Not so different from blinking compulsively, making my strange noise when I swallowed, or being compelled to wash my hands after touching anything outside my bedroom.

But the one thing I was unable to dismiss as more of my frustrating "weirdness" was that I was now aware of my heart's activity. And would remain aware for the next two decades.

✧   ✧   ✧

Over the years, I often had the sensation of my heart skipping a beat, which I figured must be normal, because I'm not dead. Instead of having a physical, I called my brother, who had seen a cardiologist within the last decade, which was close enough for me. "Does your heart ever skip a beat?" I asked.

"Yeah," he said. "Sometimes."

"And did you tell your cardiologist about it?"

"Yeah, and he said it was nothing."

And just like that, I felt two decades' worth of relief. *Why, I asked myself, had I let this bug me for so long? I should have talked about this to someone years ago. But it's so good to know I'm fine.*

Though sometimes, especially during periods of extreme stress, the skipping would be quite dramatic. There would be an instant when my heart wasn't beating at all. Like when you're on a swing and you reach the top, near the bar, and pause. My heart would skip a beat—and, and, and. And then resume. This worried me so much, I didn't dare mention it out loud to another person, for fear of making it into something real. As long as this remained something that only I was aware of, it remained possible that I was merely overly aware of my heart's normal activity.

Finally, I had a physical exam. My first in at least ten years. Dennis had insisted that I have one, not only because I was approaching forty, but because I'd lived a dangerous life, with drinking and drugs and whatnot. It almost seemed like a condition I must meet in order for our happy marriage to continue. So I made an appointment with his doctor, because I had none for myself. And at the very end of the physical, after I had even peed into a small cup and the doctor had already washed his hands, I casually mentioned to the doctor that I was aware that my heart was fooling around inside my chest.

Instead of telling me, "That's nothing," he turned his back on me, riffled through a Rolodex on the counter, and then handed me a business card: Alan Fard, M.D. Cardiologist.

It was just that simple—black type on a white card. He said, "Call him and make an appointment right away."

I took the business card home and placed it on my table, away from the other debris of my working life. It sat there in a clearing, occupying far more space than one would imagine a small card capable of. Throughout the day, my eyes would find the card, and I would be filled with a sense of impending doom. The card felt like a body I had stashed in the closet, in parts and pieces, mixed with sticks of deodorant.

"I need to call this guy," I told myself. "I'll do it first thing tomorrow morning."

Five months later, I made an appointment.

As with other doctors, I expected a wait of three weeks. Maybe four. But the aggressive receptionist at the cardiac doctor's office would have none of it. He must have been alerted by my regular doctor and wasn't going to let this wait. "Can you come in today?" he asked. I was blindsided by this question. No, I could absolutely not come in that very day. I was in my sweat pants, on eBay, looking for a coffee table. There were five hundred and sixty-seven coffee tables to go through.

"Actually," I said, "today isn't a good day. Today's just crazy with meetings. I'm good all of next week, though."

The aggressi-ceptionist said, "How about tomorrow morning?"

Fuck it. "Okay, tomorrow morning."

"Great. I'll see you here at eight A.M."

I wanted to say, "Can we make it eleven?" but I knew he'd be on to me.

I took a cab to Dr. Fard's Park Avenue office the following morning. It was a white, loftlike space with high ceilings. Against the

right wall was a boxy, blue ultrasuede sofa. Across from this, a row
of bent plywood chairs. And directly opposite the door, a glass
desk.

Behind the desk was a twenty-four-year-old Prada model. I approached him. "Hi. I'm here for my appointment."

Prada Model said, "Okay, great. Is this your first time here?"

I told him it was. And he reached behind him for a clipboard,
pen attached. "Then I just need you to fill this out, okay?"

I took the clipboard and sat.

Prada Model had shoulder-length hair, like I always wanted. And
his inflection, just hearing him speak these few words, revealed an
intelligence. He was probably not a Prada model; he was probably
premed at Columbia. A guy who had chosen medicine over model-
ing. Or perhaps financed his education with runway work.

I was dressed in cargo fatigues, a frumpy sweatshirt, a baseball
cap. It had been two weeks since I last shaved, because I was writing. And when I'm writing, personal grooming slips to the bottom
of the "Must Do" totem pole.

I glanced down and noticed my white athletic socks and brown
earth shoes. At no time in American history was this combination
ever considered "stylish" or "cool." Just owning a pair of earth shoes
could warrant my expulsion from New York City.

And I was tempted to tell Prada Model, "My beeper just went off.
I have an emergency. Can I come back at noon?" and then come
back wearing my Armani Black Label suit that I bought expressly so
I wouldn't feel like I felt at that moment. My sole emergency suit:
funerals, weddings, cardiology appointments.

I filled out the form and slid the clipboard onto the glass desk.
Prada Model said, "Thanks. It should only be a couple of minutes."

I sat back on the sofa and looked to my right: a low table piled
with magazines. But not *Time, People, Entertainment Weekly*. Only

Art in America. Perhaps the only magazine I would shun in favor of looking at a bare wall.

Then I noticed that the walls were hung with original color photographs and abstract paintings.

As I sat there festering, more of the reception area revealed itself to me. Now, instead of shapes—plywood chairs, boxy sofa—I was able to absorb another layer of fabulousness: quality. This shit was expensive. This wasn't just modern furniture plucked from an online retailer. This was furniture you ordered and then had to wait nineteen weeks to receive.

And I knew that when I saw the cardiologist, he would be impeccable. He would be wearing Armani suit pants and a Paul Stuart shirt. He would have glossy black hair and perfect teeth.

A moment later, the cardiologist walked into the room to speak to Prada Model. He walked past me and slid behind the glass desk. He was impeccable. He was wearing Armani suit pants and a Paul Stuart shirt. He had glossy black hair and perfect teeth. He was not only a handsome cardiologist, but he was a sexy cardiologist.

"Mr. Burroughs?" he said, looking directly at me. "It'll just be a few minutes. Just wait here and she'll come get you."

He spoke with a refined Middle Eastern accent. Obviously Iranian royalty, living in exile, having to now work for a living. With just a few words, he had managed to convey sophistication, competence, sex appeal, extreme wealth and power, along with exceptional taste in art and design.

If I had to have a baboon heart like Baby Faye, what better guy to do it?

As I sat there imagining a life attached to machines, my skin blue, a young woman in a white lab coat called my name.

I followed her down a wide, long hallway and into a room filled with cardiac equipment. I knew, without knowing anything about cardiac equipment, that this stuff was top of the line. No way would a doctor who owned a seven-thousand-dollar blue ultrasuede sofa buy cheap gadgets. This guy would pour over the catalogues, and he'd order the best.

She explained that they were going to perform a sonogram on my heart. First, at rest. Then, under stress.

I said, "What do you mean, under stress?" I felt like a dog being tricked into the car for his neutering appointment with the vet.

She nodded at the treadmill in the corner. I hadn't seen that when I first walked in. Automatically, my brain dismisses exercise equipment.

"We'll have you walk on that, and then we'll do another sonogram."

I could walk. "Okay," I said.

She instructed me to remove my shirt and lie on the table. Then she attached a series of electrodes to my chest and shoulders. She had me turn on my side. Then she placed the sonogram wand over my heart.

Just the process of having my blood pressure checked makes my heart beat faster. So I knew that having a sonogram would make my heart really pound. Possibly resulting in a misdiagnosis, and then an emergency heart-lung transplant, which would fail. I wondered if I had opened a horrible, medical Pandora's box. And I thought, I should have left well enough alone. Unless, of course, all was not well enough.

After the sonogram, the doctor entered the room and motioned for me to step onto the treadmill. He wore cufflinks, gold. His nails were manicured, which I saw as he waved at the treadmill. "Please," he said, as though inviting me to help myself to a buffet.

I climbed up on the treadmill, and he turned it on. It moved slowly, and I was able to walk at a leisurely pace, as though walking to the Korean market on the corner for a box of laxatives.

He said, "So you're a writer?"

I said I was.

He said, "I love talking with writers and artists. You creative types!"

He seemed to fancy himself a patron of the arts, this much was clear, judging from his modern art collection and his dreary *Art in America* magazine collection.

I said, "Well, I would think what you do is fascinating."

He said, "It's very interesting. Many older patients. You are one of the youngest."

And this made me somewhat nervous. So young and already experiencing heart trouble. Not a good indication of a long, rich life.

Then he raised the incline of the treadmill and the speed. He took my blood pressure and continued talking to me, forcing me to answer.

"Did you have a good weekend?"

I said, "Yeah, it was fine." It wasn't difficult to speak, but it did require more air than I felt I could comfortably part with. The incline made walking more difficult.

He took my blood pressure once again and then raised the incline, along with the speed. Now, I had to walk fast. And I was walking uphill. Within ten seconds, I was winded.

"Oh yeah?" he said. "So what did you do this weekend?"

I wanted to scream, "Shut the fuck up," but said, "Relaxed."

He took my blood pressure once more and, to my horror, raised the incline, along with the speed.

Now, I was feeling it. My lungs were burning, and I checked the digital readout. Two minutes, thirteen seconds. My throat went instantly dry, and my vision began to darken.

He took my blood pressure. Turned up the speed.

"This is"—I gasped for air—"really hard." I said, "I don't"—my vision was beginning to tunnel—"think I can do this."

He smiled and took my blood pressure. He was taking it every twenty seconds now. "You're okay, just keep pushing yourself."

I was going to die. He was bringing me to the point of cardiac failure, and in a matter of seconds, I was going to fall backward on the treadmill, and my heart was going to stop. I knew he must have equipment to restart it, but there was no guarantee it would start up again. This might be it.

I saw tiny pin pricks of white light, blinking in front of my eyes. Like snow on a television that has lost its reception.

My legs burned. I knew if I didn't stop right then, I was going to drop over dead.

He said, "Okay!" and turned the machine off.

Somehow, nine minutes had passed. It was impossible! How could nine minutes have passed? I'd experienced a complete, alcoholic blackout. *THANK GOD*.

I stepped off sideways, half falling. He held me up and pushed me back onto the table and into position, on my left side with my left arm above my head. The sonogram lady got her wand out. "Don't breathe deeply," she said. "It's difficult to see your heart when you take deep breaths."

I was heaving. And now I had to take shallow breaths.

She said, "Good, good, that's right."

In a moment she was done, and I was allowed to heave.

After another moment, when my breathing was normal and the stars were gone, she told me I could sit up.

"That was a dirty trick," I said.

She smiled. "Well. No, not really. We need to stress the heart to get a reading. You were really good. You pushed yourself. And you're young. It was an excellent reading."

I put my shirt back on and stepped into the reception area. Two new patients had arrived—one a fat man my own age. I was tempted to whisper, "Get out of here. Run. Go to McDonald's while you still can."

The doctor told me to return in a week for the results.

But I doubted this would be necessary. Surely, my heart had been damaged and would quit within the next few days. Didn't this always happen? Didn't people who were otherwise healthy visit the cardiologist, get a clean bill of health, and then drop dead of sudden cardiac arrest? Wasn't that almost a cliché?

As I left his office, though, a curious sensation gave me pause. At first, it alarmed me because it was so unfamiliar. I stopped on the sidewalk and looked back at the doctor's building, thinking maybe I should go back up to his office. But then it dawned on me exactly what this feeling was: health. I felt fucking great! Energized, refreshed, vigorous. All from spending nine excruciating minutes on a treadmill. Which is eight minutes, fifty-five seconds longer than I had ever managed on my own.

A week later, I returned. "No heart disease, no defects," he told me. "Which rules out a number of sudden-death scenarios."

I said, "So?"

He tossed his head slightly, in such a way as to cause his hair to sweep back. This made me feel actual pain, so extreme was my hair envy. He said, "We're going to give you a device that you will wear, a monitor. Wear it for twenty-four hours, then bring it into the office."

So for twenty-four hours, I was attached to a portable tape recorder, through a series of wires and small patches. My job was to wait for a heart palpitation, then push the button. The device was clever: it instantly recorded the preceding ninety seconds and the following sixty seconds. To catch those slippery palpitations.

I had them every day, so this wouldn't be a problem.

But. It was a problem. Because no heart palpitations came.

I was simply stunned. My own body, turning against me. Making diagnosis impossible. It seemed the mere act of seeing a (sexy) trained medical professional was enough to sooth me, make me relax, and cause my heart to stabilize.

I returned to his office with no data.

"That happens, sometimes," he said. "Okay, so here's what we're going to do." And he reached behind his chair for a box. Inside the box was another device, this one smaller. But similar. "You'll wear this for two weeks. It's the same routine. When you feel a palpitation, push the button and it will record it. But then you push this button here," and he pointed to a different button on the device. "All you have to do is dial the toll-free number printed right here on the case; then you push this button, and the information is transmitted over the phone lines to this company. Then they fax me a report."

Here I felt a mixture of feelings. Awe at the technology. Alarmed that he was so determined to find something wrong with me. Or at least that he was suspicious enough of my symptoms to keep looking. And fear that something horrible was, in fact, wrong with me. On top of these feelings, I wanted to ask Dr. Fard, "Could you just turn to the side? So I can admire your profile?" I imagined his face on a coin that I could keep in my pocket and thumb for good luck.

For the next week, I was wired to the monitor. The novelty wore off after approximately an hour. The pads itched but could not be removed. The dogs kept getting tangled in the leads, causing me to accidentally hit the "record" button and record my heart's activity. And the only way to erase the data was to phone it in.

But then the palpitations began. And I was able to record them, one after the other, and then phone them in.

On my follow-up appointment, Dr. Fard had already reviewed the data.

After another sonogram, I was sent to his office to wait for him.

Sitting there, waiting for the cardiologist, I saw myself as anybody else would have seen me: a young guy about to get a fatal diagnosis.

Instead, Dr. Fard breezed in and told me he knew what was the matter. He spit out a complicated name, which sounded like something that would absolutely require many surgeries. Then he said, "I'm going to give you a prescription for beta-blockers."

I asked him, "What causes this?"

He said, "Well, caffeine, nicotine, stress."

I thought, "Starbucks, nicotine gum, New York City."

He gave me a prescription and told me to make an appointment for the following week. He wanted to check on my progress.

Once I began taking the pills, my heart became invisible. The first night, I was stunned. All my life I'd felt my heart. And now, I felt nothing. For years I'd lived with a shoe in my clothes drier, always hearing that tumbling sound. And then somebody came along and said, "Hey, you have a shoe in here." And took it out.

On my following appointment, he suggested yoga.

I thanked him. And left the office feeling relieved and much lighter, physically.

And I was thinking about what he'd said earlier. When I first saw him. He'd said there had been no signs of heart damage. No hardening of the arteries. Which meant every potato chip and cheeseburger from McDonald's I'd ever consumed had gone clean through me. Did this not imply a certain kind of immunity?

On the way home, I bought a bag of Lay's potato chips, thick cut with sea salt. I also bought four Hostess Fruit Pies, apple flavor. I don't care for the fruit filling, just the crust. So, once home, I bit the top off the first of the pies and shook the nasty fruit slime into the sink, rinsing it down with the sprayer.

Standing there, I felt as though I'd won a stay of execution.

I remembered being twelve and worrying constantly that I would suffer psychotic episodes just like my mother. That when I turned thirty, my mind would split, just like hers. I would become two people—psychotic in the fall and winter, my old self the rest of the year. But it never happened.

And now I wouldn't have to have a heart transplant, like I was half-expecting. And then a dark and creepy feeling spread over me. Because if I wasn't going to have mental illness or heart disease, what was I going to have? What was waiting just around the corner?

I realized I was lucky. I didn't have cancer or terrible burns to try to live with. I didn't have ALS, which is the most sadistic disease I can think of. I didn't have much of anything. And it was fixed by a pill.

"Be glad you don't have a vagina," my friend, who does have a vagina, told me. "You have to have a special doctor. You have to have these awful exams where you basically get naked and then remove your dignity. And then the various parts down there can get cancer and have to get cut out. I'm telling you, having a vagina is like having a pet. Like a dog that's always chasing cars."

When she described it this way, it did seem a blessing that I was born without a vagina. I mean, I can't even handle having a heart.

The Wisdom Tooth

It had been three years since our last vacation and Dennis insisted we take some time for ourselves. He was thinking: ocean, an inn with a fireplace in the bedroom, multiple appetizers, possibly romance.

I was thinking, What about the dogs?

"They'll stay with Sheila and her family," he said, as though this were a perfectly acceptable solution.

The idea of taking a holiday sans pets was a terrifying proposition. I have come to feel something beyond love for our two French bulldogs. I have developed an unnatural dependency on them. Besides, who else will know they require somebody to put on a rubber cat head mask at least once a day and run around the apartment making deranged *meow* sounds?

"But I will miss them," I said. The simplicity of these words belied my true feeling, which was desperation.

"It's good to miss them. Because then you'll enjoy seeing them again."

I said, "But I enjoy seeing them now." I was trying to smother my panic. It's not a good idea to let your spouse know you don't want to go on vacation alone with him because you will miss the animals too much. This is exactly the sort of thing you must never do.

He looked at me in a way that suggested finality. Body, dropping through trapdoor, rope around neck. *Fini.*

He had a point and I knew it. We did need time to be together. Without a small animal, plucked from nature, between us. Whenever we get into bed, Bentley gets into bed and slides between us. Then The Cow tries to climb up on the bed, but because he's short, he only butts his head against the mattress. When I kiss Dennis, Bentley licks our faces and Cow steps on our heads.

I said, "It will be great." This was my way of saying, *You win.* And also, *I love you.*

Dennis is the person who organizes everything in our lives. To the casual outsider, it would seem grossly unfair. He owns a company, he handles all our money, he manages our lives. While I sit and write, Dennis does everything else. When I try to accept additional responsibilities, I make a mess and he has to fix whatever I broke.

So Dennis spent some time online and decided: a rocky island. An old inn. With a fireplace in the bedroom.

It was perfect.

He showed me pictures of the inn he'd found and indeed, it did appear perfect. The photo revealed a room filled with antiques, quilts and—yes—a fireplace.

However, there was something else about the inn that was not shown in the pictures online at the Web site.

Something we discovered only when we arrived.

Something that made me whisper to Dennis upon arrival, "I want to leave. Right now."

Walking in the front door of the inn revealed the innkeeper to be a doll collector.

Standing there in the foyer, on the inch-thick maroon carpeting, I stared directly at a human baby girl doll, seated in a high chair. Behind her on a bookcase, a row of little girls, all in Victorian dressing gowns and little black flats.

Now maybe I'm just ultrajudgmental, but I really feel that only two groups of people have any business collecting dolls: little girls and grown women who lost all their children in fiery car accidents.

Other than these two exceptions, doll collecting is just plain creepy.

"Welcome, please come in to the parlor. I'll give you some paperwork and then give you the grand tour and then you can get settled in your room. How was your drive, was it okay?" she asked. She was a nice enough woman. In her early fifties, short, efficient hair. Nothing out of the ordinary.

Dennis said, "The drive was really beautiful," at the exact same moment that I said, "The drive was very long." I was trying to hurry things along. I wanted to be left alone.

She looked between us, "Oh! Okay. Well, it was long but it was beautiful. Well, I'm happy it was beautiful."

I gazed around the room and my eyes stopped dead on a little boy standing in the corner. This was a particularly eerie doll. Life-sized and blond-haired and blue-eyed. I saw a little Nazi boy, pockets probably stuffed with scissors and retractable blades. My grandfather on my mother's side was rumored to be half Jewish, which practically makes me Jerry Seinfeld's brother, and thus wary of blond German boys with their hands out of sight.

All around the room, dolls. Little dolls in a display case between the windows. A doll on the sofa right next to us. Two dolls sharing a seat behind the innkeeper's chair.

And then on the tabletops, framed photographs of her own children.

As Dennis filled out the forms and made small talk with the woman, I became lost in a fantasy of the innkeeper's children. Imagining how mentally ill they must be as a result of having a mother with this curious fetish.

Did they feel like pets, her children? Did they feel competitive with the dolls? Did they hate them? Had these two boys in lacrosse uniforms never been able to invite a single friend over, for fear of shame?

A few moments later, we were all standing and she led the way into the adjoining room, where meals were served. "Breakfast is at seven," she said.

I don't wake up at seven, let alone eat. Let alone eat in a doll collector's strange house. My idea of breakfast is two Advil washed down with Coke. Not pancakes made by somebody else's mom.

"We might skip breakfast," Dennis said. "We're not big breakfast eaters."

Oh, thank God for him, I thought.

The woman's smile dropped. "Oh. You're not? Oh. Because I make them myself. Waffles. You don't like homemade waffles?"

It was pitiful. But it worked. Dennis said, "I love waffles. Well, maybe we'll have breakfast after all."

At last, she dragged us to our door and gave us the key. "If you need anything at all, just call out for me," she said.

We thanked her, then stepped inside the room and closed the door.

Dennis immediately whispered, "Holy shit."

I said, "Shhhhhhhhhhhhhhh. She's listening."

"This is really weird," he whispered.

"I hate this," I said. "I wish we were at a chain hotel. I can't stand this level of scrutiny."

And then Dennis looked crestfallen. "I'm sorry," he said. "I should have known you'd hate this place. I never should have booked a room at an inn."

I immediately hugged him and told him that it was perfect. The room, I said, was adorable. There was a fireplace! And we were on vacation! And it wasn't like we were going to spend all our time in the room.

Then I moved to the window and lowered the shade. It was early evening and I didn't like the thought of the innkeeper crouching outside the window with a doll, watching.

Dennis and I are so much alike that he was doing the very same thing, at the other window. "I bet she watches her guests," he was saying.

I love the way he thinks.

The room was decorated with original and reproduction Victorian furniture. I love antiques—slant-top Chippendale desks from the 1700s, a nice William and Mary table. But I've never been fond of Victorian furniture. Especially particleboard Victorian furniture.

But the room was the nicest in the inn. It was a room that many couples on their honeymoon occupied. And I had to wonder, was she horrified to have a couple of guys in here? Gay guys? Was she thinking, "I hope they don't get AIDS on my sheets?"

Well, I was thinking similar thoughts. I was thinking, "That bitch better not have any dolls in here. Because if I find one, I'm taking the head and leaving the stalk behind."

Which gave me an idea, so I said to Dennis, "Imagine if we went through the house tonight and removed all the heads."

And Dennis said, "Or took just the pants off the dolls, so they were all naked from the waist down."

Surely, someone had done this before us?

It's just inconceivable to me that such a doll-infested inn could remain free of such hateful pranks. Certainly, some guest before us had contemplated removing all the heads and placing them on sticks, lining the walkway up to the house? I cannot be the only person to be so tempted.

"Well, well, well," Dennis said, and I turned.

He was crouched down next to the bed, rummaging through a stack of journals. "What are those?" I asked.

"These are like guest books. I guess she just leaves them here and people write notes in them. That's what the pens here are for."

He was paging through one of the books and read, "'What a beautiful room. And such fine service. Our honeymoon was an enchanting memory which we shall soon never forget.'"

"Oh my God," I said. Suddenly, this was my favorite room in all the world.

Dennis was laughing. "Okay, okay, hold on. Listen to this one. 'Thank you so much for making our special vacation very special.'"

Dennis sat down in the chair with the journal and began to really read it, as one might read *The New York Times*. Page by page. Laughing.

I unpacked my essentials: pain killers, Nicorette nicotine gum, my computer. The truth is, I wouldn't be able to relax in the room until I was medicated, on my back, chewing gum, and online.

I was relieved—almost high—to discover that being on an island in no way interfered with my ability to check e-mail. Had I been unable to check e-mail, I would have suffered through the vacation. I'd told Dennis as much in the car, on the way up.

"But what if I can't log on?" I whined.

"You'll be able to log on, don't you worry."

"But what if I can't?"

"You will."

"But if I can't?"

And finally, Dennis had been forced to promise that if I couldn't log on, we would go right back on the ferry and then drive into Boston and stay at a major hotel. Which appealed to me, so in a way, I was hoping not to be able to log on.

As I wrote to my friend Russell in Manhattan, Dennis continued to read from the journals. Then he suggested, "Maybe we should write something."

I turned away from my laptop to face him. "Like what?"

He said, "You know, like well, we could say 'She watched us. We saw her outside. I think that's weird.'"

I said, "I have a pen right here in my bag."

But could we stop at just one message?

Could we not also write, "There's something about the dolls. One of them is different. It's hard to explain. The one in the living room, near the fireplace. She had blue eyes when we checked in, but now both her eyes are missing."

And if we wrote that, why not then write, in different colored ink, "I'm not sure, but I think I saw the innkeeper's husband masturbating in the woods. Like I say, I can't be sure. But my husband and I are packing the car and leaving. It's 2:37 A.M. I hope the person reading this is okay."

We spent the next afternoon driving around the island, making ourselves sick with real estate envy. And not just for the thirty-million-dollar waterfront homes (circa 1790), but the modest inland shacks one could pick up for an easy million.

This is the most pristine New England geography you can possibly imagine. And then, it's an island. For someone like me, somebody who has large vacant holes where character should be, the island filled me with profound need. But I was smart enough to understand that unless I, too, recorded a song that someday became a catsup jingle, it was unlikely I'd ever be able to afford living here.

But that evening, things changed, when the possibility of a lawsuit arose.

We were having dinner at the Harbor House restaurant, located in one of the large hotels on the harbor. A sumptuous luxury hotel I longed to stay in the moment we saw it.

"Sorry," Dennis said. "I didn't know about this place."

"I love our inn," I lied.

We were seated in a booth.

Probably because we were there in the off season, the restaurant was empty. Which I actually liked. I was able to enjoy the clean interior design without being distracted by the celebrities and political leaders that surely filled the place in summer.

We both ordered prime rib and clam chowder.

As I bit down on a potato in the chowder, a large cracking sound filled the empty room.

It was the sound, more than the sensation in my mouth, that horrified me.

I spit a mouthful of potato and tooth chunks into the palm of my hand. "Oh, no," I said.

Dennis, who has perfect teeth, was aghast.

I looked at the mess in my hand and there, among the half-chewed square of potato, the sprig of rosemary, the other fresh herbs, was the pearlescent cusp of my rear molar. Outside of my mouth, it was a surprisingly beautiful thing. In fact, I imagined that an entire necklace of teeth, in the abstract, would be quite lovely.

But since this was *my* tooth, suddenly outside of *my* mouth, my appreciation of the tooth's aesthetics was replaced by a more primal feeling of something at once being terribly, terribly wrong.

I said, "Oh, no."

Dennis said, "*Oh*, are you okay? Does it hurt?"

I told him I didn't know if it hurt, which was the truth. The shock of suddenly seeing the better portion of the molar I have had since forever out of context and in my hand, removed any possible pain. And suddenly, I understood exactly how women trapped beneath burning SUVs can only ask, "Is my purse still on the seat?" Because in a condition of extreme bodily trauma, the pain center shuts off. Praise Jesus.

I said, "I need to go look at this in the bathroom," and stood to excuse myself. Then I grabbed a knife, one of the wide flashy steak knives. "I'll use this as a mirror to see back there."

Dennis looked at the eight-inch blade. "Be careful with that. In fact, I don't think you should be sticking that in your mouth at all."

"It's okay," I told him. "I've done this sort of thing before."

In the bathroom, I angled the knife in such a way to reveal my tooth, minus half. It was a clean break. A shear. But it was right down to the gum line.

And now it was starting to hurt.

I returned to the table to see the manager standing there, speaking with Dennis. Just then, our meals arrived, the waitress having to deliver the plates to the table by stepping around the manager.

I explained, "So I bit down, and there was a big chunk of clam shell in the chowder. And it broke my tooth out. See?" I showed him the tooth, which he looked at, before looking away.

I slid into the booth and found I was trembling. But from rehab years before, I'd learned to look at my emotions in the abstract, to turn them over like coins in my hand and explore them. I was trembling because I was afraid, this was true. I was traumatized from losing my tooth, this was true. I was afraid because it was hard not to imagine that a ghoulishly invasive dental procedure would be required to fix the tooth, this was true.

What was also true was that as sure as I was sitting in that booth clutching my tooth, I could see myself on the witness stand, bawling in front of a jury of my peers.

"I am a public figure. An author," I would cry. "My face often appears in magazines. Young kids look up to me," I might lie, under oath. "This restaurant has destroyed my appearance."

I saw an out-of-court settlement for four point five million dollars. I saw myself waiting ten days for the check to clear and then immediately phoning somebody at a local real estate office. "I'm looking for something in the hills, offering dramatic water views of lobster pots and surrounding island."

I saw myself saying, "Mortgage broker? Oh no. This will be a cash purchase." Then leaning in and whispering, "You see, I received a large medical settlement."

Nothing impresses a person more—not fame, not an Ivy League education—than a large cash settlement, originating from a medical crisis.

If truth be known, I was sitting in that booth trembling from excitement over the possibility of owning one of the many amazing homes on this island. For this? I would happily spit all my broken teeth into a steel pail and walk around the rest of my life smiling like a crazy person and gumming steamed apples.

However, the manager appeared less concerned than one might expect from a future defendant. "I'm really sorry about that," he said. Then he left the table and returned a moment later with some paperwork. "We just need you to fill these out."

These were accident report forms. With "Accident Report" printed right at the top. As though accidents were so common in this restaurant as to warrant a graphic design firm to specially create these forms for the hotel.

A space was provided to describe the incident, so I set about writing down the details.

While consuming a bowl of clam chowder on or about 7:38 P.M. on Saturday, December 13, 2003, while seated at table seven at the subject es-

tablishment, I bit into an unskinned, quartered Idaho potato whereupon my left rear molar encountered a foreign object. Upon contact with the foreign object (which by the gross negligence of some undocumented fry cook had been included in the chowder), the above referenced molar shattered. Excruciating and debilitating pain was the direct result of the damage caused by breakage of molar. Upon inspection of the affected tooth in the men's room of the subject establishment, it was revealed that over one half of the above referenced tooth had been dislodged by the debris in the clam chowder, advertised on the menu as "fresh, homemade." Despite the physical and emotional pain that I am currently experiencing, I am as a conscientious citizen completing this obligatory form, which has been provided by the proprietors of the subject establishment. It is approximately 8:21 P.M. on Saturday, December 13, 2003, and I am on an unfamiliar island in the Atlantic Ocean. It is my hope that I may find a local dentist who can repair the decimated tooth structure, but at this late hour, it is highly likely that I will locate no such dentist and will instead endure considerable physical pain throughout the remainder of the evening (and, more likely than not, for the remainder of my vacation). Moreover, as my vacation was intended to be an opportunity to reconnect with my traveling companion, the fact that I am experiencing excruciating pain and may very well be unable to effectively use my mouth for any function other than drinking clear liquids for the duration of my vacation, may result in a loss of consortium. Clearly, long-term emotional distress is likely to result from this ordeal.

I worded the paragraph carefully, as I imagined it would at some future point in time be excerpted on CNN and dissected by a number of legal panelists.

The manager claimed the form and Dennis tucked into his meal. "The beef is excellent," he said.

Naturally, I was too distraught to eat. Would four million get a person a waterfront house in move-in condition? Or would you need to hire an architect and then gut the bathrooms and kitchen before renovating? And if so, how much would all of this cost? Would four million not even be enough for a residence in the first place? And wasn't four million the *least* amount of cash I could expect from such a devastating physical injury in a restaurant? Certainly, no court in the country would award me less, right?

I looked around the dining room. What would I give to own such a hotel? Not paralysis, certainly. But I might trade a limb. Definitely a foot. I've never understood the point of toes, so I would clearly trade all of these. A tooth was totally worth a house.

The thing is, I'd already blown my big lawsuit opportunity once. And I wasn't about to do it again.

Years before, I'd accepted a job at an advertising agency on Fifth Avenue. I'd been living in Chicago at the time and when I got the job back in New York, I spent a weekend with a broker, searching for apartments. I found one in the East Village, a studio on the third floor of a walk-up building. At the time, it cost twelve hundred dollars a month, which was one third of my pay. I'd read somewhere that the average New Yorker spends over half their income on rent or mortgage, so it seemed like a bargain.

But the best part of the place was that I could now walk to work. It was a fifteen-minute walk, with at least a dozen coffee bars on the way.

On my first day, I was walking west along Twelfth Street when I was hit in the head by a two-by-four and knocked to the sidewalk.

I was stunned by this event. Stunned, and also embarrassed to be flat on the sidewalk. So I stood immediately and saw that the wood had fallen from scaffolding attached to the building. The building itself was being renovated.

I saw this as a bad omen, but continued walking to work nonetheless. When I got to my office, I walked into the men's room and looked in the mirror. There, I saw an actual depression in my flesh in the shape of the wood.

At the time, I saw this as funny. Not as certain retirement.

It was years after the fact when I told my lawyer friend Carlos about it.

"If you had sued, you'd have won that building," he told me. "You'd have won enough money to live well for the rest of your life."

Hearing this hurt me far more than the wood had.

I'd missed my one big chance, certainly. After all, how many times can one person legitimately claim medical damages?

But here I was again, on vacation and damaged!

At the end of the meal, I was surprised to see a check delivered. "That's tacky," I said to Dennis. "They absolutely should not have charged us for the meal."

He said, "But we ate it. I mean, I did."

"Yes," I said, explaining the missed point to him, "but it's the principle of the thing. Their food has ruined my mouth. It should therefore be free. That's just the very least they should have done."

Mentally, as punishment, I added an additional two hundred thousand dollars to my claim.

The following morning, I suffered through a dawn breakfast. Dennis ate, and when he was finished with his, I slid my plate over to his side and he started working on that.

The innkeeper stepped into the room and stood at our table. "Did you have a nice night?" she asked.

Dennis explained what happened and asked her if she knew of a local dentist who might repair my tooth. She excused herself and made some calls, then returned with a name. "My regular dentist is away in Anguilla," she said. And I thought, of course he is, billionaire island scumbag. "But this doctor is supposed to be excellent."

She offered to call and make an appointment and I thanked her. I was as grateful that she would make this effort as I was that she would leave the table so we could talk about her.

"So how is it?" I asked.

"This is great. I wish you could have some."

"Yeah, me too," I said. I was glum.

Dennis felt terrible, I suddenly saw. The expression on his face, I had misread as hunger. Instead, it was failure. "This whole vacation is starting off to be one big mistake and it's all my fault," he said. "First, the awful, creepy doll inn. And then the tooth. I'm sorry."

At moments like this, I wish I could somehow open a door and have him step inside my head so that he could know how fully I adore him. After all these years with him, my feelings only become stronger every morning, when I look at him. I watch him pee sometimes and I actually sigh with joy because I won him, somehow.

Happily, GLEEFULLY, would I live in dire poverty with him, if it meant we got to live to each be one hundred years old. The next morning, a tree could fall on the top of our cardboard box and crush us both to death at the same instant. *Bliss.*

I said, "You did such a good job with this vacation. It's an adventure. You know me. You know how much I love an adventure. I don't need that many teeth. I usually only eat soft things anyway!"

He did sort of smirk at this because he recognized the truth of what I said. What does a person who swallows cream Napoleons nearly whole need with a full set of teeth anyway?

✧　✧　✧

The dentist's office was located on a commercial strip in the center of the island. And while it was a commercial strip, it was still beautiful. I wouldn't have turned my nose up at a raised ranch next to the supermarket.

He was a calm, blond man who had the look of somebody who learned to surf before he walked. And his office was impressive: sparkling new equipment and comfortable, orthopedic chairs. This was nothing like any dentist's office I'd ever visited in Manhattan. This man made my dentist seem like an angry butcher with a drill.

Unfortunately, after inspecting my mouth he informed me that there was nothing he could do. "This will need a crown, and that'll take a week or more. So you'll have to have this fixed back home."

But he reassured me that the tooth itself was stable and wouldn't fall out. And by this point, there wasn't so much actual pain, but only phantom pain. Pain I caused by imagining it to be there. So it seemed I'd be okay.

That evening, we climbed into the hot tub. One of the selling points of our room was that it came equipped with a hot tub. The hot water soothed my back, which hurts constantly. And Dennis enjoyed just relaxing with a glass of red wine.

Vacation, it seemed, had taken a turn for the better.

And for the remainder of the week, this trend continued. As we walked through the different towns, browsing in the quaint stores, I was able to eat certain foods—French fries, deep-fried fish, ice cream. A diet I hardly saw as a compromise.

We returned to New York and I saw my dentist, who was able to repair my tooth using silver. The dental bill was two hundred dollars, which didn't seem like an amount that would justify a four-million-dollar settlement from the restaurant.

There would be no beachfront house for us. No gingerbread Victorian with a carriage house in the back. No streamlined contemporary with expansive ocean views.

It took me a full week to move through my disappointment. And to help speed things along, Dennis indulged me with some of my favorite foods. One night, he even made tater tots.

Scrambled eggs, bacon, and tater tots, eaten in bed, while watching my favorite real estate show on television was a sure way to put me in a great mood.

But when I bit down on a tater tot, a chunk of tooth came out.

A chunk from a different tooth.

I said, "What the FUCK?"

This time, the tooth was near the front of my mouth. And instead of half, almost all of the tooth broke away.

By biting into a *tater tot.*

Now, I understood what was happening to me. My teeth were breaking apart in my head. Surely, I surmised, Nicorette was the cause of this. Surely, all my gum chewing had dissolved my teeth.

This would be my fantasy lawsuit.

This wouldn't be any four-million-dollar settlement. I'd own all of fucking GlaxoSmithKline for this level of carnage.

In a panic, I left a message on my dentist's answering machine. "They're all falling out. They're just breaking, one after the other. I could spit them out like corn." His office called the following morning and I was able to see him at noon.

"On a tater tot?" he snickered.

And there was no way to remain dignified.

I said, "Never you mind my culinary habits. Why? Why are my teeth crumbling in my mouth like this?"

After exploring my mouth and taking some X rays, he put a

hand on my shoulder and said, "The tooth that broke had been filled a long time ago. It was going to break any day. So this broken tooth is unrelated to the other broken tooth. It's just sort of a freak coincidence."

While I didn't appreciate his use of the word "freak," I was relieved because this seemed to imply an end to the tooth breaking. But I was also disturbed. Because all of this mouth nonsense had begun because of a simple vacation. My primitively wired brain now connected *vacation* with *severe oral trauma*.

Dennis would, from now on, have a hell of a time getting me to leave my chair. And suddenly, I felt bad.

I got *him*. And he gets stuck with *me*. How is this fair?

Of course, it's not. Which is why we'll be going to an island next year, somewhere exotic and impossibly blue, with silky sand. And then Europe. All of it, like a gulp.

We'll take in the world. Even if I have to gum it down.

GWF Seeks SAME

My friend, Christy, was a pretty, tall, blond lesbian who hated the word *lesbian*. "It sounds so gross. *Les*bian," she said, stretching the name out, emphasizing the "z" sound of the word. "It sounds like some kind of extra female part, you know? Labia, lesbian. Like, *her lesbian is infected and she has to go on heavy antibiotics*."

So Christy refused to call herself a lesbian and instead described herself this way: "I'm just a girl who likes other girls."

Then *New York* magazine ran an article about pretty lesbians like Christy who wore makeup, feminine clothes, and high-heeled shoes. Christy called me the day the issue hit the newsstands. "Hey, guess what?" she said.

"What?" I said.

"I'm a *lipstick* lesbian," she said. "It says so right here in *New York* magazine." Christy was thrilled to finally have her very own label. "Lipstick lesbian, God. Doesn't that *lipstick* word make all the difference?"

In a way, I knew what she meant. Because for many people, the word lesbian conjures an image of a manly woman dressed in dungarees with short hair, a firm handshake, and some hair on her upper lip.

"Those creatures repulse me," Christy said of this kind of lesbian. "And I don't ever want somebody to associate *me* with *them*, just because of that damn L word."

But when you modified the word lesbian with lipstick, an entirely new image came to mind. And it was an image that pretty Christy could relate to.

"I had no idea there were so many other women like me, who have Ann Taylor credit cards and everything. So if there are enough of them to write a cover story in a magazine, why can't I ever find one?"

Christy had been single for the ten years I'd known her. She'd dated many women, but these relationships lasted only a few months. And breaking up was always complicated because even after a few months, the two women often already lived together.

"What does a lesbian bring on a second date?" Christy was fond of saying. "A moving van."

I laughed at her pitiful joke, not because it was funny but because it seemed to be so true.

"You have it so easy," she said. "Gay guys can sniff each other out. You have this weird look you give each other on the sidewalk and then you turn around and talk to each other. Or you meet at the gym. Or you go to bars."

This was all true. I'd met a shrink on the street just by looking at him.

"But with gay women, it's different. Because women always check each other out. And you can't ever tell, is she looking at me because she's attracted to me? Or because she likes my necklace? And you can forget bars. All we have is the Clit Club."

The Clit Club was a bar in the meatpacking district of New York. This, together with Crazy Nanny's, comprised New York's nightlife for lesbians. While gay guys had about three hundred bars to choose from.

"And then imagine you aren't just some truck-driving bull dyke. You're pretty, like me." She smiled playfully and batted her long eyelashes. "It's just awful. You have no idea."

I'd never actually thought about the perils of lesbian dating before and now it suddenly made sense why Christy had always been single. It did seem more difficult for a woman to meet another woman, especially if you wanted a woman who had her eyebrows waxed. Not to mention her sideburns.

I suggested that Christy stop relying so much on fate and chance encounters and take her destiny into her own hands. "Why don't you place a personal ad?" I said. "That way, you can write down exactly what you want."

But Christy was afraid of personal ads. "I think they're creepy," she told me. We were sitting at a Mexican restaurant in Murray Hill, not far from her studio apartment in Tudor City. We were getting increasingly drunk on beers. And it wasn't yet three in the afternoon. "Only somebody desperate would reply to a personal ad," she said.

"But that's not true at all," I told her. "It's just another way to meet somebody. It's no big deal at all. And anyway, how would you know? You've never even tried. That's the thing about you," I said. "You're meek. You're the opposite of somebody prone to excess, like me. You're prone to invisibility. Even if another lipstick lesbian did pass you on the street, she probably wouldn't even see you."

It was a harsh thing to say but the beers had made me thoughtlessly honest. The truth was, Christy was afraid. Even to take a small, safe chance. So I pushed her more. "Just write an ad. If you really freak out, don't even read the replies. Throw them away. Besides, nobody will see your picture. They have to send you theirs first."

She looked into her beer mug and thought about this. "So, you know? You're absolutely right. You're right about it all." So we decided to write an ad, right then and there. Christy reached into her shoulder bag and removed a pen, along with a pad of note paper. "Don't you wish you were straight and had a wife?" she said as she did this. "Because she'd always have a bag with her and you'd always have a pad and pens and tissues and aspirin."

It was true. That was one thing I envied about straight guys. Their girlfriends and wives came equipped with purses.

"Okay," she said, uncapping her silver Cartier pen. "Let's see." And she began writing at the top of a clean sheet of paper.

Lipstick Lesbian seeks Little Black Dress of a girl for serious relationship and frivolous shopping.

"What do you think of that for a headline?" she asked.

"With you, shouldn't it be the other way around? Frivolous relationship and serious shopping?"

"Oh, stop," she said. "I'm very deep. But I have a playful, shopping side, too. I just want an investment banker. Or a CEO. A business executive. Or Jodie Foster."

We ordered yet another round of beers and I suggested that Christy make a list of everything she wanted in a woman. "Since you seem so specific, maybe you ought to get it all down on paper. Start with that. With the qualities she absolutely has to have."

So Christy set about making a list, which is something she was very good at. As a stock analyst, Christy was very comfortable with data and there was nothing she enjoyed more than to organize it. Her apartment was stuffed with lists. Shopping lists, to-do lists. Even old lists from Academy Award shows of years past, with her check marks next to the names of the stars she expected to win.

By sunset, Christy had filled ten pages with qualities that her potential mate would need to possess.

"Now I just need to edit this down to a simple paragraph," she said. She fanned the ten pages out on the table in front of her and studied them. "It's hopeless. I really want *everything* I asked for in here. How will I know what to cut?"

"That's the thing about you, Christy," I said. "Always thinking first of the compromise. For once, tell me, why does there even need to *be* a compromise? Just type it up and run the whole thing as an ad."

She was horrified. She just stared at me as though I had suggested she shave her head and put a bull's ring through her nose. "But that would be so long. It would take pages and pages. It would cost thousands of dollars."

I took a final gulp of beer and said, "So?" I wiped my mouth across the back of my hand and smiled at her.

And she crinkled her eyes up, leaned forward, and said, "But that's crazy."

And I told her, "For once in your life, Christy, stand out."

Two weeks later, I picked up a copy of *New York* magazine and turned to the back, where they run personals.

Right away, I saw Christy's ad. It stood out from the others, all right. I felt pretty confident that nobody would miss it.

Christy's ad was the first ad on the page and it began on the upper left hand corner. The headline was ordinary enough: Attractive Lipstick Lesbian Seeks Same.

What set the ad apart from the others was that there were no others. Christy's ad was so long, it extended for all six columns, filling the entire page of the magazine.

In it, Christy conjured her ideal woman. "Somebody who is comfortable in a pair of faded jeans, walking along the beach. But someone who also likes to dress up in Armani and enjoy dinner out at a fine restaurant. You are a woman who has a successful career that you love, but you don't work so much that you have no room left over for a serious relationship. You might be a banker or a lawyer, a doctor or a business owner. You don't smoke or do drugs or drink to excess."

Christy even suggested that her future mate might ". . . enjoy the color blue as much as I do. And if you're like me, you probably don't care for green at all, which I consider to be blue poisoned by yellow."

Then there was this: "Hopefully, you have a strong, defined chin or are at least willing to have a weaker chin surgically corrected. In other words, I'm looking for a woman who wants to be the best she can be, and is honest in her self-appraisal and willing to do what it takes to improve areas that need it. Spirituality is good, too."

And suddenly, I felt guilty and embarrassed for her. Instead of coming across like a confident woman who knew exactly what she wanted, as I had expected, Christy would seem like a control freak who wouldn't let so much as a freckle pass by her without scrutiny and judgment. "Freckles are okay, but not ideal. A few freckles sprinkled across the bridge of the nose are one thing, but please, no full-face freckles. Which means, probably, no redheads."

Again and again, Christy emphasized that she didn't want to hear from any woman who might be considered "butch." She wrote, "You should be strong, confident, and self-assured. But in no way should you be considered masculine. Think: Sigourney Weaver not Chastity Bono. Yes, you wear jeans. But are they a pretty size four? Or a solid ten? And if they're Wrangler's, this ad probably isn't for you."

She closed with a request for a photograph "not taken by a photographer. Just an ordinary picture. So I can see what you truly look like, without the aid of professional lighting."

Not only was the ad mortifyingly specific in what was and was not acceptable; not only was it horrifically shallow; not only was it the entire page—but it was my idea. Her other friends would tease her, make her see how truly abhorrent it was, and then she'd blame me and make me pay the three thousand dollars the ad had cost.

Christy called an hour later. "I'm not sure this was such a good idea. Have you seen it yet?"

I decided to remain upbeat and optimistic. Three thousand dollars would buy a lot of drinks. "Yeah, I saw it. It's fantastic. It's like modern art, right there in a magazine."

"Yeah, but I don't want modern art. I want a girlfriend."

"Don't be so wary," I told her. "Let's just wait and see what happens."

The following week, Christy called me at my office. I was in the middle of a new business pitch, and I had to be called out of a horrid brainstorming session to take her call.

She was nearly in tears. "It's been a week and I haven't received anything in the mail from my ad. Nobody answered it. I wasted three thousand dollars and I'm going to be a spinster."

I reminded her that only a few days had passed. "You have to give people time. First, they have to read the ad, and that could easily take a couple of days," I said. "And then they need to think about their reply, write it out, write it again. Go hunt for a good picture of themselves. And then stick it all in an envelope and mail it to the magazine. Then the magazine has to sort through all the mail and forward it on to you. I wouldn't be surprised if it takes three or four weeks, honestly."

"God, why can't you be a girl," she whined. "You're so logical and level-headed. And you've got a great advertising career. I want a girl version of you."

Christy had never seen my apartment. We'd known each other for nearly ten years and she'd never seen the inside of my apartment, which was filled with alcohol bottles, dirty clothes, and empty Chinese food containers. "Oh, yeah. I'm a catch," I said.

"You are!" she said. "And why am I the only one looking for love? You should place an ad, too," she said.

"Nah, I don't have time," I said. I didn't tell her that I *did* place ads. All the time. I went on AOL and wrote personal ads when I was drunk. Sometimes I was an Asian businessman looking for a wife. Sometimes I was a black girl looking for a white man. And sometimes I was a gay guy who wanted to meet other gay guys interested in becoming straight. I placed ads as a postoperative transsexual seeking marriage. And as somebody who was a dwarf, looking for somebody of normal height. Writing personal ads was my drunk fun. It was the solitary, intoxicated equivalent of throwing eggs through the open window of a passing car on the freeway.

Christy's drought ended in the middle of the following week when a large parcel arrived from the magazine. Christy called and said, "You have to come over to my apartment and help me go through these replies. It's like Christmas!"

Because she lived only a few blocks west, it took me five minutes to get to her place. We sat cross-legged on the floor drinking wine and reading the letters.

"Oh, God. Look at this. *Look at this*," she said, furious, clutching a photograph in her hands. She whipped it around for me to see.

The picture was of an attractive woman standing on a breakwater. The rocky shore made me think the picture had been taken on the East Coast—Martha's Vineyard, Cape Cod maybe. The woman in the picture was pretty and she was smiling. "Yeah, so?"

Christy scowled. "I specifically said no redheads."

The woman in the photograph had red hair. Her face was freckled. "Oh, come on," I said. "You can't be that way. She's beautiful, look at her. You'd never in a million years guess she was a carpet-muncher."

Christy sucked in air through her teeth. "Don't *say* that, that's disgusting. Ick, don't ever call it *that*."

"Well, you're being ridiculous. What does her letter say? Here, give it to me." I reached for the letter, grabbing it out of her fingers.

I scanned the first paragraph and said, "She sounds nice. She works as a nurse. That's perfect for you. You need a nurse because you're always worried about having cancer or a brain tumor."

"Exactly why I *don't* need a nurse," she corrected. "A nurse will only make me worse. Because they know about all sorts of diseases I haven't even heard of. Plus, hospitals are filthy. I don't want my girlfriend bringing home all those sick people germs. I can't imagine being touched with those awful fungus-fingers. And besides, nurses get paid in dirt. I don't want to be the one who always has to pay for dinner, who always has to front the money for the airline tickets."

At this rate, Christy would end up in Lesbian Limbo: on the futon sofa alone with a tub of Hood ice cream and surrounded by rescued cats in various stages of feline leukemia. A nightly Sigourney Weaver movie would be followed by something starring Jodie Foster. Probably *The Accused*, because Jodie drinks and dances. For mysterious reasons, her testosterone level would soar. I said, "You are being crazy picky. Christy, she's pretty. And she's a nurse. Do you know how hard nursing school is? It's like medical school. So she's obviously smart. And she looks fantastic with red hair. Red hair is great. It's *rare*, and therefore superior. You need to get over some of these weird phobias of yours."

"*No*," Christy said. "I've got over a hundred replies here. I get to be choosy at first. If I get desperate, I can always fall back on one of the redheads. Here, give me that," she said, snatching the letter and picture out of my hand and placing them in front of her on the floor, off to the side. "We'll make three piles. A no pile, a maybe pile, a yes pile."

Into the yes pile, Christy placed a letter and photo from a woman who lived on the Upper West Side. I took one look at the picture and would have placed her right at the bottom of "no." She was a dark-haired, sneering woman. Her face was painfully angular and she had deep little lines between her eyebrows from constant frowning. Thin, tight lips were pressed into what she must have considered a smile. I could easily imagine her saying, "A funny thing happened when I had my dog put down the other day." In her letter she said she was a divorce attorney and that she "passionately loved" her job. I think it's great to love what you do for a living. But when your career involves tearing apart marriages, maybe "love" isn't the word you should use to describe it?

"No, she's good," Christy insisted. "Because look," she said, pointing with her long, deep red fingernail to the woman's face. "See how she has sort of a bump in her nose?"

I picked up the picture and studied it hard. As somebody who had worked in advertising for so many years, I was accustomed to scrutinizing visual images, searching for imperfections. I didn't see the bump she was talking about. "Where?"

"Right here," Christy said, sliding her fingernail a millimeter to the right.

And yeah, I could kind of see what might have been a bump. Maybe. "Okay, I guess I see the bump. So what are you saying?"

"Well," Christy said, "I call that a Jew nose if ever there was one. And my friend Ann in Chicago said that Jews make the best girl-friends because they are very loyal and they like to shop. They're supposed to be fun is what I've heard."

Then she lowered her voice, as though there were other people in the room, and she asked me, "Have you heard that, too? Is it the same with boys? Are the Jews good as boyfriends?"

I said, "You know what? You are veering dangerously close to being a dumb blonde."

She just smiled. "Better than being a diesel dyke," she said, turning her red lips into a smile.

All together, we ended up with five people in the yes pile, nine in the maybe, and the rest were no's.

As I was standing up to leave I asked her, "So what do you do now?"

And she said, "Well, I'll start calling them. I need to hear their voices on the phone. And then if I like what I hear, we'll meet."

It never occurred to Christy that any of the women might not like *her*.

Another envelope with yet more responses arrived the following week. And by this time Christy had eliminated all but one of the previous batch of women. "And she sounds really good," Christy said of the final remaining contestant.

"Which one is she?" I asked.

"The one you didn't like. The one you said looked like a bitch. You know, the Jew."

Christy made arrangements to meet the woman in person at a bar on the Upper West Side, near the woman's apartment.

"I won't make the dinner mistake again," she told me. "The night before last I had dinner with this woman who *sounded* really good. Her letter was great, her picture was great, we spoke on the phone. And she told me the most amazingly sad story about her childhood and I ended up being on the phone with her for like four hours." She paused, as though she was embarrassed to tell me something. "At one point, I even cried. I mean, it was a very sad childhood."

"Yeah?" I said.

"Well, so then I agreed to meet her for dinner down in Tribeca.

And I'm sitting at the bar waiting for her to show up. I'd only seen the one little picture of her but she was very pretty. And in walks this *creature*. I'm not kidding. She was this total bull dyke monster from hell with short, spiky, awful hair and a mustache and jeans and a man's shirt and boots. It was horrifying. She came right up to me at the bar and sat down."

I tried to repress my smile.

"It's not funny. It was one of the most mortifying experiences of my life. Because everybody was looking at us. Then this thing had the nerve to tell me that she had cut her hair and apologized for not telling me. God, I wanted to say, and you changed your sex without telling me, too. So anyway, I couldn't just leave, so I had to wait for the table, then sit down and have dinner with her. And watch her chew her steak like some big cow with ten stomachs. So no more dinners, ever. Only drinks."

I said I thought that was a wise plan.

"Yeah, so tonight it's just drinks. If it's great, terrific. We can have dinner. And if it's awful, I only have to sit through one drink and then I'm free."

As far as I was concerned, Drinks Only was such a basic concept of personal ad dating. Because people are always very different in person than they are on the page, on-screen, or on the phone.

Once, I answered a guy's ad. He was an anesthesiologist and really handsome, too. We met for drinks and got along. So we decided to stay for dinner. Then about halfway through he whispered, "Hey, I got something I want to show you." I waited for him to show me whatever it was, but he said, "No, under the table. Look under the table. I don't want to pull it out."

I looked under the table, as casually and normally as possible, and he was holding a bottle of Johnson's Baby Oil.

"I was thinking after dinner, we could, *you know*."

"No," I said. "I don't know. Why are you carrying around baby oil?"

"I'm really into it, man," he said. "I love the smell, I love how it feels. I was thinking after dinner, we could go back to my house and, you know, be babies."

Which just goes to show you: even if you follow the Drinks Only rule, you can still get screwed.

"Well, good luck on your date tonight. I hope it goes well."

"Thanks," Christy said. "I'll call you."

And she did call, just a few hours later. She was manic with excitement. "Oh my God, it's her," she said. "It's totally her. I'm sure of it."

"Her who? What are you talking about?"

"I'm talking about, I met the woman I'm going to spend the rest of my life with, *that* her."

Apparently, they'd had a marvelous time. Sitting at the bar and saying terrible things about every other woman in it. Then talking about their career ambitions, movies they both didn't like, and, of course, how awful lesbians are, in general.

A few times, though, the date kicked Christy in the shins. "I said something, and I guess I said it too loud. So she sort of kicked me and said, not so loud. So that was a little weird."

I said, "Yeah, that's more than a little weird. That's pretty screwed up, don't you think?"

But Christy was determined to let it slide. "It's no big deal. I mean, I probably was talking really loud. You know me. I get excited."

But kicking somebody? To get them to lower their voice?

"I will say, though," Christy finally admitted, "that Melissa's a bit of a cunt. That's her name, Melissa. She's cold, is what most people would say. But I love cold. People say Jodie Foster is cold, and God,

I would love to be her girlfriend if she would have me." It was interesting to me, this universal worship of Jodie Foster among lesbians.

Then Christy said, "I need to do something special. Send flowers. Like people used to do. It was just such a perfect date, I want her to remember me."

I suggested that she instead arrange another date for the following week.

"Next week! Are you kidding me? I want to be living together next week," she said, only half-joking.

Then I got an idea. "Why don't you send her some roses?"

"Oh my God, that's a brilliant idea," Christy said. "That's so romantic and old-fashioned. I was thinking of sending her an orchid, but roses are much better, more old-fashioned. Oh, I bet she'd just love that."

I said, "Yeah, but not just roses. Send a lot of roses. I mean, if you *really* feel strongly about her, you should send, like, a dozen dozen roses."

"What do you mean, a dozen dozen?"

"I mean, send her *twelve* dozen roses."

"Send her a hundred and forty-four roses?" Christy said, a worried edge to her voice.

"Yeah," I said. "It'll be great. I mean, maybe she's received roses after a date or on her birthday. But not a dozen dozen roses. You can be sure nobody has ever made *that* kind of gesture before. Come on, little invisible ghost girl, be dramatic for once. You're crazy about her, right? So let her know in a big, dramatic way."

Christy said, "I don't know about that. That seems sort of weird to me. Like, maybe it's just too much."

I pressured her further. "Look, you've already spent three thousand dollars. Why blow it now? This will just cost a few hundred dollars more. Go ahead. Be bold."

She said she'd think it over.

✧ ✧ ✧

Christy called me the next evening, sobbing. "I think I fucked up," she said.

"What do you mean, you fucked up? What happened? What did you do?" I asked.

"Well, I did what you said. I sent a dozen dozen roses. All white. I ordered them last night when we hung up and they were delivered late this afternoon. And then Melissa called me really upset. She called it an 'excessive gesture' and then she said she was so upset she even called her shrink. And her shrink told her not to have any more contact with me because I was sick." Here, she sobbed harder. "She said they arrived in a cloud of tissue paper and that the part-ners in the law office all came to see them and she had to lie and say she'd won them."

I thought, *Oops*. "Why don't you call her and apologize?" I sug-gested. "Tell her you had a really great time and that you just got carried away. Or screw it. Just tell her the truth and blame it on me."

"I can't," Christy said. "She said if I contact her again she'll file a restraining order against me."

I felt responsible for this mess. I'd made her write the scary ad. I'd made her send all those flowers. The least I could do now was point her in the right direction. "Why don't you go take a look through your no pile?" I said. "Maybe you missed somebody."

Christy sniffled. "I guess I could. But I can't stand that she thinks I'm sick. And so does her shrink. Two people I don't even know think I'm sick."

"You're not sick," I said. "You're just more romantic than most people. You need to hold out for somebody who is just as romantic as you. Go through your no pile."

"Okay," she said.

✧ ✧ ✧

Five years later, Christy and her girlfriend, Allyson, celebrated their anniversary by renting a car and driving to a small, rocky beach in Rhode Island.

It was the very same beach where Allyson had once had her photograph taken, years and years before. A photograph she then mailed away to a perfect stranger, who'd placed the longest personal ad she'd ever read.

When Allyson and Christy first started dating, I teased Christy. "Isn't she the original no? The girl with the red hair and the freckles?"

"Oh, yeah. I guess she is. But you know. You can't have everything. It just seemed like dismissing somebody because they have red hair was an excessive gesture."

I said, "Like the roses."

She turned to me and glared.

Mint Threshold

It was a low point in my career when I found myself as the sole copywriter on the Junior Mints account.

"The concern is," the account executive explained, "growth. How do we grow this business? Because our consumer research shows, people have a mint threshold. And they're just not willing to cross it." He frowned when he said this. Worry was etched on his forehead. Poverty, global warming, the threat of terrorism. I wanted to laugh. And then scream and punch my eardrums out with pens.

I hadn't been on the account for one week and already the phrase *mint threshold* was being bandied about. This was, I felt, a bad omen.

I was in the first of what would be *many* Junior Mints meetings. Far more meetings than one would expect of a product that is eaten entirely in the dark.

"Movie theaters, obviously are *very* important, consumption-wise," the client said, as though ticking off items on a list. "And . . ." But then he stopped. Having apparently reached the end of his list.

"Well, what I'm saying is that moviegoers are a primary target for us."

And I thought, You're paying a Madison Avenue advertising agency countless millions of dollars a year to tell you this? Don't you already know this?

He added hurriedly, as though just remembering, "And Halloween." He smiled. "Yeah, can't forget Halloween. That's a real big one for us. Real big."

Oh yes, I thought. Must not forget Halloween.

In fairness, the client appeared nice enough. A tall man with red hair and a pencil mustache, he had kind eyes. While not what I would call a dynamic leader, at least he wasn't bitter and outwardly hostile, the way many clients could be. He was polite. This was saying a lot.

Once, a client told me to imagine his product in a brand-new way, in order to energize the brand. "Think of it as a dick. And make people want to suck it."

The Junior Mints brand manager was a relief after that.

But still there were concerns. "So one thing does really worry us," he said.

I wondered if this was not, in fact, why he had been hired by Junior Mints in the first place. What better career for a worrier than as the marketing manager of a lackluster candy brand? "How do we deal with this mint threshold issue? Because if it truly can't be crossed, well, that would seem like big trouble and maybe our sales goals aren't realistic and need to be adjusted. Except I'm not in a position to revise those sales goals. So somehow, we have to meet them. If it's at all possible. *Somehow*, we've *got* to get people across that mint threshold."

The account executive said, "We will find a way!" He displayed a pumped energy and enthusiasm that collided with the worry and dread hovering in the air. The result was lightning in the form of "Absolutely!" and "This is going to be exciting!" comments from around the table. And, just as after a thunderstorm, there was a sense of relief, a decompression.

The Junior Mints man smiled for the first time and leaned back in his chair. He glanced down at his hands, noticed they were clenched into fists, and then stretched his fingers over the arm of the chair. He said, "Maybe I will have a little coffee, after all."

Later, in my office, I discussed the project with my art director, Ann.

"So what can we do for dusty old Junior Mints?" she asked.

"Well, I guess we could do something with the name."

"Oh yeah," she said. "That's a good idea. That's what we should do. Pretty much, that's all we *can* do."

We could take the name and visually illustrate it. Perhaps we could build a campaign around "Junior." Or "Mints." Or even just "mint." I said, "Refresh . . . mint. Know what I mean?"

"Got it," she said. "That's what we'll do. We'll do a montage spot. So, like, we'll see somebody in a convertible reach into the glove compartment and pull out a box of Junior Mints. Then we'll have a super over it that reads, 'compart . . . mint.' And then maybe we'll show somebody on a beach." She paused. "Or maybe not a beach because the chocolate melts. But maybe on a roller coaster. And they pull a box out of their pocket. Maybe a kid pulls a box out of his pocket."

And I said, "Yeah. Excite . . . mint."

"Yup," she said.

"And we'll just take it totally out of the movie theater environment, because they already own that."

Ann added, "Or maybe we could do one. Like, at the end of each spot. We could always end in a movie theatre and say . . ."

And together we said: "Entertain . . . mint."

We began laughing hysterically. We hunched over, clutching our stomachs and gasping for breath. It was as though we had been told the funniest joke in the history of the world that, for safety reasons, had not been revealed until now. We were laughing because the idea was so stupid and obvious and we had finally hit rock-bottom and were full advertising whores. "Ninety seconds," I said, finally catching my breath.

"Damn, we're fast." She blotted her eyes with a tissue.

"Let's go to a movie," I said.

"Okay," she said. And then, "What's today? Tuesday?"

"Yeah," I said.

"Okay, so then what do you think? We'll show the account people ideas on Thursday?"

"No," I said. "We'll tell them on Thursday that we're *close* but need the weekend."

"Okay, that's good. We'll show them Monday."

"Yeah. But we should have a couple of other ideas that they can kill."

She said, "Exactly."

Just then, one of the account executives came into our office. "Hey, you guys." Then he smirked. "Why are your faces red? What, do you have a suntan lamp in here or something?"

"Nothing," Ann said. "So what's going on?"

"I just spoke with the client. And he said they'd like you to tour the factory."

The pleasant, professional expressions on our faces froze in place. Touring a client's factory was akin to spending the afternoon with the parents of the world's ugliest baby and being forced to endure eight hours of home movies.

"Really?" I asked. "Because I don't know that we really need to see the manufacturing process. I think it's a pretty straightforward brief."

The account executive said, "Well, technically we don't have a strategy yet, so you have nothing to execute against. So the thinking is, we'll tour the factory tomorrow. Then we'll create an advertising strategy by Thursday. Client will sign off on Monday. And you guys will then work and have things for Wednesday."

I pointed out that this gave us two days to create the advertising.

"Yeah," he acknowledged. "I know, the timing kind of sucks."

But we all knew it didn't really matter. Because we'd start working immediately and wouldn't even glance at their strategy. We all knew that there would only be so many ways to skin this mint cat.

The Junior Mints factory was in Cambridge, just outside Boston. Home of Harvard University and M.I.T.

Our client met us at the front door of the huge building. "It's really nice that you could come. I think you'll find it very helpful."

We smiled and agreed that it would be very helpful indeed.

But once we got onto the actual factory floor, it became immediately clear that a "factory" campaign was not to be in Junior Mints' future. Sometimes, if a company has a particularly unique factory, it's interesting to show the inner workings. Like, if a car is truly handcrafted, you might want to show the craftspeople stitching the leather. Often, when all else has failed, a creative team can present a "factory campaign" to a client and it will be bought, simply because it features so much footage of the product and often many of the actual employees.

But the Junior Mints factory appeared to me to have been created in the 1940s and was, miraculously and mysteriously, still continuing to chug out the minty pellets. Gigantic machines, presses, mixers, and conveyer belts that should have malfunctioned and died decades ago continued to manufacture the delicious treats.

As the client led us through the various areas of construction, my eyes watered from the overpowering mint concentrate that permeated the air and nearly made my skin bubble into blisters.

It was mint hell.

And any moment, my eyes and ears would begin to bleed.

Nonetheless, it was mildly interesting to learn exactly how they got that minty cream into a chocolate shell-ball.

The mint part, it turned out, was not somehow injected into the chocolate, but was formed as a round white marble. A hard marble. Then the marble was placed into a mixer and sprayed with chocolate. Then these pellets were thrown into a gigantic cement mixer tumbler thing where they were polished. Enzymes in the mint marble denatured over time and made the center soft and creamy.

But if you bit into a factory-fresh Junior Mint, one fresh from the tumbler, you could actually lose a crown.

To amuse ourselves, we checked the floors for signs of rat hairs, broken teeth, fingernails. But we found nothing. The factory, although apparently ancient, was tediously spotless.

The next day, we saw two movies back to back. Then we popped into the office to check voice mail. At four, we left the office for the day.

The day after this, we drew storyboards for our concept. I also created another concept based on the aroma of mint and chocolate together. These commercials featured a woman "like Jessica Lange" speaking to the camera, talking about how she loves the aroma of mint and chocolate. She says that after she's finished a package of Junior Mints, the "fumes" that remain in the box make her hungry for more ("So she successfully crosses the mint threshold").

We created this campaign just so somebody could kill it. It was born to die for a greater cause, like Sylvia Plath.

We did nothing the rest of the week, nor Monday and Tuesday of the next. Then we presented on Wednesday and the account executive pronounced we had "nailed it."

The account team spent more time discussing why our campaign was so smart than we had spent conceiving it.

And then a few days later, we presented it to the Junior Mints client.

✧ ✧ ✧

With a campaign for Junior Mints, based on using words that end with "mint," there's not much to explain. Especially when the type used in the commercial matches, exactly, the Junior Mints logo. Hammer to head.

And yet, the client was perplexed.

In total, we took him through the storyboard six times. And each time, I read the script slower and slower until I at last felt I was giving street directions to a dog.

"So. Then. You. Will. Have. These. Words. Come. On. The. TV. Screen. When. We. See. The. Scene. Is. That. Correct?"

I looked him in the eyes and I said, "Yes."

And he said, "But. When. Will. We. See. The. Mints?"

And I said, "Within. The. Context. Of. The. Scene."

And he said, "Within. The. Context?"

And I knew I'd blown it. One should never use words like *context* when speaking to a client responsible for a product that costs less than a dollar.

After the presentation, the client stared at the boards, all fanned out on the table in front of him. He scratched his head. He pondered the meaning of a picture showing a woman reaching into the glove compartment of her car and pulling out a box of Junior Mints, the word "refresh . . . mint" printed below the picture.

I said, "It's refreshing. Because she's in a convertible. And that's refreshing because of the wind. And it's refreshing because of Junior Mints. Because of the mint. People think mint is refreshing. And then we tie it to Junior Mints by using the *mints* part of the Junior Mints name."

After a few moments of silence, where the account executives all exchanged doubtful glances, the client spoke up. "Oh!" he said. "Okay."

And just like that, he got it.

But then: a problem. As always happens.

"But would the convertible be red, like you've drawn it here?"

Ann answered this question. "It doesn't have to be. I just made it red because, well. No. It can be any color."

"Could it be white? Like the box?"

I said, "Yeah. It can be white."

I hated him now.

Then he said, "When does she bite the mint?"

Ann and I looked at each other, very quickly. Communicating through our well-honed advertising telepathy. We hadn't actually imagined that anybody would ever eat the product. In our minds, everybody in our commercial had reached their mint threshold a long, long time ago.

"She could bite the mint at the end," Ann said.

This made the account team smile. One of them chimed in. "Right at the end, for emphasis. Like an exclamation point at the end of the spot."

The client, though, wasn't buying it. "Well. Why couldn't she bite the mint at the beginning? So we get the product in there sooner?"

I remained quiet for a moment because I could not risk opening my mouth and having "Now, listen here you stupid motherfucker" come out.

"I think it's best," I said, "if each person bites the mint at the end. Because if they bite the mint before we bring on the '. . . mint' word, we lose the point. And if we bring the '. . . mint' word on too soon, before the action gets a chance to play out a little, we haven't established the concept. And I think viewers will get lost."

"That's a good point," the account person said. "I agree with that. So everybody will bite the mint at the end of the scene." He made a note on his legal pad. This note would later that day be typed by a secretary and delivered to everyone's desk with CONFERENCE RE-

PORT stamped on top. Along with CONFIDENTIAL in bright red.

The client had another idea. "Do we even need the car? Couldn't we just have the people standing somewhere? Maybe in a grocery store, in front of a display of Junior Mints? And then we could super those '. . . mint' words as they ate the mints?"

As diplomatically as possible I said, "Seeing many different people eating Junior Mints inside of a supermarket is not going to be very interesting to people."

And the client looked at me as though I had just told him that his deformed, four-eyed child was deformed and had four eyes. "Well, why not? Why wouldn't that be interesting? I think it would be very . . . motivating."

I wondered if he'd earned an MBA just so he could say the word *motivating* at this very meeting.

"Well," I said. "I think if you step outside of the Junior Mints shoes, and you then step into the shoes of the average consumer, who is home with her two children, with a meal to prepare, with career obligations in the back of her mind, with a husband, I think you'll appreciate that consumers are not waiting impatiently for the next Junior Mints commercial to come on the air. And because there is not much interest, we have to earn their interest. By entertaining them, however mildly. Which is why we have those cute little scenes. And the small bit of cleverness with the '. . . mint' words."

The client became defensive. "Well, I do think people are waiting to see some ads for Junior Mints. I disagree entirely. We don't have a presence on television. So when somebody sees the Junior Mints brand name flashed on the screen for a good fifteen seconds, you can be sure that's going to get a lot of attention. Yes. That's going to get talked about. Because people just don't expect Junior Mints to be advertising on television. They are used to encountering the product in a movie theatre. Not when they're home, relaxing and watching some television shows. Seeing Junior Mints like that, in the context of relaxing and watching some good shows, that's what will make people want to have a Junior Mint. Not seeing somebody in a convertible open up a glove compartment or seeing all this complicated typography on the screen."

It was at that moment I finally reached my mint threshold.

And thankfully, the account executives stepped forward to take over. They said the words most soothing to a client: "That's a testable proposition. We produce some test spots and put them in front of consumers. Get a handle on how consumers really feel about the advertising."

This translates to: We could make a cartoon version of the commercial and then pay people in sandwiches and cookies and diet soda to watch the cartoon and tell us if they like it or hate it, and if they like it, we can then turn the cartoon into a real commercial, and if they hate it, we can start over.

All of this would cost many, many tens of thousands of dollars and consume months of our time.

But the client nodded. Yes, the client thought, this is good. We will produce a test spot, and then study it as though it is a silver box that has arrived from space.

The client was not happy, but the client was now calm.

I was silent.

The account executive to my left passed me a note. I opened it and glanced at the text: *Never have so many worked so hard for so little.*

I wrote a note in reply, passed it. *I want to punish them.*

And in response to this she sent me a final note that defined the meeting, our lives at that moment, my career, her career, the known universe.

The note read, simply: *Debase-mint.*

Locked Out

There's probably not a connection, but when I started drinking again, my apartment wandered back into squalor. I'd cleaned it when I got home from rehab. But after my thirty-second birthday, the bottles and filth started to collect.

It's hard for people to imagine modern, urban squalor. They picture clothing lying over every surface, lots of magazines, massive piles of paper. In other words, people see something very similar to their offices at work.

But the reality was more organic. A layer of newspapers and magazines created the foundation of the room, the primary floor covering, much like wall-to-wall sisal. To this layer, two years of debris was added. And walking paths were created.

So when I showered, I often dried my feet simply by walking across the floor to my bed, allowing the water to be absorbed by the newspaper. Which caused them to stick to the floor, cementing them in place.

Because I stored my H&R Block tax documents in the oven, and kept boxes of color film, socks, and underwear in the refrigerator, I never cooked. I didn't even own a fork. Instead, I ordered in.

Rarely did I remove the food containers, still containing food. These were discarded on the floor, or left on surfaces, such as the kitchen counter or my computer desk, behind the computer. After a period of a year, the food materials in the containers hardened and shrunk.

I was also in the habit of blowing my nose on the same T-shirt. It was a tissue you could wear!

My life was simple then: go to work, come home as early as possible. Walk three blocks to the liquor store and buy two bottles of Dewar's scotch. Go to the drugstore next door and buy two packs of Marlboro Lights, two containers of white Tic Tacs, one liter of Poland Spring water.

Many times, I would buy two sandwiches for dinner. Usually sliced steak and cheese on a baguette from Dean and Deluca. If not this, something from Subway.

I rushed as I bought the sandwiches, eager to be home. I hated to be in public where I felt I was looked at, sniffed, and judged.

Once home, I filled my crusty Santa mug with scotch, lit a cigarette, and and the night began.

I always spent my evening online. I read personal ads, visited random links, looked at books on Amazon. Often, in the depths of my drunken stupor, I wrote personal ads. And would then wake the next day to find a mailbox full of replies. Of course, it would be impossible to actually date any of these people, especially since most of them thought I was an attractive transsexual in Minnesota.

On Saturdays, I often forced myself out of the apartment for an hour or two. But I made certain I returned by twelve. By doing this, I was able to begin drinking at noon, but also tell myself it was okay because I'd been out all day.

One afternoon, I was walking through the East Village. I was killing time, checking my watch and walking into various shops, intending to buy nothing.

I crossed Second Avenue and saw a bus. The bus was parked, empty. A sign taped to the rear window read, "This school bus has been searched for sleeping children."

And I thought, now what does that mean?

Like many things in our culture, it felt vaguely litigious. Placed there at the express direction of a city attorney. Certainly, there had been meetings about the sign. Conference reports. Endless e-mails. "Subject: City Bus Sleeping Children Signage Meeting Rescheduled."

It reminded me of an advertising story. When I was working on an airline account, the ad agency created a strategy based on customer service. To imply that the airline's care for their customers somehow surpassed other airlines'. But I heard a story from an art director. He told me that the airline management was nervous about this strategy because they weren't sure they could substantiate it. As an example, they relayed a story of a paraplegic woman who was left on the plane after it landed. The flight attendants failed to help her off. So she had to crawl out of her chair and use her elbows to shimmy across the floor, and then slide out the door. Airline management was worried that if the agency went ahead and created advertising based on a strategy of their customer service, somebody would reveal the paraplegic story to the press, all the advertising would have to be trashed, and they'd have to start over again, with a new strategy. Probably something price-based.

The school bus sign made me happy. And I found myself thinking of how, in so many ways, lawyers have touched our daily lives.

I've often been tempted to swallow a bottle cap. Just so I could inflict enough damage on my body to be awarded a fifty-million-dollar settlement.

As a reward for observing that there is no "do not swallow" warning on the caps.

Checking my watch, I saw that it was now eleven-thirty. Close enough.

Because I'd stocked up on alcohol and cigarettes and mints the night before, all I needed was to stop at the store on the corner of Third Avenue and Twelfth Street and get some magazines.

After doing this, I walked back to my apartment and reached in my pocket for my keys.

And here I encountered a surprise: no keys.

I checked the other pocket. Nothing. I thought, Didn't I bring them? I must have brought them.

I am one of those compulsive people who never loses things like keys and wallets because I check my pockets for these items every four minutes.

And yet, here I'd apparently left my apartment without them.

Fact: Upon locking yourself out of your apartment, you will immediately need to use the bathroom.

Fact: And then you will stand in place and watch your door. You will just stare. As though rebuffed by it. As though it has done this to you.

I, with my salad bar of insecurities, stood there looking at my door and feeling rejected by my apartment. And as somebody who could then not even manage to pay my phone bill, I had no clue what to do about the situation.

And then I saw something in my head. My mind basically handed me a slip of paper with a note. I remembered the "24-Hour Locksmith" stickers that covered the aluminum mailboxes in the foyer. I'd seen them every time I checked my mail for the three years I'd lived in the apartment. And until this moment, they had never contained meaning. They had merely been trash, stuck to the wall.

I walked downstairs and looked at one of the stickers. I tried to memorize the number, but while alcohol has spared my long-term memory, my short-term memory has been destroyed. I could no more remember those seven digits than I could remember the phone number of the third guy I ever dated.

And I didn't have a pen. So I began peeling the sticker back, being as gentle as possible, so it didn't tear.

I managed to get the essential portion of the sticker free—the number. And I took this with me outside, in search of a pay phone that worked.

Now that everybody carries cell phones, the phone company doesn't maintain their pay phones anymore. And you could just forget the enclosed boxes. Those were no longer possible for a number of reasons: price of real estate, danger of fingers broken in bifold doors, resulting in lawsuits, and the fact that homeless people could sleep in them, upright.

Still, I was able to find a pay phone in the lobby of the movie theater and I called the lock guys.

"We can be there in eight minutes. Please wait in front of your building," the dispatcher said.

Sure enough, a few minutes later a big Greek hunk with a tool belt showed up in front of my building. It was the first time in my life some guy showed up at my apartment looking much better than I expected.

"Hi," I said. "I'm locked out."

"I know," he said. "I recognize the look."

I was intrigued. "What do you mean, the look?"

He said that people get this look on their faces when they're locked out of their apartments. He said it was something like panic, combined with guilt.

I said, "And also having to take a leak."

He said, "Yeah, everybody says that."

Then he said, "Let's go."

So I took him upstairs to my front door and he began hunting for a power outlet for his drill. But there was no power outlet. Immediately, my hopes crashed.

But then right away he unscrewed the light bulb and began wiring up his own outlet. And within a minute, was hitting the trigger on his drill. I was impressed.

He began drilling through the lock on my door. He said, "These Medico locks take a while. Like, twenty minutes."

I'd had the locks replaced when I first moved in. I wanted safer locks. But had I known that I, myself, would someday need to break into my apartment, I would have left the old, crappy locks in place.

The noise was terrible and made my brain itch in a most unusual way. Normally, I was not one to draw attention to myself. When I heard people outside my apartment, loitering in the hall or opening their own doors or knocking on somebody else's, I froze in place in my little nest and began taking shallow breaths. I didn't want to be heard. If somebody knocked on my door, I wanted to give the impression of not being home. I didn't want somebody to say, "Come on. I know you're in there. I heard you moving around a second ago." But now, standing here with the Greek Lock Man, who was making so much noise, it was likely that people would open their doors to see what the terrible, invasive metallic sound was and they would see me standing there in front of my apartment.

But nobody so much as cracked a peek through their door. And this relieved me and made me love, even more, the aloof nature of the city.

"This is a devil of a lock," he said. "This is going to take longer than I thought."

There was nothing I could do but stand there and wait. Remain in a position of suspended animation.

After an unknown period of time, but one that felt similar to an hour, the lock was disengaged. And without ceremony, the locksmith opened the door.

"Holy shit, you've been robbed!" he shouted as he stepped in to my apartment.

I hadn't thought this far in advance. I somehow hadn't imagined that he would actually open my door and walk in and see my mess. I made a mental note: always think a few steps ahead, never be surprised.

My mind engaged with a swift lie. "No, that's my brother. I was in L.A. for a month and my brother and his girlfriend stayed here and they left the place like this. Now I have to clean it up and then I have to go find him and kill him."

The locksmith, though, gave me a look that told me he didn't believe my story. He also gave me a look I had not seen before. It was a face drained of respect and then replaced with pity and fear.

I paid him. He left.

I now had one old, very questionable deadbolt on my door. In order to replace the lock, I would have to clean the apartment. As this seemed insurmountable, I knew then I would live with this one meager lock. My door could now be opened by anybody with a shoulder and a bad mood.

Inside my apartment, I closed the door and sat at my desk chair—actually, a chair made for outdoor use. And I was washed in relief.

When I was a child, when my parents would scream at each other and I was terrified, I would sit in my closet. I would tuck myself under a mound of clothing and stuffed animals so that if somebody came looking for me, if they opened my closet, they would not see me. And there, in my closet with my face pressed to the smooth oak floor, I felt a similar kind of safety.

Forty minutes after being let back into my apartment, I was on

my way to reaching my "place." My Place was reached through alcohol. A certain amount of alcohol was needed to reach this Place.
The amount depended. If I was lucky, I could get there on half a
bottle of Scotch, and then the remainder of the bottle and whatever
else I drank after this was merely enjoyable. But until I reached my
Place, I was anxious.

My Place was where nothing surrounding me mattered in the
least. Where there was no stressful advertising job in the morning
and there would be no fumes to explain on my breath. My Place
was a safe, warm zone where anything was possible. Where the debris around me became not filth, but insulation.

I was living in a tiny apartment, in a city crammed with millions
of people, and not one of them was thinking about me or wondering where I was or needing me for anything. And this knowledge
made sliding into my Place possible. There were no snags.

But as I continued to drink, I felt frustrated, as I was not reaching my Place. Instead, I was bothered by the locksmith, the man
who had seen inside me. And I couldn't stop myself from seeing my
apartment from his eyes. How shocking it must have been. How
frightening.

And I thought back to the early summer. When something was
wrong with the smoke detectors in our building and they kept going off for no apparent reason.

The first time this happened, I was startled awake at noon by a
pounding on my door and a commanding voice, as one imagines
the voice of God, "New York City Fire Department, open this door."
And how at that moment, I was in my bed, pee-stained and despicable, and I knew that if these men broke down my door and saw
me, they would call an ambulance. They would be so shocked by
the sight of a human being living in this nest they would think, *Emergency medical attention required.* And how I felt the terrible crush of
knowing everything was going to end now. But instead, the firemen

turned away from my door and they walked down the steps and I could feel them gone. I could feel the absence of their immense energy. But they might return. Maybe with larger axes.

So I dressed quickly and left my building and walked around the neighborhood for four hours, until I felt it was safe to return.

I thought of this and how the next time I heard fire engines whining down the street, I immediately left. Much better for them to break down the door and find the mess and nobody in it. I remembered walking down my own street and seeing the fire department inside my building and wondering, have they broken down my door?

And then, somehow, the alarms in our building were fixed and the firemen stopped coming.

So I was thinking all of this as I sat there at my computer, drinking, and I could not get these intrusive thoughts out of my head, and therefore could not reach my Place.

After finishing the one bottle, a liter, I moved on to the next. But now, I had no spare, full bottle on my kitchen stove. If I finished this bottle and needed more, the liquor stores would be closed and I would be out of liquor and would have to drink beer from downstairs at the twenty-four-hour market.

I was drunk enough to be unsteady when I stood. And drunk enough to be loud in my apartment, speaking to myself. But I had not reached my oblivion. The warm Place where I felt safe, cocooned. Where I felt no strings pulling me in any direction. Where I could float and explore. And now, after having been let into my apartment, after having the lock cut away like a tumor, I was still locked out from my Place.

I felt suddenly sober.

I sat on the edge of my bed and turned on the television. I was numb, vacant. I needed the television to wash over me.

A documentary was on the Discovery Channel.

It was about Eisenhower, a man I've considered for less than thirty seconds my entire life. I watched for almost an hour.

Eisenhower said, "Every gun that is made, every battleship that is built, every missile that is launched, is a direct theft from the people who are hungry and starving in this world."

When I heard this, I had to get up and go to my computer, so I could write. Because I was overwhelmed with the truth of that statement. And the fact that I'd never think of such a thing. I thought, There is a complexity to life that I often overlook. There is a depth of thinking, there is a richness. I am skating on the surface. Especially by drinking. Completely by drinking.

I suddenly wanted to quit my job and go to school because I didn't feel I had any richness or knowledge in me. But then I thought maybe I did but I just ignored it. By drinking.

I realized it was as though I was standing on a lid, trying to keep it pressed down against the forces that were trying to open it, explode it open, and I am padlocking that lid with alcohol every single night and distracting myself with the Internet, with fantasy log-cabin shopping, with "Will I have alcohol breath?" With building up the drunken courage to walk across the street to McDonald's at midnight for take-out.

I understood at once, I am not living, but actively dying. I am smoking, living unhealthily. I'm shutting down.

I need to go the other way, inside.

And it was so clear to me what I was doing. It was suddenly perfectly clear.

I understood, *I need to write*. Live here, in my words, and my head. I need to go inside, that's all. No big, complicated, difficult thing. I just need to go in reverse.

And not worry about what to write about, but just write. Or, if I'm going to worry about what to write, then do this worrying on paper, so at least I'm writing and will have a record of the anxiety.

And then, instead of sinking into my drunk place, I felt something else: alive.

I felt ignorant, self-deprived, incredibly isolated, deeply and profoundly lonely and missing people, absolutely starved for affection, physically weary from alcohol, very depressed about my physical appearance, my weak muscles. Hurt and angry and sad and still tied to my dead friend, Pighead. But alive.

For an instant, I could see myself living in a small, inexpensive college town someplace. Maybe the Midwest. And I would own a futon, which I would place on the floor. And a desk, or maybe just a folding card table. And a computer. I would get a gym membership and eat rice and beans every night. And I would write. I would write every day, all day. I would get a part-time job, something that paid my low rent and afforded me my rice and beans but not enough of a job to distract me.

And as soon as I saw this life, I realized I was making it more complicated than it needed to be. I didn't need to move to a small college town. I could just begin writing, right now. Here, in my hovel.

I could clean it. I could take everything out so it was an empty shell.

But, of course, I was drunk. I was drunk while I was thinking all these things and even though I believed everything I'd realized, I knew it was dangerous to make plans under the influence of alcohol.

So I went to sleep. I turned off the lights, shut down the computer, crawled into bed, and emptied my mind.

In the morning I was hungover.

My skull felt too small to contain my swollen brain. The first emotion I felt was depression. *Look at this mess.*

I didn't have the energy or motivation to clean. I remembered my thoughts from last night, though. I remembered understanding that I need to go in reverse. Go inside, instead of always living outside, on the surface.

So instead of folding all the debris in the room into huge plastic trash bags, instead of giving myself a clean slate, I just sat down. And I wrote:

"You exposed your penis on national television, Max. What am I supposed to do?"

The line came to me automatically. I didn't look for it. It was simply there. So was the line that followed: "I didn't expose it, Howard. It just sort of . . . peeked out."

A show host on a home shopping channel being confronted by his boss, after the host's penis slipped out from beneath his robe on the air, in front of millions of viewers. Sooner or later, this was bound to happen, wasn't it? On live television.

Silly. It made me laugh. I hadn't laughed for a year. I kept writing.

I wrote until seven that evening. Then I drank. But I never reached my Place. Instead, I thought about what I'd written during the day. I went to bed.

The next day, I wrote more. I started drinking later in the evening and I drank less.

By the third day, I wrote until midnight and I didn't drink anything at all except lime seltzer water.

By the seventh day I had written a book. At least, I thought it might be a book. It contained one hundred and fifty pages and they were in order. That's more than a monkey could do.

I called it *Sellevision.*

I did not drink.

And it occurred to me that perhaps losing my keys had been a bit of good luck. Because for the first time in my life, I had the feeling I was home.

Getting to No You

I never had anxiety about turning thirty. "The Big Three-O" did not loom over my head, deeply dreaded. I couldn't have cared less. I hadn't noticed any difference between twenty-eight and twenty-nine the next morning. So why would I notice anything at thirty?

But when I turned thirty, something was indeed left behind. Suddenly, inexplicably, a piece of me went missing. The very piece responsible for breaking up with a guy if he turned out to be a freak.

Literally overnight, I went from somebody who was a pretty good judge of character—somebody who was able to go on a date or two, and if I didn't feel the chemistry, kindly back out—to being a sucker, unable to think and act for myself.

Now, I found myself having third, fourth, fifth dates with people I didn't care for. Even people that I loathed and wished would get caught in a grinding, malfunctioning escalator.

Alex had placed a personal ad and I'd answered it. We exchanged a few e-mails and finally met for coffee in the East Village. There was nothing new in this. I was a well-oiled dating machine. The cafés might be different each time but the process was always the same.

I walked in and scanned the room for his face. This could sometimes be tricky because people often sent you pictures that had been taken years before. Or they'd sent you that one picture in a thousand where they looked pretty normal. Good, even. Many guys with advanced computer skills used Photoshop to embellish their images, making noses slimmer, chins more defined, cheekbones higher. Personally, I felt such digital imaging to be dishonest and would never do that to one of my photographs. The most I would do was use the shadow tool in Photoshop to bring out the muscular rips in my stomach, which were honestly there. Beneath the fat.

Alex saw me first. "Hellooooo!" he sang, rising from his position on the secondhand sofa, the furniture of choice for trendy East Village coffee bars. "I'm Alex. You must be Augusten. You look just like your picture."

I wanted to say, "And you look nothing like yours," but instead smiled politely and shook his hand.

In his photograph, Alex looked like a dark-haired, complicated man with soulful eyes and a playful smile. But in person he simply looked vapid and dysfunctional.

He was also much taller than I expected. At least six-four. Normally, I don't have anything against guys who are taller than I am. But in this case it was a problem. Because it meant there was simply too much of him.

"Come have a seat next to me," he said, leading me back to the sofa. He'd created a sort of urban nest there, with his knapsack, the *New York Times*, and a copy of *Time Out* magazine. His coffee was three-quarters full and there was a fresh pack of Marlboro Reds on the table.

I wanted to leave. I wanted to say, "Would you excuse me while I go to the men's room for a second?" and then climb out the window and run.

Instead, I found myself sitting next to him on the sofa. Sitting so close our knees touched. "This is nice, isn't it?" he said, smiling in a wretched, *aren't-I-adorable?* fashion. He glanced at our legs, first mine, then his. "It's nice to touch," he said.

I hated him. I hated all people who assumed immediate intimacy. While I'm not somebody who eats with his arms protectively encircling his plate, I do maintain a certain distance, at first. I'm from New England, from a dysfunctional home. I'm not Mediterranean in the least, holding any hand I can grab and kissing everybody's hairy cheek. There is a little German in me, therefore I don't do cuddly.

I had assumed that my need for civilized distance was obvious from my body language alone—leaning away from him, arms crossed over my chest, nose upturned. So I hated him for not seeing this and for assuming I was fully delighted to sit thigh-to-thigh with him. But I detested him for other reasons, too. Reasons I couldn't yet articulate, but which were very real. Animal reasons. Something said: *he's wrong.* Not just wrong for me, but somehow wrong. He's broken. Defective. I was raised around severe mental illness, so I just knew.

Alex said, "Do you want some of my coffee?" offering me his cup. Then, seeing my expression said, "Or would you like your own?"

I said, "I'll be right back. I'll just get a double espresso."

I was glad for the chance to get up from the sofa, to be alone once again. And now I had the chance to revise our seating arrangement. To sit further away from him on the sofa. To sit at the other end.

I got my espresso and felt slightly pained that it was not okay for me to simply leave. But then, why wasn't it? Why couldn't I return to him and say, "You know. I'm sorry. But this isn't going to work. I'm too crazy. Something's wrong with me and I can't go through with the date." Blame it all on myself, my inadequacies, which was the right thing to do and probably the truth to boot.

Why did I have to sit back down on the sofa, closer than I wanted, by accident? And, with my thigh once again touching his, say, "So. What have you been up to today?"

This one question released a torrent of information.

"Well, God. Today has been just crazy!" he said, smiling wide, almost laughing.

I nodded and said, "Really?" My expression was one of condescending reserve. *Tell me about your crazy day, mentally challenged little boy.*

"Oh, God. Totally crazy!" He said again. Then he had a sip of coffee. "Not that I need any more caffeine. God, I've had ten cups already."

Here, he laughed and touched my shoulder. "Not really ten. I'm exaggerating. But close!"

He spoke of daily life with a manic excitement that I didn't like. Be excited when you encounter cosmetic surgery mistakes. Be excited when a birth defects marathon runs on The Discovery Channel. But don't be excited because you had some coffee.

"So then first thing this morning, I had a little setback, so to speak. I mean, not that you need to know this up front, but I am a very *regular* person, if you know what I mean." He blinked in a way I imagined he assumed was slightly flirtatious, but which was in fact not flirtatious on somebody who is not a sixteen-year-old girl and has never been one.

"But I was *constipated*. God, I hate that word!"

Anybody else could have left at this point. When you begin discussing toilet intimacies on the first date, you have failed the first date. And yet I sat there, listening. Nodding, as though fascinated. I said, "Really? I'm sorry." The only thing more pitiful than talking about your bowel problems is hanging around while somebody else talks about theirs.

"Yeah, so. What are you gonna do? And so then, I had to go with my friend, Heather, to take her cat uptown to the ASPCA. She loves it so much, God, it's like her daughter. But she can't keep it because her building doesn't allow pets and the landlord found out, yadda, yadda, sad story."

I said, "Why didn't she place an ad in the paper? Why did she bring it to the kennel to be exterminated?"

He shot a look at me. "Don't say that. That's terrible. They won't put that cat down. Trust me. That cat is a winner. Somebody will adopt her in a heartbeat." But suddenly, he didn't look too sure. To make him all the more *unsure*, I simply shrugged. "If you say so."

It was time to leave. He was insufferable, had toilet problems, looked demented to begin with, and now he was the accomplice to a cat killer. Yet did I leave? No, I sat there. And I thought, What has happened to me? Why am I not rising up off the sofa? Why am I not leaving?

Jesus, hold my hand.

It was as though I had begun taking a new medication and one of the side effects was inertia. And yet, nothing had changed. I had crossed from my twenties into my thirties. One day, a new decade. But everything else was the same. And yet it seemed that the part of me that would never put up with shit like this, was putting up with shit like this.

"So after that, we went to Barney's because I needed some shoes. You like?" he extended his left leg, turning his foot right and left at the ankle. The shoe was tacky, white, and open-toed. "These were eighty percent off!" he said, positively delighted. They were a shoe buyer's mistake and they were on his feet. And his toenails were long. They were simply overlooked, forgotten. He'd decided to wear the new shoes, tonight, on this first date with me, a person he had never met. And it didn't occur to him to trim his nails so that they did not curl over the toes. Again: a sign of mental illness.

"So then after that we grabbed some lunch. And oh my God, the waiter was cute. Actually," he said, looking at me a little sideways, "he looked a little like you."

While he intended this to flatter me, it instead made me picture him being assaulted by Rottweilers on the way back to his apartment. Cornered and quivering in his new white shoes.

The remainder of the date continued in exactly the same fashion. In great detail, he outlined his week. Then he told me a little of his family history, which included an older sister he wasn't close to because she didn't "get" him, a father he'd never felt affection from (surprise, surprise), and a mother whom he adored.

"So tell me about you," he said, letting air out along with his words. He was tired from talking. An hour and a half had passed.

I hesitated. I wanted him to have no part of me, not even my information. "Well, I work in advertising. I write. So that's me."

"I love that ad for the car, where the guy is upside down? Did you do that one? That is a funny ad. When I was in Paris the year before last, I was watching some television in the room and my God, those ads are so racy over there. They aren't afraid to show boobs and butts and things. The French are so much more evolved than we are here in America, even in Manhattan. And you can just forget about that area in between here and L.A.," he said, waving his hand dismissively at the majority of the country.

When you insult the Midwest—land of corndogs, casseroles, and all my favorite packaged food products—you insult me.

Finally, I was able to say, "Well, it's been really nice meeting you, Alex. But I'm going to have to run. I'm tired today and I need to get home to pay some bills." This was a lie. I never paid my bills; all my accounts were in collection. I couldn't tell him the truth, which was that I had to get home to e-mail my friends about how horrible my date had been.

"So listen," he said, grabbing my arm. "I want to do this again. I want to see you. I think we obviously have a lot of chemistry and I think it would be great to see each other soon. So what do you say? Dinner on Friday?"

Not a chance. "Um, sure, I guess," I said.

And why did I say that? Mentally, I was removing my own shoe and hitting myself in the forehead. I was hitting myself hard, drawing blood with the heel. What was the matter with me?

"Great," he said. And then added, "I've got to dash. But this was great fun. I had a grand time."

And he was gone. As though it had been his idea to part in the first place. And now I had another date with him. Something was wrong with me.

Thirty was a disaster.

On Thursday he left a message on my answering machine, giving me his address and telling me to come over at seven. From there, we'd go to dinner at a restaurant in his neighborhood. Which was also *my* neighborhood, but he called it *his*.

I arrived at his apartment five minutes early, and before hitting the buzzer, contemplated turning around and leaving. And then I wouldn't pick up my phone and eventually he'd get the message and go away.

Instead of doing this, I rang the buzzer.

His apartment was blue, even the ceiling. A dark, blackish blue. With black trim.

Two rooms: the main room, a tiny bedroom. The queen bed filled the space, and on the bed he had a madras bedspread, along with two neck pillows. These were the grain-filled pillows that lesbians and soft blond men from Amherst, Massachusetts, slipped under their necks. Something chiropractors try to foist on you. Give me down. And give me Polaroids of the fifty geese that had to die in the process.

The main room was surprisingly spacious. It was small, but sparsely furnished. There was a tiny table in front of the window, with one chair. A loveseat. No television. A four-shelf bookcase. I scanned the titles and saw that they were all self-help books from the "spiritual" genre. Vague, foggy tomes about healing, guidance, acceptance, and instinct. *Release of the Heart* caught my eye. Had he been a good guy up to this point, these titles would have made me instantly, deeply suspicious. But as I detested him already, the titles merely caulked my feelings into place.

"Sit, sit," he said, patting the sofa.

I felt compelled to obey. Actually, I felt compelled to push him back against the wall and then run, but instead I sat.

"I'm always a little nervous when somebody new comes into my space. I get, I don't know, self-conscious. I guess because I have spent so much time and emotional energy on the place. Decorating is a huge interest of mine. Oh my God, you have no idea. It's just, like, I should have been a decorator."

Nothing in his apartment was remotely tasteful or in any way co-ordinated. Even the small black mat—which I assumed to be de-signed for use in front of a bathtub—was askew on the floor, dusted with white lint, strands of things.

"Because it's like, when I show you my home, I'm showing you myself."

Clearly, he was steering me in the direction of a compliment. But I wasn't going to give him one. Not even on the bones of the apart-ment itself, which is the only true compliment you can pay some peoples' apartments, when desperate. Instead I said, "Really? You *are* interested in interior design? That's very surprising."

And he said, slightly on the offensive, "Now why is that so surprising?"

And I said, "Well, judging from your books," and I pointed to the bookcase. "You strike me as a more spiritual man."

He relaxed into the sofa. "It's true," he said. "But spirituality and aestheticism are not mutually exclusive."

Then, to my horror, he said, "*You* are deeply intuitive. I can't believe you said I'm spiritual. Because oh my God, you have no idea. Do you want to know something?"

I did not.

"I am *very* spiritual."

Now, instead of being psychologically queasy, I was physically so.

"In fact, I'm in the process of accepting a new spirituality. It's so hard to put this into words." With his hands, he made a box in the air in front of himself.

"I'm moving, I guess is the word. I'm evolving, that's a better word. I'm evolving into a space where I have adopted a new set of beliefs that are just, for me, you know, very true."

The man needed a laxative on many levels.

"I'm converting to Sufism," he said. He looked at me expectantly.

I said, "Oh. Really. I guess I'm not terribly aware of what that even entails."

He said, "You sit right there. I want to share something with you."

And he got up from the sofa and disappeared into the bedroom. Now, alone on his ratty sofa, I truly had the chance to leave. It would be what? Five, six steps? And then a twist of the deadbolt and I'd be gone. I had to leave. I had to leave now. It made no sense to suffer through this date. I knew I would never, ever see him again. It had been a terrible mistake to have this, a second date. And I could no longer sit passively and allow myself to be hijacked by somebody. Especially somebody who repulsed me.

He entered the room wearing a dress, of sorts. It was thick cotton. Embroidered. It was a dress, but then not. It was a smockish thing. It had fins, almost. It was unusual. And yet familiar.

And he began to spin. He began to spin around in the center of his blue room, and the dress, it blew out from him. He was a top. A spinning top.

He stumbled. Onto the floor. He was on the floor. He was laughing with apology.

"I'm not even supposed to be doing that part yet," he said. "But I can't help it! I just love that. But it's hard," he said, rising from the floor, breathing heavy. "It's much harder than it looks."

"What are you doing?" I said, not absolutely masking all of my horror.

"Don't you recognize it? I'm going to be a Dervish. A Whirling Dervish."

People in Manhattan convert to Judaism. They do not convert to Whirling Dervishism. It isn't done. Only richly skinned women with exotic names can do this. Gay guys from the East Village with blue apartments, terrible shoes from Barney's, and thumb rings cannot do this. Call me a bigot. But it's not allowed. Somewhere, I was certain, this was in fact written.

"I still get dizzy. But apparently, that goes away. Once you really make the right connection. Once you're, you know, doing it for the right reasons. I shouldn't be doing it to show you. I should be doing it to connect to my God."

Finally, much too late, my personality came back to me. It was like waking from a nap and remembering an important call you had to make. It was the feeling of, "How could I have fallen asleep? How long have I been out?" Instant mental clarity, combined with the desire to wipe something away—sleep, behavior.

"You remind me of Circle Dog," I said. I said this thoughtfully, not smirking. But then I smirked. It was automatic. And once I smirked, fuck it. I laughed.

Alex smiled, too, but his was unsure. He was on the other side of the smile, being smiled at, and he knew it. And it made him briefly, instantly unsure.

"I had this dog once," I said. "I bought him from at a pet store on the Upper East Side. He was old, for a puppy. A year and a half. And all he did was run in circles. I'd trip over him, because he circled my legs. And to get him off me, I had to walk over to the dining table and transfer him over to one of the legs."

He was looking at me now, serious.

"But night and day, all that dog did was circle. I guess from being trapped in a dog kennel for his whole life and just walking around and around in that little cage. Anyway, after a month, he'd driven me nearly crazy. I knew I would throw him out the window. I mean, he was adorable. But he was just so ruined. And something about him going in circles, I don't know. My brain, my own problems, whatever, I am not equipped to deal with something that goes in circles. I go in so many circles myself. So I had to put an ad in the *Village Voice* and find him a new home. And I did, too. Some nice guy from Brooklyn took him for his mother."

"How do I remind you of this dog?" Alex said. He was pissy. His words were floating in piss.

I stood up. I needed to be near the door. The door was my friend.

"Well, it's just that I guess you remind me of him because seeing you do your circles, you know. That's the obvious connection, I guess. But the other thing is that you were both just so completely wrong for me."

"I don't agree," he said, popping the words from his mouth. "You're wrong. I *do* think there's something between us. There's obviously something between us. I think you're just afraid."

I said, "You know. Here's the thing. We just met. Okay? There's no chemistry. We met and I didn't like you, but for some reason I went on a second date. And now here we are. And I can't even finish the date. I can't date somebody who is studying to become a Whirling Dervish. That's one thing. And that's a big thing. I guess I'm just shallow in that respect. But the other thing is that there's just something about you."

I didn't finish the thought. I said, "Look, I'm sorry. I know what an asshole I must seem like. Must be. And I'm sorry. I'm sure you're a nice guy." I unlocked the door myself.

"Wait just one minute," he said. "You're not walking out of here like that. How dare you? How dare you!"

I left the apartment. He called after me. "Asshole!" But I smiled as I walked, bounding down the stairs, on my way to freedom, happy to be single, happy to be thirty and able, once again, not to get all caught up in somebody else's spinning around.

Kitty, Kitty

I really wanted a dog when I got out of rehab, but I knew I had to start making smarter choices. So I bought an orchid instead of a puppy, figuring that if I needed practice keeping something alive, first I should start with an item that would look good on the coffee table as opposed to something that would chew it. I knew it would be years before I was allowed to have another dog. Because I'd had one once before in Manhattan. And I had been very, very bad.

The last time I wanted a dog, I was a drunk. But even as a drunk, I knew better than to get a dog. So I bought an expensive acoustic guitar instead. The guitar salesman gently stroked the inlaid wood of the tapered neck and said, "I bet you've been dreaming about this baby your whole life." I told him, not really. I said I didn't play, but how hard could it be? "I don't think there's a dyke alive who can't play 'Constant Craving' on a guitar," I joked, but he didn't seem to think this was funny. Still, I bought the Martin and a pile of songbooks, too.

I kept the guitar for a month, halfheartedly attempting to learn "Stairway to Heaven," and then I decided that I had no need for a guitar, as I never sat around campfires or attended political rallies. So I took the guitar back to the store where they gave me an eighty percent refund. Then I went into a bar and had a few beers. And the next thing I knew, I took a cab over to the AKC Puppy Center on Lexington Avenue and bought a soft-coated Wheaten terrier.

I did know that you're never supposed to buy a puppy from a pet store. And the reason is that you support the puppy mill industry. A puppy mill is a disreputable breeder who churns out puppies the way Nabisco churns out Oreos. Often, the dogs are inbred and have health problems. But all of this knowledge evaporated once I went inside the pet store and saw the adorable puppies. A rational person would have seen the filthy cages where the dogs were kept and known better than to slap down his credit card and take one home. But I saw the filthy cages and thought, *I must save one.*

I named him KittyKitty. Because he looked like a kitty. But twice the size. And he was so gentle and sweet that for the first two weeks I thought he might be mildly retarded. His kind brown eyes were always half-closed and he licked my hand, even after I pulled it away. His little tongue just continued lick, lick, licking the air. It was endearing, but also a little pathetic. Yet I knew I'd made a good purchase because he was almost no trouble at all, like a potted cactus. He made less noise than my answering machine, and housebreaking was easy because my floor was already covered with magazines and foreign newspapers, which I couldn't read and only bought because I was pretentious.

But by the third week KittyKitty became alarmingly energized, as if awakened from a long, deep hibernation.

When he wasn't barking at the exact frequency that causes windows to shake, he was leaping from the sofa to the floor to the chair and then running full speed down the hall to the front door, sliding into it and knocking the jackets hung on it to the floor.

He also liked to grab his rawhide bone in his slobbering maw and then shake his head violently from side to side until the bone flew out of his mouth and sailed across the room, smacking into the glass door of the microwave.

By the time KittyKitty was six months old, he was at least twice the size of a normal soft-coated Wheaten. Friends told me, "Idiot, you shouldn't have bought a dog at a pet store. Those puppy-mill puppies have all sorts of problems." It was too late to take him back and get a Philippe Starck armchair, so I was stuck with him, even if he eventually reached the size of a Great Dane and grew a second puppy-mill tail.

One morning I took KittyKitty to the Tompkins Square dog run. This is a fenced-in portion of Tompkins Square Park in the East Village that is blanketed with cedar wood chips. The inside of the fence is lined all the way around with benches so you can sit and read the paper, talk to other dog people, or work on a mental assignment from your therapist.

The dog run must have seemed like a wonderful idea, there on the city planner's desk as a blue and white sketch. The reality, however, was quite grim. The designers hadn't taken into account the possibility of eventual rain, and its effect on dog shit and wood chips.

First of all, KittyKitty was terrified of other dogs, so he immediately ran underneath one of the benches, cowering in the soft mud. There, he whimpered and shook with fear, taking small breaks from his terror to lick the dirt.

With the help of the freeze-dried liver treats that magically caused him to obey me without question, I finally coaxed him from beneath the bench. He immediately started running, then a couple of other dogs started chasing him and he had no choice but to keep going. This is good, I thought. He's getting socialized. So I had some time to sit back and absorb the park. And as I sat there looking around, it dawned on me how disgusting the park really was.

There was smooth, creamy dog shit everywhere, blended into the cedar chips like some kind of awful urban casserole. And because of the recent rain, there were deep ruddy puddles of muck scattered all over, which the dogs just galloped straight through. And the people on the benches, upon closer inspection, seemed to be pretty okay with all of this. People who, themselves, looked to me just one step above plant life, happily sat with their feet pressed deep into the stew. Women with dog-hair-covered sweatshirts French-kissed unfamiliar dogs that came up to them. Men sporting needle tracks picked dropped food items off the ground and ate them.

As I sat there thinking hateful things about the other people, KittyKitty ran into one of those festering sewage puddles and started to frolic, like a hideous little imp. His stump tail was wagging and his tongue was hanging out and he was stomping his little feet in the puddle, splashing around. The other dogs kind of backed away. As if the puddle was too gross, instinctively, for even them.

So I ran over to him yelling, "Fuck! No! Hey, no! Get out! Fuck!" Briefly, he glanced up at me. Then he paused and began to drink the liquid in the puddle. As I got closer, cleverly trying to hide the leash behind my back, he looked up at me, tongue still in the water, and bolted. He was immediately tackled by a German shepherd with a missing rear leg. They wrestled and the shepherd chased KittyKitty into another sewer puddle.

Meanwhile, a new woman entered the dog park. She was very SoHo, with her blunt cut and tiny fringe bangs, which were so ugly as to be considered "modern" and therefore stylish. She wore her Sunday blacks and large hangover sunglasses that covered the entire top portion of her face. She walked her calm and beautifully groomed Golden Retriever to a far bench where she unfastened him and then sat down with the *Times*.

Unfortunately, KittyKitty, who was standing about thirty feet to my left, was watching her, too. And as soon as she sat and her dog wandered off to squat politely in the corner, KittyKitty's rear engine rockets ignited and he blasted off in her direction.

Like a car accident, it happened in slow motion. Just as she was bringing her inevitable Starbucks Decaf Skinny Soy Venti Caramel Macchiato to her lips, she paused and saw the manic, filthy, shit-covered animal raging toward her.

At the same time, I began to run. But in the opposite direction.

I turned around just in time to see KittyKitty leap up onto the woman's lap, sending her Starbucks cup arching through the air.

She recoiled and screamed, shielding her face with both hands.

I moved toward the exit, thinking I'd just leave. This was my first, true instinct. I would just leave the park; abandon KittyKitty and the SoHo woman. The whole incident would be something I innocently witnessed, as opposed to indirectly caused.

Instead, from the deep recesses of my lower brain stem, some vague sense of morality and responsibility surfaced and took control of my nervous system, propelling my legs in the direction of the fiasco.

"God, I am so sorry," I said as I approached.

She was standing now and frowning, trying to shake the wet, sloppy shit water off her clothes.

KittyKitty began to hump my leg. Quickly, I snapped on his leash.

"I don't know what to say," I said. "He's a puppy, he's . . . I should have been watching him closer. I am so—"

"It's okay," she said. And then she chuckled with the forgiveness that only another dog owner could possibly summon. "Don't you sometimes wish you had a cat instead?"

I laughed, as well, because I was relieved that I could leave and would not have to retain an attorney.

I walked KittyKitty home, bitching at him the whole way like a welfare mother, then threw him into the tub and washed him four times with Liquid Dial antibacterial soap, using the hand-held shower massager set to PULSATE partly because it rinsed well, and partly, I had to admit, as punishment. Of course, he saw this not as punishment, but as delightful fun. And he tried biting the water as it pulsed, snapping at it while his tail stump revolved happily.

Later, as I sat on the floor drying him with a towel and he licked my wrist, I thought, I wish I could take him back to the pet store. Like shoes that just didn't fit.

When KittyKitty was dry and fluffy, I took a Polaroid of him. The flash made him blink and he got stuck blinking, so to break the circuit I handed him a freeze-dried liver treat, which was probably a mistake because now he'd associate blinking with treats. Dogs learn in very direct ways, I've discovered.

By the time he was a year old, KittyKitty was the size of a Labrador. Even shaving his long, fluffy hair down to stubble did little to decrease his bulk. I wouldn't have minded his size if it went along with obedience, but KittyKitty had no sense of obligation to me or the words that fell out of my mouth.

"Sit" could possibly get him to look at me. "Stay" would cause him to follow me, sniffing at my front pocket. "No" caused him to bounce up and down off the floor with a look of loony excitement. I hired a dog trainer who claimed, on the phone, to have trained a number of unruly dogs belonging to very famous people.

But even she was powerless over KittyKitty. She eventually pulled the puppy mill line out of her hat. "You really shouldn't have bought a dog from a pet store. They have so many insurmountable problems."

Alone with my insurmountable dog, I began to think of how I

could dispose of him and continue with my life. Could I give him to my brother? I called and asked, pushing KittyKitty's positive qualities like a used car salesman. "He's really affectionate and he loves water."

"Is that the same beast you complained about last month? The unruly terrier?"

I said that it was the same dog, but that he was much better now. Trouble-free, I said.

"Then why do you want to trade him in?"

"Because the apartment is too small."

"Well, I can't take him out here. We've got cats that don't like dogs."

My father couldn't take KittyKitty because of allergies that he seemed to develop while speaking with me on the phone.

Adding to my stress was the fact that my downstairs neighbor began pounding on his ceiling—my floor—with some sort of stick. KittyKitty would merely leap from the bed and land on the floor and within five seconds I would hear, *ker-thump, ker-thump, ker-thump*. One morning there was a note taped to my front door. *"Christ, what are you doing up there? Could you PLEASE have A LITTLE respect for your neighbors and not play FIELD HOCKEY in your fucking apartment?!?"*

I started desperately searching for an exit sign to dog ownership. He belongs on a farm chasing rabbits, I reasoned, not in a studio apartment with an alcoholic.

I came across "Animals, laboratory" in the yellow pages and thought maybe this might be a noble option. KittyKitty could unknowingly further science, through the testing of shampoo and makeup.

On the other hand, I could simply walk him downstairs and loop his leash around the wrist of some homeless guy sleeping off his morning six-pack.

In the back of my mind, of course, was a thought I did not dare give voice to. It was so despicable an option that even I was incapable of considering it.

Until, that is, I had a few drinks. Then suddenly, the previously unthinkable became the quite doable.

I reasoned that giving KittyKitty to the ASPCA was no different than making a contribution to the United Way. It was a charitable act. And considering I had paid over a thousand dollars for him, it was a generous charitable act.

Perhaps, in the end, he would even turn out to be a tax deduction.

Besides, some good-hearted person would surely adopt him. It was only the older, mixed breed dogs that got "put down."

So at noon on a Saturday, quite drunk, I tricked KittyKitty into the backseat of a cab and took him uptown to the ASPCA.

To my surprise, the woman at the intake desk was extremely friendly and welcoming. Perhaps vacant and spoiled alcoholics constantly brought their purebred dogs here when they tired of them.

In a gesture of compassion, I asked, "Do you think somebody will take him?"

The woman knelt down and KittyKitty jumped up onto her knee and licked her face. "Oh, absolutely. A beautiful dog like this? He'll be gone by four o'clock."

I briefly considered adding, "Because when I found him on the street an hour ago, well, I wanted to take him home but my landlord doesn't allow pets so I didn't know what to do." Thankfully, I just nodded my head, handed her the leash, and left feeling utterly off the hook.

But then I realized what I was doing. "Wait a minute," I said. "I can't do this. I'm a fucking monster. I can't take my dog to the ASPCA."

She looked at me and smiled a little. Not a large smile, but one that was small and contained pity. She said, "You know, normally I would have to say I agree. This is not the place to leave a dog. I would tell you to place an ad in the paper. Be responsible and find the dog a loving home." She knelt down and KittyKitty licked her face. "But this is a beautiful dog. And I'm going to personally make sure he finds a very good home. And he will never get put to sleep because, before that happens, I will take him home myself."

I felt profound relief. But still guilt. That I was even here was beyond deplorable. I was an alcoholic who had raised a dog and was now giving him away. What was the matter with me? She answered this question herself.

"But you, I think, have bigger problems."

I looked at her, unsure of what she meant. And yet, absolutely sure.

"You're an alcoholic. And someday you will look back on this moment and you will realize, this was your rock bottom. It won't be a dramatic day where you wake up in a gutter. It will be today, giving away a dog because you can't take care of it because you're sick."

I said, "How do you know all of this?"

She said, "My name is Susan. I have seven years, one day at a time. And it takes one to know one."

I said, "I'm a horrible person, aren't I? I'm cruel and I'm selfish and I'm awful." My bottom lip was, to my horror, beginning to tremble.

"No," she said. "You aren't. You're a drunk. So why don't you get out of here and go to an AA meeting."

I nodded and left.

As punishment, I forced myself to walk five blocks south before hailing another cab to take me back downtown.

Once downtown, I gathered KittyKitty's few belongings, including his doggie bowl and his rawhide bone, and I threw them into a garbage bag.

Then I sat on the edge of my bed and sobbed. KittyKitty would be okay. I knew this because I believed the woman.

And I'd never been mean to him. I'd always been sweet.

But I gave up on him. I raised him, then gave him away to a crazy place. And somewhere in the gin-soaked back of my mind, this glowed with the familiar. Because the same thing happened to me as a kid.

It scared me to realize this. To know that I could treat another living thing, a KittyKitty, in the same way I was treated. There had been no learning, no evolution. There had been simply programming.

And then I thought, maybe seeing for myself means something, makes a difference. Maybe this insight alone is like the ape-to-man chart they show you in school. Maybe I was slumped over before, dragging my knuckles. But now, right now, maybe I am just a little more upright.

This was my hope.

Peep

Almost nothing thrilled me more as a child than to share dinner with the family down the street, the Hendersons. Mrs. Henderson was a bleached blonde who always had a cigarette dangling from her lips when she brought the ham or the meatloaf or the shepherd's pie to the table. And she, herself, never sat at the table, but on a tall stool pulled up next to the counter, a plate balanced on her knees. Mr. Henderson always sat at the head of the table and the two Henderson kids—who were both younger than my eight years—sat on either side. They almost never said anything at all. Because Mr. and Mrs. Henderson spent the whole dinner yelling at each other.

I always had the same seat—a rock about forty feet from the sliding glass door of the dining room, in their backyard at the edge of the woods. But with my brother's binoculars, it was almost as though I was there. Better, even. Because if I had been in the actual room, there is no way it would have been okay to really get in close and watch Mr. Henderson chew a piece of ham, to see the mashed potatoes blending in his mouth with the peas, the glint of silver from one of his many fillings sparkling through the chewed paste. And then to watch a partially chewed pea shoot out of his mouth and hit his daughter on the forehead when he screamed "Fuck you!" at his wife.

The Henderson children were shy and quiet at school. Sometimes, I was tempted to reveal that I knew more about them than I ought to. I fantasized telling Sally, "You look like a girl who eats a double helping of carrots. Your skin is so orange I bet you glow in the dark." Because I knew that her brother hated carrots and always let her eat his serving, which she did, happily. Or maybe I could whisper in Sean's ear, "You know, your mom is a slut. Everybody knows it." Because that's what Mr. Henderson called her, a slut. Sometimes he even called her a "dirty" slut. But he always ate her candied ham, even sucking on the cloves. So how much of a slut could she really be? I had no idea, of course, what a "slut" was, but I knew it was bad because he only said it when he was screaming.

I also knew that my knowledge of the Hendersons' most intimate lives must remain my secret. And if there was one thing I was good at, it was keeping secrets.

For example, even though I was just dying to tell somebody, I never breathed a word about Mr. X, who lived up on Highpoint Hill and read *Playgirl* magazine while he sat in his car, parked in the garage. He kept a copy tucked under the seat. I was just itching to come up to him and his wife when I saw them in town and say, "Hey, Mrs. X! You're so lucky! I wish *my* father would read *Playgirl*. But he's not interested in *anything* good."

So how perfect that I would end up living in New York City, in the West Village in a small one-bedroom apartment in the rear of the building. The apartment overlooked a courtyard with low bushes and skinny city trees. On the other side of this courtyard was another apartment building. With windows. And directly across from my living room window, and down two floors, lived Saturday Susan.

I never knew her real name. But she became Saturday Susan because Monday through Friday I almost never saw her. Sometimes, she might pad into the living room in her nightgown and turn on the television. I would watch her watch the television, see the cool blue light play across her expressionless face. Sometimes, she ate ice cream from the container. But that was it. For the most part, hers was a window not worth watching.

Except on Saturday nights.

When Penis Man came.

And suddenly, Saturday Susan was out of her normal sweatpants or threadbare nightgown. And she was dressed in a black skirt and heels. A sexy, gauzy blouse. Her hair was styled, blown into position, sprayed in place.

The action began at around seven in the evening. This is when Saturday Susan began to pace her apartment. She fluffed the pillows on her sofa, rearranged items on the coffee table, and paused frequently to examine herself in the mirror. I couldn't see the mirror, only her posing before it. She practiced everything, from laughter to coy flirtation.

This went on for hours. And I was there for all of it, my drinks lined up like soldiers on the floor beside me. Sometimes I had a bowl of chips and some guacamole dip. When I had to pee I would say, *"Shit!"* out loud and then run to the toilet, pressing on my abdomen to make the stream flow faster.

As the evening wore on, Saturday Susan's pacing became more frantic. Candles that had burned down would be replaced. Her skirt would be changed, yet again. Chewed-off lipstick would be reapplied. And then finally, some time after midnight, Penis Man would arrive.

Always, she ran to the door and then stood on his feet when he entered the room, wrapping her arms around him. She was like a Newfoundland with this greeting. Pure exuberance. Kiss, kiss, kissing his mouth as he gave her his cheek and slapped her on the ass a couple times.

For all her preparation and anxiety, the remainder of the evening was relatively anticlimactic. Penis Man tossed his overcoat on a chair and then slipped out of sight, possibly into a bathroom. Quickly, she undressed, folding her clothes into a neat pile and tucking them out of sight. She left her panties and heels on, but not her bra. Sometimes she pinched her nipples. In the same way one might pinch one's cheeks to infuse them with a natural, rosy color.

While he was still in the bathroom, she took this naked time to pose in front of the mirror. Quickly trying to determine the most natural pose. Hands behind her back? No, scratch that. Hands on hips? Too dominating. Eventually, she settled on the sofa, legs crossed, her body angled toward the door through which he would reenter the room.

And when he reappeared he was always naked and sporting an erection. His comb-over was in place and he made an effort to suck in his remarkable belly.

The sex happened on the sofa and it was fast. Missionary position, with her legs in the air. I kept careful notes. Normally, he reached climax after eleven humps. The longest he'd ever lasted was forty-two humps, but this was after they shared a rare bottle of wine first. The quickest: five humps.

There was never any foreplay. No kissing. No touching. He simply climbed aboard and humped away. When he was finished, he climbed off her body and used the hand towel he'd brought with him from the bathroom to wipe off his penis. Oddly, he often spit into the towel, as well, before tossing it next to her on the sofa. Then he went back into the bathroom and she was alone.

While she was alone, she quickly slipped her underwear on, then a robe, which she'd obviously stashed nearby for just this reason. And she paced. I could see her look up at the ceiling and say something to herself. Was she saying, "Why?" It looked that way.

When Penis Man came back into the room he was dressed. More than this, his hair was wet; he was freshly showered. He was ready to leave and she hugged him again, standing on his shoes, her doggie style. And then he left and she would be alone in the apartment and she would sob.

She spent the next three hours doing nothing but sitting on her sofa and crying as the candles burned lower and lower.

And this is how it was, every Saturday.

Over time, I developed an affection for her. And a loathing for Penis Man. I felt she was too good for him. Dressing up as she did, just for his arrival. And then being so excited when he finally showed up, probably late. And then putting up with that terrible sex. I imagined he was married. She'd no doubt gone against the excellent advice of her girlfriends and was dating a married guy. And now she was miserable and I wanted to help.

Many times I thought, maybe I should send her some flowers. I could walk to the Korean market on the corner and buy her a bunch of tulips. She lived only one street over, directly across from my own apartment. I could easily figure out exactly which building and apartment was hers.

I could buzz all the buzzers on the front of the building and surely somebody would answer, "Yeah?" I would then say, "I forgot my key, I'm your neighbor upstairs. Can you buzz me in?" Somebody would.

And then I could find her apartment and leave the tulips.

I realized it was risky. The following Saturday she would say to him, "Thank you for the flowers, they were beautiful." And he would think, *What flowers?* But would he actually *say* this? I didn't think he would. I imagined Penis Man would say, simply, "You're welcome," and kiss her on the forehead.

It just seemed to me that she should *get* something from the asshole.

But then I had a more devious thought. What if I left the flowers? But with a note. A note that read, "I love you. I need more of you. I need seven days of you. Marry me?"

Surely, she would confront him about this note. On Saturday when he arrived, she wouldn't have candles burning. When he came through the door she would say, "What did you mean? Are you serious?" She would be so stuffed with hope that I'd be able to read her face from across the courtyard.

And this, he wouldn't just let go. "What note? What flowers? What are you talking about?" He would think, *Crazy woman.*

This would break them up. I knew it would. He wouldn't show up anymore once his Saturday fuck started playing games with flowers and notes and marriage. He wouldn't be back the next Saturday. I was sure of it.

And she would be heartbroken. But then, she would move through it. And wouldn't she be better off? Without him? I felt certain she would.

I desperately wanted to leave her the note. I disliked Penis Man enormously. I felt protective of Saturday Susan, as though I was watching over her.

Of course, technically, I wasn't watching over her. I was merely a Peeping Tom with alcohol breath and corn chip crumbs on my shirt. *But still.*

It never occurred to me that it was in any way wrong to watch her life. Any more than I felt it was wrong to spend all day watching Uma Thurman walk around her penthouse apartment on Fifth Avenue.

Of course, when I signed on as an associate creative director for the ad agency, I didn't know my office overlooked the actress's apartment. But had I known, I certainly would have slashed my salary in half just to get the job.

It took me exactly one day to spot and then recognize Uma. She was sitting on her sofa, which was positioned across from a black grand piano. She was barefoot and reading a script.

"Oh my God," I said to my art director partner. "Is that Uma?"

She approached the window. "Where?"

I pointed to the top floor of the building across the street. "Right there, see?"

She studied the woman and said, "Yup. That's Uma. Funny. Okay, let's get back to work."

But I would never be able to do any work in that office again. Because, look! Uma has gone to the window to smoke a cigarette!

It pained me that I could see so little of her space. Was limited to Uma activities that occurred only within the first ten feet of the apartment. All the good stuff, the back-of-the-apartment stuff, happened out of my sight.

Although on my second day something quite wonderful happened. When I looked out the window and into Uma's place, the furniture had been rearranged.

Uma was now sitting on a chair that I was certain had been in a different place the very day before. And the sofa, too. And the piano. Everything was different. Uma was a furniture rearranger. Just like me!

I felt bonded to the acclaimed actress. Positive that we would be close, close friends.

I began staying late at the office. Until ten, eleven at night. I would have given both testicles and possibly an arm to see Uma stick her finger down her throat and then throw up a sandwich. Or maybe? Do something really Hollywood, like dump a bag of coke out on the coffee table and snort it up with a hundred-dollar bill. But none of this happened. The most exciting thing Uma ever did was pick up the phone, read a script, or have a cigarette.

At least the woman at the Northampton, Massachusetts, state fair could smoke a cigarette with her pussy.

Uma didn't even do that.

Impossibly, I became bored with Uma and her shockingly un-eventful life. "Jesus, Uma. At least get a kitten," I said, finally yank-ing the cord to my blinds and letting them slam down against the windowsill.

And then I thought, What if Uma had seen me gawking at her? A rich and powerful celebrity, she could easily have hired some-body to arrest, if not kill me, as I probably deserved.

And this made me think of how dangerous peeping can actually be. I thought back to my very first peeping experience and how it nearly landed me on Alcatraz.

I was nineteen and living in San Francisco.

My apartment was on a tiny alley of a street, in the North End, near all the tourist shit. It was a street that even long-time residents of San Francisco had never heard of. Because for one thing, long-time residents of San Francisco wouldn't want to live in the most touristy part of the city. But it was such a tiny street and it ran di-rectly into an area containing subsidized housing.

One evening, after consuming a box of California white wine, I strolled downstairs and stood in the alley. I was going to walk to the store and buy more wine, but something in one of the windows of the subsidized apartments caught my eye.

It was a ratty sofa, with a big-ass ugly magnolia print. A sofa so hideous that I, at nineteen, couldn't imagine what kind of person could have it in their home. And then I noticed that a lump of pillows on top of the back of the sofa moved. And then I realized, those aren't pillows but a bulldog. And this drew me closer to the window.

I have always had a fierce connection to dogs. More so than with humans. Whenever I see a dog, I am compelled to communicate with it.

The dog was an English bulldog. One of my favorite breeds. Every breed is one of my favorite breeds when I see it. But English bulldogs are one of my favorite breeds even when I don't see one.

It was at window height, so somehow it was elevated. Was it on a table? Or—impossibly—sleeping along the back of a sofa? This would have made the most sense, visually. But how could it rest along the narrow back of a sofa?

I whistled. Just a quick note.

Nothing.

I whistled again, and saw the right ear, closest to me, twitch. The dog was in profile to me and remained so. But the ear, it definitely twitched.

So I whistled once more, but in a pattern. A burst, then three long notes, then another burst.

The bulldog's head turned.

I whistled again. I waved.

The dog was looking. To the right, to the left, everywhere but at me, the source.

I whistled as loud as I could.

The dog saw me.

Two car doors slammed, one after the other.

Almost immediately, two men were standing beside me. I turned.

A badge was flashed. "San Francisco police officers, undercover," they said. And indeed, the badges looked authentic. So did the suspicion in their eyes.

"Who are you trying to contact in the building?"

I was too stunned to even reply. I said, "What?"

"We've been watching you for the past five minutes. You're obviously sending a signal to somebody in the housing project over there. Who are you trying to contact? Are you looking for drugs?"

At this stage in my life, I was absolutely not looking for drugs. I was nineteen, working at my first job in advertising; I was aloft.

I said, "No, I'm trying to get that bulldog's attention, see." I pointed. The dog was gone.

"Well, he *was* there," I said.

Then I said, "Look, I'm serious. There was a bulldog in the window and I was trying to get it to look at me. I'm not buying drugs. I'm an advertising copywriter. I can prove it."

They were looking at me with a higher degree of interest.

I must have reeked of cheap white wine.

I repeated the copy from my latest Beef Industry Council ad, which I recalled verbatim. "A lean, three-ounce serving of beef has no more cholesterol than chicken—without the skin. Stunning, but very true. We have other facts that would make your grandmother spin. Consider this: Beef is fast. You can cook a roast so fast . . ."

I continued to recite all the words from every beef ad I currently had in production.

One of the cops said, "Is that true? Beef has no more cholesterol than chicken?"

I said, "Yes, it is true. That's the thing people don't realize. They think beef is just horrible, but it's really not." Then I added, "True, you don't want to eat a steak so big it touches both sides of the plate, but—"

He interrupted. "Hey, that's funny. A steak that touches both sides of the plate. That's really funny. I can see it in my mind when you say that."

"Thanks," I said. "I was actually testing that line out on you right now. I was thinking of using it in a print ad. Anyway, no, it's true. Beef isn't unhealthy. But you have to trim the fat and remember that a serving is three ounces."

"So what's that?" the cop said. "That's, like, a very small steak. I always get the sixteen or twenty-two-ounce sirloins."

"Well, three ounces is the size of a deck of playing cards."

"Oh, so that's how they do it," he said. "They call that a serving. Shit, that's not even an appetizer."

Then, suddenly aware that I was not chatting about beef with a couple of guys on the street, but technically being interrogated by police officers, I said, "So wait. Listen. I'm really not buying drugs. I don't ever do drugs. I'm against them. Although I drink more than I should, but I don't ever do drugs. I was really just looking for the dog. I like dogs more than people. I don't tend to like people very much."

And the cop said, "No, we know. We can tell. It's okay. So what about hamburger? Is that bad?"

I said, "Well, hamburger is tricky. Which is why we can't ever make health claims about it. Because there's a lot of fat in hamburger meat. So we go after more of a craving angle, you know? Like, sometimes you just have to order a burger, even though the trendy restaurants are all pushing radicchio."

"Well, everything in moderation," said the cop.

"That's the thing, really," I agreed.

And then they left. "Be careful," one of them warned before stepping back inside the unmarked police car.

I went back to my apartment and deadbolted the lock. Even though I hadn't been looking for drugs, I felt exactly as though I had been. And was just lucky to be free.

I vowed to never, never look in another person's window. Not ever. No matter what. And for a few years, I didn't. I even kept my blinds closed.

But then I left San Francisco and moved to New York. And in a city of so many millions of people, it was just impossible to keep my eyes to myself.

Taking Tests, Taking Things

Sara Lee Chocolate Chip Cheesecake drove me from the advertising industry.

The Sara Lee clients were nice enough. In fact, I was fond of them. I even thought the Sara Lee product itself was good. I believed in what I was selling, which is highly unusual in advertising. So it wasn't entirely the cheesecake's fault.

The problem was me. I was out of ideas. I was spending hours at my computer, sorting through old files on my hard drive, searching for dead concepts I'd tried to use on other brands and Frankenstein-monstering them together into new work for the cheesecake.

That was a cool technique I'd tried to sell those tampon people. Or, Why couldn't I just substitute a cheesecake for this personal lubricant? All it needs is a new voice-over.

But in the end, I knew that this hideous fusion approach was destined to fail. My job was to think of fresh, new ideas. Even when I didn't feel like it. And if I couldn't think of fresh, new ideas, I needed to leave the business. Or at least take a vacation. After all, it had been five years since I'd had five days off in a row.

I said to my boss, "I think I need some time away from the office. I mean, I'm scraping the bottom of the barrel, in terms of ideas."

My boss was an Evangelical Christian, deeply philosophical, who seldom lost his temper and almost never swore. He said, "Well, keep scraping. Because whatever muck you come up with, we need to stick on TV for this fucking cheesecake."

So I grabbed my pad of paper and my thick black markers and I got back to work, trying to pinch out a turd of an idea.

What I came up with was not so much an idea, but a collection of words I knew the client would like to hear, along with a visual technique that featured a smiling child, shot from an unusual perspective. It was an idea that I had to romance, as I presented it. Because on paper, there wasn't much there.

But sometimes a lack of an actual idea is a good thing in advertising. Because the creative director or the client can then superimpose their own idea onto yours. Much like transference, in psychotherapy.

"Oh, I get it," my boss said. "So it's sort of like a visual representation of what it *feels* like to eat the cheesecake."

That sounded pretty good. I said, "Yeah! That's exactly what I had in mind."

The commercial made it through the various layers of the ad agency, and finally to the client. The Sara Lee people liked the commercial very much. Because it was mostly food footage, which could be shot inexpensively in a local studio. And a little outdoor footage with a child, which did not get in the way of the food footage. And because the "live action" footage of the child would be colorized in postproduction, given a warm chocolate color, there was no danger of them having to pay for a weather day if we ended up shooting under overcast skies.

So I'd succeeded. The commercial would be a dreadful embarrassment to me and would invoke scorn from my peers. But I'd bought myself a little more time in the business. Thinking, which was the hard part, was over. Now, I could coast on commercial production. *"No, I don't need to look through the camera. Just make it pretty."* And that was the next best thing to a vacation.

So I spent my mental energy contemplating alternate careers. Trying to visualize my escape hatch from the business.

But what, exactly, was I qualified to do?

And the answer was absolutely nothing.

Because I had no formal education and didn't know basic math, I couldn't even operate a cash register, so even a Gap sales position was out.

What internal reserves did I have that could be tapped?

That was easy: rage.

So what could a person with no education, zero skills, but an endless reserve of bottled rage *do* to earn money?

And this is when I decided I would become a police officer for the City of New York.

Unlike many people who become cops, I didn't have fathers and brothers and uncles who'd been on the force.

But I had, over the years, had a number of positive experiences with men and women in uniform.

The first time I snorted cocaine, when I was sixteen, was with a female police officer. She had just bags and bags of the stuff, and she even snorted it in uniform, though without her hat.

Many years later, I dated a cop from Brooklyn. The thing I liked about him was that he was an honest, no-bullshit kind of guy. When he was with me, he was *with* me. He wasn't looking around the diner, scoping out the other guys. I never suspected that he was secretly dating someone else on the side. If my cop wasn't with me and he wasn't at work, I knew he was home with his trusting wife and two young children.

These experiences taught me that law enforcement offered great latitude as a career choice. It accepted many different kinds of people into its ranks.

Certainly, if a coked-up chick from western Massachusetts and a sexually confused adulterer from Brooklyn could be cops, so could a mediocre advertising burnout.

So I bought a book, *The Police Academy Entrance Examinations: Study Guide and Test Questions.* And I began to study it at night, after work.

Never a good student, I found myself most attracted to the practice exams, as opposed to the actual words one is supposed to read before taking them.

I figured cops were born. Not made. Besides, one look at the questions and it was pretty obvious that the police academy did not have the rigorous intellectual standards of a Yale or Columbia University.

It seemed even *I* would be able to pass *this* exam.

So I spent an hour and filled out the first of the tests. After this, I graded myself. And to my real surprise, saw that I had failed. Out of all the questions on the exam, I got a pitiful smidgeon of them correct.

Helpfully, the book provided the answers, along with the reasons why any given answer was correct.

One of the questions asked, "The traffic lights are broken and you are directing traffic. A pedestrian approaches you and asks for directions. Do you:

A. Ignore the person and continue directing traffic.
B. Stop directing traffic and answer the person's question.

C. Answer the person's question but continue directing
traffic.

D. Tell the person you cannot help them because you are
directing traffic."

The obvious answer was A. *Ignore the person and continue direct-ing traffic.* Clearly, if the traffic lights are broken, a car accident is an imminent threat.

But the answer was B. I was expected to stop directing traffic and answer the person's question.

This seemed not only contrary to common sense but just plain stupid. To stop directing traffic and have a little chat with an ordi-nary person could lead to death. So I read the explanation and dis-covered that the number one priority for a police officer is his relationship to the public. The police officer must, at all times, demonstrate to the public how much she respects them.

I thought, oh, that's hogwash.

The next question was even more obvious. It asked, "A store owner has failed to clear the sidewalk in front of his building of ice. Do you:

A. Remind the shopkeeper that he must clear the sidewalk
of ice and then walk on.

B. Remind the shopkeeper that he must clear the sidewalk
of ice and wait while he does this.

C. Fine the shopkeeper for having ice on his sidewalk and
then make him remove it while you watch him."

The obvious answer was C. I would fine the shopkeeper for breaking the law. And then I would stand over his sorry ass while he removed every fucking ice crystal.

But again, I was wrong. According to the entrance exam, I was to remind the shopkeeper of his duty to clear the ice, and then simply *trust* that he will do this, as I *walk away*.

I failed other questions, as well. Many of them involving guns and when to brandish them. My instinct was always have your gun in your hand. Especially when you are telling somebody to do something.

But, in fact, the police academy discourages this. They feel your gun should rarely, if ever, be brought out of its holster. Most certainly not when children are involved, which is exactly when I saw myself using my gun most often. A truant teenager loitering outside a movie theater is going to be far more motivated to return to school when he has the barrel of a .45 pressed against his cheek.

So I had to ask myself, what was my motivation for becoming a cop? And the answer was to say I was a cop.

I simply liked the idea of wearing a uniform, carrying a gun, and walking around in a cocoon of safety and authority. I liked thinking about how much fun it would be to pull advertising account executives over in their BMWs and give them speeding tickets—at gunpoint—for going four miles per hour over the limit.

I smiled when I imagined myself being the ultimate party pooper, arresting kids on the NYU campus for smoking a joint. And then pocketing the joint for myself, for later.

Plus, I already had a little experience in the security industry. I'd been a store detective at a crime-infested eastern Massachusetts department store when I was eighteen.

And oh, how I'd cherished that job.

I spent six hours every day—often skipping lunch—upstairs alone in an office. Here, I had a bank of television monitors that accepted feeds from cameras located throughout the store. Each camera could be individually operated with a joystick. So I could follow people. And then I could zoom in.

I watched men pretend to scratch their ankles, only to slip a pair of needle-nose pliers or a screwdriver into their socks. I saw single mothers tuck lipsticks and batteries into their babies' diapers.

Frequently, I saw other employees stuff eyeliner, gum, and candy bars into their pockets.

And the manager who hired me used to walk through the store pocketing razor blades, toothpaste, and combs, winking at the camera every time.

I was even allowed to smoke up there in the office, so it was like being at home. Actually, it was better than home, because there was nothing this good on *my* television.

It was the most supreme form of entertainment one can imagine. If only I'd had a special red button that I could push to release furious Dobermans into the store.

But as with every job, it wasn't *always* exciting. Sometimes days would pass when the most interesting thing in the store was a crotch or two.

But for the most part, this was a town of crooks, delinquents, and frauds, and I was in charge of security at their own hometown department store. And my feeling was, *If you're even remotely sexy, you can steal.*

But in truth, I let even the ugly ones get away with it because I was petrified by the thought of going downstairs, flashing my cheap tin badge, and confronting one of these desperate criminals.

The only glitch—and it was a small one—was that I shared this job with another store detective. A local guy who was enrolled in the police academy for the following year.

His name was Shaun, and even though this name brings to mind

images of a soft, pornish man, Shaun was a soulless geek with a machine heart, a flattop haircut, and black, narrow eyes.

While I sat at my screen, using my joystick to make the camera
move up and down the legs of the college soccer players when they
came into the store, Shaun used his camera to track young mothers
stealing small jars of baby food.

Worst of all, he then went downstairs and nabbed them.

The process was this: Bring the "suspect" upstairs into the
brightly lit detaining room and interview them. If you found the
goods on their person, you were to call the police and the store policy dictated that charges would be pressed.

That was far too complicated, as far as I was concerned. For
three dollars an hour, I'd watch people shoplift. You bet. But if you
wanted me to then go downstairs and confront them—and often
they were men nine times my size—that was going to take another
two hundred dollars an hour, along with a shotgun and a bottle of
vermouth.

Every once in a while Shaun would come up to me and say, "So,
how many did you get today?"

I'd say, "Well, none. But I'm looking."

And he'd say, "That's good. Keep it up. It takes awhile, but once
you see your first shoplifter, your eyes learn real fast. And then it'll
come easy. Don't be too hard on yourself," he'd say. "It took me a
couple of weeks before I started seeing them, too."

I didn't dare tell him that I saw somebody shoplifting every
thirty seconds.

When Shaun asked me what I was going to do with my life, what
my "plans" were, I always tried to give as vague an answer as possible. Because I had no idea. And it was humiliating to be asked by
somebody who had a very firm idea, and not only that but an en-
rollment date.

"I can't wait to get out there on the highway," he told me. "I may not be able to make the world a safer place for the kids I'll eventually have, but I can make these here streets a little safer."

Shaun stopped liking me so much after a month.

"Come on, man," he'd say. "We're a team and you're not holding up your half of the bargain."

"Yeah, but check out the pumped chest on that dad down there. The one who just stuffed the blowtorch refill down his pants," I didn't say.

In truth, I felt for the shoplifters. Especially the mothers taking baby supplies. And, okay, I could see that maybe it was good to confront the old man with the seventeen Seiko watches strapped to his wrist. But the old woman, swiping a fifty-five-cent package of tissues? To carry with her to the funerals of all her old friends?

No. I wasn't going to take another lap around the fire lake in hell for punishing some tissue-stealing old lady.

Not only would I not apprehend these people, but I would prevent Shaun from doing it, too.

If Shaun got a little too suspicious about somebody I knew was stealing, but felt was entitled to steal, I would simply throw him a red herring.

"Shaun. Look! See that?"

And he'd come running over to my screen.

"What?" he'd say, pressing his pointy rat nose at the monitor.

"That guy there. He just took something. I couldn't see what it was, but he jammed it up his shirt."

And Shaun would fly out of the room and down the stairs and thirty seconds later, I'd see him on my camera, as he approached the man.

Unfortunately, this is exactly how Shaun lost his job.

I'd sent him downstairs to follow a guy who'd "taken something weird, I think it was a cassette tape or something. And tucked it into his underwear."

I lit a cigarette and watched on my monitor as Shaun went downstairs and got into an argument with the man.

Then Shaun decided to prove his point. He reached forward and stuck his hand into the man's pants to pull out the cassette tape.

But instead, he found only a penis.

Unclear Sailing

Marblehead, Massachusetts, is known as a "coastal town," which means "the narrow streets are cut through the rock so you are always in danger of falling onto jagged shards and being swept away by Poseidon." Curiously, this increases the property values. Expansive, cedar-shingled homes dot the landscape. Sailboats outnumber seagulls, especially in the summer.

It would appear there's a law that allows only Saabs, Volvos, and BMWs. And in the winter, the owners must fix Christmas wreaths to their grilles. Anybody who dares present a Star of David on their lawn will certainly have their home burned to the ground.

Need I mention that not one black person lives in Marblehead?

At least, not when I lived there, at the age of eighteen. I had just graduated from a computer programming trade school but had decided two weeks before graduation to "get into advertising."

So far, I hadn't had any luck.

I'd thought up a few ads, typed them up, and stuck them into a three-ring binder. Then I'd phoned ad agencies in Boston and asked to show my portfolio.

Four agencies had agreed, and all four told me to go away within ten minutes of staring in horror at my mistyped, messy pages.

So I decided to hone my entrepreneurial skills and secure my own accounts. At eighteen, I could pass for twenty-four, which seemed more than old enough to start my own ad agency. Right here in Marblehead.

And I'd start with a sailmaker, a company that made sails for sailboats and the seventy-five million yachts crowding Marblehead Bay. They occupied an impressive loft building, so surely they'd offer me a fortune.

I presented my sweaty self to the receptionist. "I'd like to speak with the owner, please."

She said, "I'm sorry, the owner is unavailable. I'll get a manager for you, if you like."

This was as good a time as any to get familiar with corporate bureaucracy. I nodded.

She waved me toward a sofa. "Have a seat."

A moment later, a startlingly blond man in his early thirties appeared. His hair was streaked almost white from the sun; even the hair on his arms was bleached beyond color.

"Hi. I'm Cliff. What can I do for ya?"

I told him that I was starting an ad agency and that I would be honored if he would consider giving me his account, as my first. And that if he did, I would service it for just two hundred dollars a month, which I was positive was many hundreds of thousands less than his current ad agency in Boston charged. And then, somewhat embarrassed, I told him my name.

Cliff smiled. He said, "Wow, you sure talk fast! Why don't you come back to my office?"

So I followed him down a long hallway of polished wood. The

walls were lined with artful yet repetitive photographs of yachts cutting through ocean.

Cliff sat at the chair behind his desk and said, "So you're going to start your own ad agency, huh?"

His face was so open and friendly, I was tempted to tell him my entire life story, including my recent failure to get a job in advertising. But instead I swallowed and said, "Yes."

He looked apologetic, shrugged his shoulders and said, "To tell you the truth, we're pretty happy with our existing ad agency."

I deflated. Of course he was happy with his current ad agency. I was an idiot to even try this stunt. I shrank back against my chair.

"But if you're looking for work . . ."

Well. Maybe just for a *few* months. Until I could save enough money to start my own empire. I said, "What kind of work?" Knowing he would say, "Janitorial."

"We could use a new sail cutter," he said.

And because he hadn't said the word, "toilet," I was puzzled. "What's that?

Cliff explained. "Sail cutters take the canvas and use a pattern to cut the shapes that then get sewn together into the finished product. The sail. To be honest with you, it's hard work. But there's a lot of opportunity to advance."

I'd never in my life been offered a position so quickly. The usual process involved filling out an application, waiting two weeks, then being rejected. And unlike any other position I'd applied for, this one did not involve a deep fry bin.

"Yeah?" I said. I was doubtful. "Does it not pay any money or anything? Do you have to, like, volunteer for a while?"

Cliff laughed. "Of course it pays. Seven-fifty an hour."

More than three times what McDonald's offered. And *they* didn't even want me.

But I did have a small amount of pride. "Well. I really want to start my own ad agency. Eventually, at least. But I guess I could do that on the side and cut some sails."

"Yeah!" he said. "You could!"

"So. When would I start?"

He clapped his hands together. "How about right now?"

And now I was even more suspicious. I'd never heard of a job that you started the day you applied. Without even applying in the first place.

But maybe this was how things were done here in Marblehead. After all, for all he knew, I was a local boy, whose dad owned a brokerage firm in Boston. Maybe I was raised in Marblehead and our fathers were in the same French Lit class at Harvard.

I said, "Okay. I'll do it."

Cliff stood. His striped cotton oxford shirt was crisp, even at three in the afternoon. And his khakis were pressed. I noticed, too, that he wore no socks. Just bare, tan feet slipped into white-soled topsiders.

No mustard stains on him, that was for sure. How hard could this job be?

All the managers I'd known—Ground Round, Woolworth's— had sweated profusely and smelled strongly of alcohol.

I followed Cliff as he gave me a tour. Here are the restrooms. The time clock, please punch in. This is the vending machine. These are the corporate offices. That over there is a client showroom.

"And here's where you'll be," he said, opening the wide door of a freight elevator we were on to reveal an enormous room, empty except for walls of windows, overhead lights, and fabric on the floor.

"This is where we do the actual cutting," he said.

On the floor, men leaned over gigantic panels of white canvas. These were twenty, thirty-foot sheets of the brightest white fabric, made brighter by the sunlight that flooded the place.

The room was so huge that many sails could be spread out like this on the floor at once. And then dozens of people could busy themselves around them.

There was an almost holy quality to the room. The respect the men had for the sailcloth could be felt in the air.

I followed Cliff to the far corner of the room where he introduced me to three guys. These were Cliffs in miniature—all blond, all handsome. The oldest was probably twenty-two. We were peers. But grade school was as far as I'd made it academically, so I was uncomfortable around them and unsure how to behave. I was fine around people who were much older than me. Because I wanted to please them.

But I didn't know what to do around these three guys my own age.

"Hey," they each said, nodding.

I said, "Hey" back to them. Like a monkey staring in a mirror. I said "Hey," instead of the more formal "Hello." Or worse, "It's just wonderful to meet you," which was actually the first phrase that came to mind.

Then Cliff began speaking in tongues. "Start him off with a tri-Radial Spinnaker for a thirty-footer. If that goes okay, get him on a vertical batten mainsail for in-mast furling."

"Will do," one of the guys said, whose name had simply bounced off my forehead.

Cliff grabbed my upper arm and gave it a squeeze. "So, great. This is really exciting. You'll do a fine job and I think you'll have a terrific time here with the guys. And don't sweat if it's a little confusing at first. It'll take you a couple of days to get the hang. But, like I said, I think you'll do a fantastic job. And if you have any problems or if you need anything, you know where to find me." He smiled, revealing flawless white teeth, and walked away.

I watched him as he strode toward the elevator. *Is that it?*

"So it's pretty easy," the guy said to the back of my head.

I jerked around to look at him. "I'm sorry, what's your name again?"

"Chip. Anyway, it's pretty easy. Here, why don't you just watch me for a few and then I'll let you loose? But to be honest, I think I'm gonna start you out on a simple jib."

I didn't know what a jib was, but I liked that he described it as simple. And I also liked that all I had to do was watch. Maybe I could stretch this watching thing out all week, then quit and collect my week's pay.

"Come with me," Chip said. And I followed him across the floor of the loft and into a storage room filled with bolts of cloth. The bolts were huge—over ten feet long—and stored on shelves, ceiling high. Chip removed one of the bolts and told me to grab the other end. I did, but just barely. It was heavy and I was weak. Which instantly made me feel ashamed. Because I struggled so obviously to keep my end of the fabric bolt off the floor, I felt the words "pansy cake" etching into my forehead with an electric knife.

Now, I was not only overwhelmed but horribly self-conscious. This combination had the effect of generating static electricity in my mind. At that moment, I couldn't have named the color of the sky.

"Bring this out here," he said, and I had no choice but to run, struggling under the weight of the canvas, to keep up.

After we got back to the main floor, Chip unfurled the bolt of fabric, allowing a good twenty-five feet. He used an industrial blade to cut the fabric from the bolt, stepping on the back of the roll so that he kept the face of the fabric clean.

"Never," he said firmly, "step on the fabric. Always, *always* step on the opposite side of the roll, here. You don't want sneaker marks all over it. Ever."

And at that moment, I was cursed to a career, however brief, of sails covered with a tango of my footprints.

Then, to my utter horror, he removed a calculator from his pocket and set it on the floor.

The only use for a calculator that I'd ever had in my entire life was to use it to spell the words "Shell Oil" upside down.

"Basically, it works like this," he said. "We make custom sails. So you gotta know about the boat before you can make a sail. I'm gonna have you work on a sail for the same boat we're working on right now. So here's the deal." He turned to face me. "Shapes for different types of sails might look the same, but there are small, important differences for every boat. You know, like the sheeting angle, spreader length, and spreader locations. These are added so that we can develop the proper twist distribution for the sail to make sure it'll trim correctly around the individual rig."

I noticed that while his teeth were just as white as Cliff's, they weren't as straight. My teeth, I knew, were neither white nor straight. And this is all I was thinking as he continued to speak ancient Greek.

"So basically, we're looking at four different steps, two-dimensional measurements, three-dimensional shapes, panel layout and calculation, and nesting for cutting."

He squatted and removed a small pad of paper and pencil from his back pocket. Then he began to sketch some terrifying figures.

"First thing to do is input the two-dimensional numbers. The luff, leech, and then foot for what we call *mainsails*. Okay? And luff, leech, and foot"—he scratched the side of his nose with the eraser of his pencil—"or luff and clew positions for the headsails. Then we just fill in the specifics for head width, roach, leech hollow, and the foot round. See what I mean?"

I did not see what he meant, but I nodded, which meant, *I see that you have a large Adam's apple and I am very tempted to reach over and touch it.*

"So now we need a three-dimensional profile for the sail. We apply the mast bend for our mainsails. The headstay sag for headsails? This calculation we get based on the size and the geometry of our sail, along with wind force for the range of the sail, and the headstay tension."

He'd filled the page with sketches and numbers. Abstract lines and angles. A horror of mathematics.

"We define the sail shape for a few different cross sections of the sail. You know, in some ways this is a lot like certain aspects of automotive design or, probably, aviation engineering. But anyway, so these cross sections. At each of them we figure camber, which is the depth of the sail taken as a percent of its width, right? Then the distance from the leading edge right here"—he tapped his drawing—"to the point of maximum depth. The rate of the curve at any given point in the cross section. Entry angle and exit angle, then twist. This is the way to get a smooth, organic flow to the sail."

A tune was beginning to form in my head, but I couldn't quite place it. It was from a movie I'd seen recently. And the name would come to me at any moment.

"So, you got that?"

I said, "Um. I don't know."

He stood, smiling. "Yeah, I know. It might sound a little confusing at first. But believe me, you'll get it. So why don't we do this? I've sort of sketched out a simple pattern for you here. It's a jib. Just follow what I've got down here, it's just cutting, I did all the figuring out. And then call me over so I can take a look. Okay?" He smiled.

At least he was friendly.

"Okay!" I said. By raising my voice, I figured I might pass for a confident person.

He slapped me on the back and then walked away and I had the crushing urge to pee. What just happened?

I had no idea what to do. Was this a situation where one should walk away? Or just run?

Or, or. *Or* should I just take a look at what he drew and see if I could figure it out?

So I glanced down at the paper he'd given me. And there, among the numbers and the lines and the strange mathematical symbols that I vaguely recognized as geometry—about which I knew not one thing, including the names of basic shapes—I saw what resembled a sail.

It was pointy on top, with two long lines going down. And then a flat base. At the heart of all his gibberish was the same little sail I'd drawn myself with crayons a hundred times as a preschooler.

So. Yeah. I could do that.

I looked at his drawing one more time. And then I looked at the cloth on the floor of the loft. And then I looked at my hand, which was somehow holding the cutting blade.

And I shrugged. And I began to cut.

Because there was a fixed amount of canvas on the floor, I assumed that this was the height he wanted the sail to be. So I started at the flat end where he had trimmed the fabric from the bolt, and then worked my way up from there, cutting away the sides of the fabric and then tapering to create a point. I had to hack some extra fabric away at the top. But in the end, it was pretty much a point.

And yeah! It was a sail. It looked just like his picture.

Just as I had long suspected, a person didn't really need math for anything anyway. Maybe some people did. Some *limited* people. But I was smart and resourceful and I was able to take a sketch and turn it into reality because I understood his vision.

I decided it was time to show him my work, so I walked across the floor to where he was working on a sail of his own. I felt much more confident now. Almost a little cocky. Because I'd accomplished something.

Chip was on his knees and looked up. He said, "What's up? Got a problem?"

I smiled and said, "Nah. I finished that one. Do you have another one you want me to work on?"

He stood. "What do you mean, *you finished it.* That's impossible."

"No," I said, slightly less confident now. "I finished cutting it out. Your drawing, it was really good. It was very clear. So I finished it. I used to cut people's hair and stuff sometimes. So I'm pretty good with, you know, cutting. Pretty much."

Chip said, "I need to see what you did. How could you have finished that jib in less than"—he glanced at his watch—"in less than nine minutes?"

I walked toward my sail with Chip just behind me. But before we even reached it, I began to worry. Because from this angle, approaching it from this other direction, it didn't look quite so much like what he had drawn. In fact, I could see clearly that my two cuts along the sides weren't exactly straight. But then I remembered, these things get sewn. So it's okay. Somebody can fix it.

"Holy Christ," he said. "You've just ruined a ton of fabric. What the fuck do you think you're doing? What the FUCK?"

"I had to eyeball it," I said.

"You WHAT?"

I said, "I had to eyeball it. You know. Look at your picture and then just try and copy it."

"I do NOT understand this. Why did you do this? How could you do such a thing? All you had to do was use some basic geometry. *Jesus.* This doesn't make any sense."

I shoved my hands in my pockets and looked down at the floor. "I don't *know* geometry," I said, now defeated. Seeing clearly how stupid I was. How delusional. "I don't know any math at all. I can't even add."

I glanced up at him and he was staring at me in disbelief. "Are you for real?"

"I tried to make it look like the picture. I guess I don't belong here."

"No, I don't suppose you do belong here, you retard. Why don't you get the hell out of here. You stupid little faggot. Go. NOW."

So I didn't have to say good-bye to the other guys or even him. I just walked across the floor.

Because Chip had been shouting, other guys had stopped working and were standing to watch me.

To save face, I walked across the floor, making sure to step across every sail in my way. I tried to hold my head high, as though I had just been promoted and would, within weeks, own the entire company.

I imagined firing all of the Chips and Cliffs and Biffs, one blond head at a time.

UNDER NEW MANAGEMENT, a sign out front would read. I would then hire all the losers and winos and misfits. And we would make a new kind of sail. The kind that maybe doesn't work as well, but was built by hand with great, white hope.

Moving Violations

Druggy Debby could do this thing with her really long, uncommonly dexterous tongue. This was clearly a genetic gift, although of debatable value. Nonetheless, she could extend her tongue and then roll the edges inward, like a tortilla, creating a point at the end. And then she could cram this point way, way up her nostril.

As if this alone wasn't reason enough to be best friends.

But there was more. She was incredibly funny, but in a way that made you say, *"That's horrible,"* before you laughed until you accidentally farted.

And then a split second later, she could be your mother. Tender and nurturing and chopping vegetables and chicken for soup, while she passed you a joint. Debby was usually buzzed, though seldom wasted. Thus her nickname. Which was given to her in high school and probably harsher than warranted.

She was surprisingly intelligent. Which sounds like a mean thing to say except it's not, really. What I mean is that Druggy Debby had an intelligence that surprised. You could hand her your broken radio and she'd pull a screwdriver out of her hair and have it fixed for you in five minutes flat. And then she'd tune it to the only station in western Massachusetts that played punk rock and Etta James. A station you'd never heard before, even though you'd lived there your whole life.

She knew things. She knew how things worked. Druggy Debby truly understood Einstein's theory of relativity and described the world of quantum mechanics as "all about potential, dollface."

We became friends in the summer of 1983. As fate would have it, we both ended up as waiters at the new Ground Round restaurant in Northampton, Massachusetts. We became friends because we both applied for jobs the Monday before the restaurant opened. There were eight or nine of us sitting around a pushed-together table and filling out applications.

I was trying to think of how I could flesh out my answers for the section labeled "Experience." Because while I'd had a lot of *experience* in my seventeen years, none of it would be required as waiter, and some of it could even land me in prison.

"What's the matter with you? Why are you staring at the application?" she asked.

I turned to see a girl with blond hair, streaked blue. I said, "I don't know. It's this part, *experience*. I don't really have any."

She glanced around the table, saw that everybody else was busy writing. Then she whispered, "Bullshit. Of course you have experience. Everybody does. Look, what can you do?"

"I don't know," I said. "Nothing. I mean, I've never had an actual job. I've done things. But weird things, you know. Things people haven't even heard of, let alone talk about, *let alone* on a job application."

Debby said, "I know exactly what you mean. Like?" she continued. "Okay, so like, I am double-jointed in strange ways. I can bend
my wrist, well, like this," she said, bending her wrist back so that
the tips of her fingers touched the top of her forearm. "Okay? And I
can do splits, but, like, totally flat. And I can cross my legs over my
head. All this weird shit that's useless. But look, see what I did?" She
gently nudged her application, causing me to glance down at it.

There, under Experience, she'd written, "Senior Contortionist,
Toronto Council of Arts for the Handicapped."

"What does that mean?" I whispered through the smirk that had
formed on my face.

"It means *shit*. I made it up. But see, what are they gonna do? If
they ask if I was really a senior contortionist, all I have to do is bend
over backwards and touch the top of my head to the floor, which I
can do. Plus, they'll see 'handicapped' and that will just really freak
them out. You cannot fuck with the handicapped in this country, or
with anybody who even *knows* somebody who is handicapped."

I smiled at her. "That's pretty good," I said, impressed.

"I'm Debby, by the way," she said, smiling back.

"Augusten."

Then I wrote, "Crisis Management Caseworker, Northampton
Society for the Mentally Ill." "My mother is psychotic and gave me
away to her shrink, and sometimes we take her to a motel so she
can break the furniture there, instead of at home. She's been that
way my whole life."

"Perfect," Debby said. "How can they argue with that?"

We filled out the rest of our applications without saying anything more, only passing each other the occasional smile or know-
ingly raised eyebrow.

But we were friends now. We just were.

Half an hour after everybody handed their applications to the
manager, he stepped into the rear, out of sight. The bunch of us sat

around the table in slow, awkward silence. "Did he say we should just sit here?" somebody asked. Somebody else got up to make a call from the pay phone.

A few moments later, the manager returned. "You're all hired," he said.

After work, Debby and I would drive in my 1972 Chrysler to the Good Tymes Restaurant and Cocktail Lounge on Route 5. Although I was underage, Debby was twenty-one and beautiful. It was the beautiful part that got me drinks. One waiter was a skinny, very tall man with dark straight hair and oily skin. We called him Rat Man.

He had a hateful expression, with his eyes squinty and his mouth in a snarl. Except when Debby entered the lounge and then he brightened. Which was, unfortunately, a gruesome thing to see. Because when he smiled, his lips peeled back to reveal yellow, crooked teeth, with what appeared to be a full extra row on top. But his eyes softened, the nasty glint becoming something akin to warmth. Clearly, he was dopey-crazy for her. So when we ordered drinks, he nodded and stepped behind the bar to make them. Then he brought them to the table and set them down before us. Every time, he looked at me in a way that made me understand I was only drinking because he liked Debby. And she looked back at him and smiled in a way that told him she thought he was simply adorable and quite near perfect.

And then we drank while he sat at his bar smoking and openly watching her.

Each night, we drank through our tips. The bar closed at eleven, but he often let us stay until two, especially if Debby let him feel one of her breasts under her shirt, which she was happy to do as a sort of public service.

I liked this about her. She was enormously generous. And I do think she truly enjoyed his attention.

But unfortunately, Debby wasn't as good with her customers as she was with the Rat Man at the Good Tymes Restaurant and Cocktail Lounge.

Within a month, she had begun snapping at them nightly. She simply lost patience with the endless requests for a baby booster seat, an extra glass of ice water, more catsup for the French fries, and "real tarter sauce, not this shit from a can."

Finally, one night Debby lost it.

The restaurant was divided into a "family restaurant" on one side and a bar with tables on the other, with the kitchen in the middle. Most nights we worked together in the family restaurant portion. But one Friday night, Debby got stuck in the bar, covering for another waitress who was out for two days, having an abortion (her fifth).

At around ten-thirty, a dozen UMass students—all guys—came in and sat at a table she hadn't had time to bus. Immediately, they began demanding service.

"Bring us some pitchers!" they shouted at her. "Pitchers of Bud!"

Debby walked over to their table and as she told me later, "I told them I needed to see ID from everybody and then one of them started giving me trouble. Saying things like, 'Knock it off, bitch, just bring us the beer.' And the table was a mess, so they started picking up plates and just shoving them on the floor. And I told them again, I need to see some ID. And the asshole guy, he stands up and he unzips his jeans. Then he pulls out his cock and starts waving it at me. Says something like, 'Does this look like the dick of a fifteen-year-old to you, waitress?' This really pissed me off. So I reached up under my skirt and I pulled out my tampon. And I just hurled it at him, smacking him in the chest."

As Debby recounted the story, she laughed until she was sobbing. "But my God, you should have seen how that shut them all
up. Here's this big fat pig of a linebacker with a tampon stuck to his
shirt, then—splat—on his shoe!"

After pulling this stunt, Debby untied her mandatory apron and
walked out, but not before emptying the apron pockets of cash,
which she crammed in her jeans.

It was a great story and I admired her. And I also felt a little en-
vious. Because that bloody tampon had been a secret weapon. And
every woman had one. But only a woman like Debby would be
brave enough to use it.

Within a week, Debby found another job across the bridge in
Amherst. And this job suited her personality much better. She
worked the night shift at a twenty-four-hour photocopy store.

University Copy was located down an alley, in the basement of a
building. Bicycles were chained to a rack next to the door. And to
get inside, you had to walk down a flight of stairs. But far from being dark and creepy, the copy shop was at all times brightly lit by
overhead lights. Machines hummed and chunked along, creating so
much noise it was actually peaceful. Sweating college students ran
from machine to machine, wiping their foreheads on the sleeves of
their rolled-up oxford shirts.

A bulletin board inside near the door was layered with fliers.
"Lead Singer needed," "Futon For Sale—almost new," "1967 VW
Bug Runs Great." Sometimes I would go to the shop at five in the
morning, an hour before Debby's shift ended, and read the ads.
They fascinated me because they were each a portal into a different,
possible life. For example, what if I were to tear the phone number
strip off an ad reading, "Become a Massage Therapist"? What if I
took the course and then got myself a little table? I could take it
around from apartment to apartment, putting my hands on people's
thighs and calves, pulling their toes. Surely one of the people at-

tached to one of these toes would somehow change my life. Maybe
I would end up falling in love with some guy whose lower back I
rubbed?

Or I could study yoga. Or adopt a wolf hybrid. Or learn American sign language, something I'd always wanted to do.

But more than reading these fliers and imagining my new possible life, I loved sniffing Debby's hair when she got off her shift.

"Why do you *do* that, you perv," she would say, laughing and
pulling away from me.

I couldn't help myself. The copy shop had the most intoxicating
smell—sweet and chemical. It reminded me of huge English papers, diagrams of the known universe, graduate studies. Because I
had no education myself, I had developed something of an education fetish. I found nothing sexier than a pair of gold wire frame
glasses and a physics student behind them. And this aroma soaked
into Debby's clothes, especially her hair. So the instant we walked
out the door, I grabbed handfuls of her hair, inhaling the fumes.
Like a teenage junkie with his airplane-model glue.

Debby was usually wired after working all night. So instead of
wanting to just go home to her apartment and sleep for the next
seven hours, she usually wanted to go for a drive.

And this became our routine. I'd meet her at the copy shop on
my free days and we'd climb into her car, a hand-me-down white
Toyota Corolla from her mother. We'd roll the windows down immediately and then take off. Drive for hours, talking at all times,
hands going in and out of a giant bag of candy corn next to the
gearshift between us.

Usually, we'd take the highway. Interstate 91. Sometimes south
to Hartford. Or north, all the way to Vermont.

Once, we were driving and a black Ford Bronco cut us off.

"Hey! Asshole," Debby said, jerking the wheel to the left to avoid
smacking the side of his truck.

He hadn't used his blinker.

And Debby was a stickler for blinkers. In fact, she obeyed every traffic law to the letter. If the speed limit sign read "55," Debby would go 54.

Sometimes she would make comments out of the blue like, "Always leave three car lengths between you and the car ahead. I'm just saying. Always do that. But anyway, what about the guy's chest hair?"

Because Debby was such a thoughtful, responsible driver, it enraged her when another driver was careless.

"If that jerk wants to kill himself, fine. Let him. But he's not taking me with him!"

Because of this, because she cared about her life and because other people were "variables" to her, Debby took certain measures that went somewhat beyond normal highway safety.

The thing is, Debby was really a teacher at heart. Even though her hair was streaked with blue and she had a definite wild side, which often involved Quaaludes, cocaine, and pot, Debby's heart was in exactly the right place.

So she took to carrying a stack of images, mounted on foam board and placed on the backseat within easy reach.

The images were taken from magazines, enlarged at the copy shop, and then copied in vibrant, true color. Then they were spray mounted to stiff boards, as would be used in a presentation of some sort.

When somebody misbehaved on the road—tailgating, passing on the right, tossing garbage out a window—Debby would say, "Quick, grab a shot."

And I would turn around and reach into the pile for one of the boards. I never looked to see which board I was grabbing. For as different as they were, they were all basically the same.

I would then hold the picture against the window and Debby

would either speed up to pass the offending car, or she would slow down so they could get a good look.

The images were all hardcore pornography.

And these were not pictures torn from the pages of *Playboy* magazine. These were far more graphic, triple-X shots from Dutch and German porn magazines, often sadistic.

One image—a personal favorite—was a shot of a woman squatting. Pressed against her vagina was the snout of a German Shepard.

Even the crudest, most hardened trucker would stare slack-jawed at that baby.

But just a simple picture of a black penis entering a Caucasian vagina was enough to cause many mothers—Jesus, those kids aren't wearing seatbelts!!!—to pull their station wagons over to the side of the road.

Printed under each pornographic image was a phrase:

Use your blinkers when changing lanes!!!
You are a Careless Driver.
Get some Road Manners.
Stop Tailgating.
Don't Pass on the Right.

But because we grabbed the pictures quickly and without looking, often a tailgater would get a cum shot with the words "NO PASSING ON A SOLID LINE" printed beneath it. The system wasn't perfect. But the point was unforgettable. At least the driver would understand he had done something terribly wrong.

Single guys on motorcycles who made leering, sexual gestures at pretty driving Debby were in for a special surprise. For these men, there was a special board, alone on the seat next to the others.

This was a photograph of foreskin "docking," where one man slips the end of his penis into the foreskin of another, as the men stand face-to-face. Looking at such an image, cropped so close, it was a strange, entirely unfamiliar thing, though unmistakably sexual and offensive to most.

Nothing could make guy on a Harley fall behind faster than ten seconds of this particular image.

"See, the thing is," Debby explained, "people don't even think. They just pull in front of you and think nothing of it. But then all of a sudden, they see the car they just passed coming up behind them. And they maybe expect the finger. So they smile. You know, they laugh to themselves. They think, fuck you. Too bad I passed you. Speed up next time. But then they see not a middle finger, but a naked woman with a pound of hotdogs stuffed up her anus, and this cancels every other thought. All of a sudden, they are being assaulted by the most stunning image they have ever seen, directly after they have done something bad, as a driver. So they make the connection. Even if *they* don't make the connection, their brain *does*. It's Pavlovian."

She really had it all figured out.

And it became a source of great entertainment for us. And soon enough, we stopped waiting for people to cut us off, we went looking for them.

Debby would light up a joint and we'd go hunting.

"Did that moron just change lanes without using his blinker?" she'd say.

"Which moron?"

She'd point. "That one. In the blue Ford Fairmont. Five cars up. I swear he just changed lanes without using his blinker. Quick, grab one of the shots."

She'd speed up and I'd make eye contact with the driver.

When you pass a car, the driver tends to look at you. But if you don't look away, neither do they. On the sidewalk, people look away. But in cars, protected by steel and glass and speed, people aren't as afraid of unfamiliar instant intimacy. Of course, eventually, the driver will look away from you and back at the road.

But if you suddenly show them a photograph of a woman giving a blowjob to a midget, they won't look away at all. They will open their mouth and look harder.

Horns will blare, as their car weaves.

In all our miles of doing this, for the year we were best friends, not one person ever gave us the finger or mouthed the words "fuck you" through the windshield. Simply, everybody was too stunned. More surprising, we never caused an accident.

Unless you consider the red Chevy Vega that gently sideswiped the Texaco tanker an *accident,* but I don't. They bumped, a few sparks sprayed off the metal, and then the car straightened itself out again. The Vega driver had thoughtlessly tossed a plastic bag out the window which became snagged on our windshield wiper. I'd flashed the driver a photograph of a nun taking it up the ass.

Of course, there were unexpected side effects of this behavior.

Debby and I both became utterly immune to graphic and violent pornographic images, which is maybe not the best thing. And because we were so busy looking for moving violations, we didn't talk as much in the car. We watched. Which became addictive.

But perhaps the most lingering effect was this. Even today, I can't see a car run a red light without instantly having an image flash into my head of a man's erect penis, penetrating a watermelon.

You've Come a Long Way, Baby!

More than watching *The Brady Bunch* or *Gilligan's Island*, more than going out to dinner at The Hut, the Polynesian restaurant at the bottom of the Hotel Northampton and having sweet and sour chicken and a coconut drink with a paper umbrella stuck in the straw, my very favorite thing as an eleven-year-old was to watch channel twenty-two late at night and catch black-and-white movies from the forties.

I felt a powerful attraction to these movies. It was a response I never felt watching tawdry, contemporary *color* films. I mean, sure, I'd go see *Smokey and the Bandit*. But it didn't make me melancholy, and long to live in a decade past.

What I loved most about movies from the forties was that people spoke slowly, and in complete sentences. The scenes were long, with very few edits. The story was clearly and specifically drawn, with each step provided for the viewer.

Today, watching a movie from the forties is like watching a movie made for the mentally impaired.

Refined gentleman, speaking to woman: "Claudia, is that a candle in your hand?"

Pan around the room to Claudia, holding a candle. "Yes, Hollander. This is a candle. And it is in my hand."

Pan back to Hollander. "But . . . if you don't mind my asking, why? Why are you holding a candle in your hand?"

Zoom in on the candle in her hand. Linger on the unlit wick.

Cut to a wide shot of Claudia holding a candle.

Cut to Claudia's face, as she speaks. "I'm holding a candle in my hand because . . . I'm going to place it on the table, right here in one of these beautiful silver candlesticks. Would you care to help me light it?"

"Light that candle there in your pretty hand? Once you've placed it in the beautiful silver candlestick? Why, Claudia. I'd have to be positively mad to refuse an offer such as this. I would be most delighted. Please, allow me the honor."

Cut to Claudia, smiling. "Oh, Hollander! That would be delightful. Yes, please do. Please help me light this candle. It will make the room positively glow."

Watching these old movies made me sad that everything had changed so horribly. Now, we had loud electric typewriters and frantic game shows. And everything was so pointlessly *fast*. There was even a newfangled machine that could answer your phone for you, in case you were just too busy using your fancy electric typewriter to pick up the phone yourself with your old-fashioned hands. *Good God.* Was this progress? Was this evolution? I didn't think so.

Along with my fixation on these old movies, I loved old *Life* magazines. Especially the cigarette ads.

These ads made smoking seem glamorous. Lean against a fireplace mantel and light up! Or push your chair back from the dinner table and have a smoke. Cigarettes were for people who contemplated. Who *experienced* life.

Of course, I knew I'd probably never smoke. My parents were smokers, and they made smoking seem the opposite of glamorous. Still, you never knew. What if in the future I met somebody that I thought was glamorous and exciting and *they* smoked? If it ever became necessary for me to begin, I'd better be damn ready and already know my brand. It was exactly like standing in front of the mirror and practicing my smile and laugh, in case I ever became a movie star.

So I spent hours tearing ads out of magazines and gazing at the photographs, trying to imagine which lifestyle best represented me.

Out in the first round was Tareyton. These ads featured unattractive people with black eyes and bent cigarettes. I didn't like the black eye campaign at all. That was just plain stupid.

Kool had a nice name. But I didn't care for green.

BelAir had a breezy, pale blue image that appealed to me. It made me think of Georgia, my grandparents, palm fronds glancing against the hot glass. So that was a possibility.

Camels had long been a favorite animal. They were cute, and they were mean. A better combination I could not imagine. I put those at the top of my list.

Eventually, I had a stack of cigarette ads stashed neatly under my bed. I took the stack out every night, and studied each ad as if trying to glean hidden information. In time, I felt, one of these ads would speak to me and I would understand which brand would be mine, if I were a smoker.

Marlboro? No. I loathed the Wild West. I'd sooner watch the snow static on a television set than a John Wayne Western.

Winston? Again, no. There was a kid named Winston in my school and he was always trying to get everybody to eat his nose pickings.

I did like the look of those Eve cigarettes, especially the fanciful, colorful illustration of a flower garden right there on the pack. But even I understood that to smoke such a cigarette could be life-threatening, and for reasons having nothing to do with cancer. If any of the boys at school ever caught me smoking an Eve, I'd be dead.

Finally I made my choice: Camel unfiltered cigarettes. Not only did I like the animals, but the cigarettes were medicinal. Their ad featured a doctor standing at the head of a dining room table, around which guests were seated, having just finished a meal. The doctor appeared to have walked into somebody's home right off the street. And was now dispensing medical advice. "For Digestion's sake smoke Camels!" read the headline.

One Saturday, I rode my bike to South Amherst and walked into Brook's pharmacy. Stepping up to the counter I said, "A pack of Camel unfilters. I think that's what she said. Is it unfiltered? Is that right? She smokes the short ones." I was attempting to play young and dumb, in no way a stretch for me.

The clerk, probably a college kid from one of the surrounding schools, said, "Who's this, your mother? Are these for her?"

"Yes," I said. "I'm pretty sure she said unfiltered, but I don't want to get the name wrong. She'll be mad, and I'll have to ride all the way back down here."

The clerk then smiled and said, "Unfiltered Camels, yup. That's the name. Must be a tough woman, your mother."

"Oh, she is," I said, nodding with wide, sincere eyes. "She can be as mean as a snake. And she said if I mess up, I'll get my backside slapped into the next county."

My ruse worked. I was handed the cigarettes.

Then I tucked them into the elastic band of my socks and rode my bike home, grinning the whole way because I had successfully played the role of Obedient Normal Boy, Running an Errand for His Mother. I'd found that if I simply acted stupid, people never suspected I was anything but. I could buy *Playgirl* magazine if I also asked for a box so I could wrap it up and give it as a present.

So I enjoyed Camels. Not smoking them, but just knowing I had them. Just in case. Camels, the cigarette for people who wanted to be healthy.

I had, I felt, poor health, as evidenced by my weekly allergy shots and my hypersensitive disposition. Plus, my stomach caused me endless trouble because of the Betty Crocker frosting which I enjoyed eating from the tub with a spoon.

Camels promised to improve my life. And it was my firm belief that they already had.

Of course, I also realized that smoking was mildly dangerous. Both of my parents smoked and yet they were well-educated people who tried frequently to warn me of the dangers. "Don't you grow up and smoke like I do," my father often said, coughing blood into his handkerchief. "It's a bad, bad habit." Then folding the handkerchief and sticking it back in his pocket, thus ensuring I would never use a handkerchief my whole life.

And while I did believe that smoking was bad, I also believed that perhaps his brand—Benson & Hedges—was the real problem.

So while certain aspects of smoking might be bad, I did feel that if you stuck to brands that were around in the forties and fifties, you were fine.

And eventually, I did take up smoking. I met somebody who smoked and because she was the coolest person I'd ever known, and because she made smoking seem like freedom, I smoked, too. I smoked throughout my teenage years. Though I eventually got sick of picking flecks of tobacco off my tongue and switched over to Marlboro Lights.

By this time, my delusions that smoking was healthy were gone. I knew smoking was dangerous. But I figured, better to smoke a "light" than a regular.

By the age of thirty, I was smoking three packs a day, while working out in the gym compulsively. I'd wisely gone through rehab to stop drinking. But this had only increased my intake of cigarettes.

Everybody in recovery smokes. If you don't like smoking, don't even bother trying to get sober. Just stay drunk.

So while I worked hours every day, polishing my body, I would light up the instant I left the gym.

But all those years of constantly inhaling toxic smoke had left me damaged. I coughed all the time. I got winded if I climbed so much as a curb. And everything in my tiny apartment was either yellow or smelled yellow.

So finally, when I was thirty-three, I decided to quit.

My resolve was fierce: I'd been a hardcore, bottle-of-scotch-a-night drinker and I'd gotten sober. Damn right I can quit smoking!

My resolve remained iron-strong for the entire first hour without a cigarette.

But after about an hour and a half, I was ready to slaughter my neighbor and drink his blood.

After four hours, my throat itched. And I was coughing more than ever before. It was like I was being tickled from the inside, in a place I couldn't scratch. Oh, but a cigarette could scratch it.

Finally, I went downstairs to the pharmacy and bought a box of nicotine patches. And also a box of nicotine gum.

I went back upstairs and peeled two of the adhesive patches off the plastic strip, placing one above my heart, the other on my neck, on top of the carotid artery.

First, I felt a tiny tingle. I pressed my hands against both patches, trying to push the nicotine into my skin faster.

And then, relief. A strange feeling, quite different from smoking. It was the lessened desire to smoke. It was not the addition of a substance into my body, but the subtraction of a need.

I opened the box of Nicorette gum and was surprised to see that it came with an audio cassette.

I tossed this, along with the directions and warnings, into the trash, and tore two pieces of gum away from the pack.

I began chewing the gum. It had a strong, chemical taste. And then a moment later, it slightly burned. Like pepper.

The chemical taste increased.

And I began to feel something going on in my stomach. Like extra acid being made. Or a hole forming. Something was going on. Then I started to hiccup.

I loved the gum.

I could stop smoking.

The patch removed my deep cravings. And the gum gave me the sting, the control that I needed.

Between the three of us, I would be smoke-free.

Many years later, I was still smoke-free. And, of course, entirely off the patch. And, of course, not at all off the gum. In fact, I chew more Nicorette now than I ever did. Each month, I chew slightly more.

And it's expensive stuff. I pay—in an average Upper West Side pharmacy—$85 for a box of 165 pieces. I buy two boxes a week. Which works out to about $680 a month.

In other words, I chew a Mercedes Benz SL500 lease payment each month. And walk everywhere.

My partner Dennis says, "You've got to stop with the gum. It's out of control."

To which I reply, "I know." Chomp, chomp, chomp. "It's totally"—chomp, chomp, chomp—"gonna make my jaw fall off like Lucy Grealy."

Lucy Grealy's memoir, *Autobiography of a Face*, is about her experience with cancer, which left her facially disfigured, without a lower jaw. I can't bring myself to read the book, even though everybody says it's brilliant. Because I know if I do read the book, it will happen to me.

This is how my mind works, unfortunately.

For similar reasons, I never owned ashtrays when I smoked. Because, I figured, cancer only kills those who are smokers, and if you don't have an ashtray, how can you be a smoker? Therefore, cancer only kills people who own ashtrays. So instead I used almost empty Snapple bottles. I never drank the Snapple. I just poured most of it down the drain, leaving just enough at the bottom to piss out the cigarette.

So I continue to chew, always nervous that somehow, something is seeping into my jaw bones and will cause them to break away.

Already my teeth are yellow, which I blame on the stuff. The gum itself is yellow. So it must stain your teeth, right? Something they don't tell you in the little information kit they give you, which I finally broke down and read.

But I chew much more of it than a person is supposed to chew. Thirteen hundred pieces a month.

However, I am not alone.

Many times, I see a person chewing gum. I'll be in a store and I'll see them chew. And then suddenly, stop. This is called "parking" in Nicorette lingo. It's where you stop chewing and park the gum between your cheek and your gums, for nicotine delivery.

If I see somebody chewing gum who suddenly stops, I know it's okay to talk to them.

"Nicorette?" I'll simply say, nodding.

Every time they nod back. "Yup."

"How long?" I ask.

Sometimes they say, "Four." Or sometimes, "Five." And either way, I know they are speaking in *years,* not weeks or months.

It seems to me, nobody who goes on Nicorette gum ever goes off. In this way, we are the first test subjects. In twenty years, if Nicorette must say in their advertising campaign, "Long-term, heavy usage may result in bone loss and skull cancer," we will be the reason why they know this.

But still. It's better than smoking.

From what I know, which isn't much, there's no evidence that chewing the gum, even in huge quantity, is bad for you. Certainly not as bad as smoking.

So why does the stuff taste so bad? And why is it so expensive? They should be dropping this crap into the streets, out of airplanes. Everybody who smokes should be chomping like me instead.

Except a few people I know, I would like them to continue smoking.

But most people, they need to chew, too. They even make the gum in normal flavors now, like mint. Though I still prefer Original Dupont Chemical flavor.

Although I admit: Nicorette in any flavor lacks the glamour of smoking that got me hooked on nicotine in the first place.

After making love, a couple might lean back on the down pillows, and one of them might pull out a cigarette from a pack, light it, and hand it to the person next to him. Who would then take a drag.

And there's not a person in their right mind who could criticize this. It's a classic Smoking Moment, one of the few that make cigarettes so alluring.

Never will you see this same couple in bed, leaning back against the pillows after sex. And one of them reaching into his mouth to remove a well-chewed piece of gum and handing it to his partner.

And this is the flaw of Nicorette. It's not sexy. It's Drug Company Boardroom.

But still. At least I'm not speaking out of a surgical hole in my neck, like a lot of smokers.

So I guess instead of sexy, I get to be alive, and with one fewer hole, maybe for a little while longer.

The Forecast for Sommer

Some little boys grow up with divorced mothers who cycle through lots of different men. ("Get your new uncle Hank a beer.") My situation was similar, except Hank was Polly and Nancy and Betty and Virginia. There was Claudette and Marie and Runa, a revolving door of women friends stumbling into my mother's life and careening back out.

Sometimes, a woman would remain friends with my mother for years. But sometimes, just for a few months. Or even weeks, which was how long it took for my mother to cycle through her complete personality. And after seeing "all of her," many women didn't want to stick around for the encore.

My mother described her personality as "large." But in today's terms, she would be described by a clinical psychologist as "manic depressive, psychotic."

She'd be fine for nine months, the time it takes to grow a baby. And then her little fetus of mental illness would pop out, fully developed, transforming her into a woman who tore her life to shreds, for the sake of her art.

There is no denying that my mother possessed some sort of genius. Some of her early poems were quite simply ordinary words, combined in startlingly new combinations. Her paintings, too, transfixed me. It was the eyes of her paintings that made me know, even at the age of nine, that they were good. I figured, if I could see the soul of a person in his or her eyes, and those eyes happened to be made out of oil and pigment, then that must be a good painting. It just must be.

She was large, my mother. In general, she was large. But when she became manic, she became huge. She wouldn't fit into the box of her house, or the box of her life. Lids blew off everything.

The women grabbed their scarves and ran.

Some of them were fellow graduate students at the University of Massachusetts where my mother was earning her M.F.A. Others she met at readings given by some of her favorite poets: Maxine Kumin at Amherst. Anne Sexton in Boston. Mary Oliver at Mt. Holyoke.

I was certain my mother's friend Sommer wouldn't be around long. She was a meek little creature in her twenties, to my mother's late thirties. She had thin, long straight hair and a vague chin, qualities I associated with insecurity and not genetics.

Where my mother was a woman who played opera at full volume, Sommer was a woman who listened to the silence of the walls. Sommer liked white space and my mother liked wild, swirling colors.

I was certain she would flee the moment she saw the shift in my mother's eyes. The way the weather changed around her irises, the still green becoming something raging, the black striations seeming to widen. As a child, it terrified me to see her change. She became a woman unfamiliar, living in my mother's body. A shell, a husk she'd taken to occupy.

The temperature in the room—any room my mother occupied—increased. Her body heat filled the space. I would sweat. My mother was able to reset all our thermostats with her mind.

My parents had separated, my father living in a small apartment on Lincoln Avenue in Amherst. He was near the university, where he taught. My brother was living in Sunderland. I was living with my mother in our long, red house in the woods.

The first time I saw Sommer, she was blowing across the surface of her tea and I thought, "That's a bad sign." Anybody who couldn't handle scalding tea would certainly fail here, with my mother, with us.

My mother was holding one of Sommer's poems, reading lines from it into the room. She was saying, "You see? You see here, this rhyme? You've forced the word to make the rhyme, but lost the point. I would forget about rhyming entirely. I think it's stronger without. You can get the music some other way."

Sommer blew on her tea and then took a quiet sip. Her face revealed nothing: was it too hot? Just right? Her expression remained something I couldn't measure.

I was accustomed to reading faces in order to understand things. I was illiterate with Sommer's mask.

"But this," my mother said. "This one is wonderful. It is true." And she read another line.

"Which reminds me," my mother said, rising from her chair. The paper fell from her lap, sailed to the white shag carpeting. She strode across the room, down the hallway, into her office.

I was alone with Sommer. It was night. The large windows of our living room no longer revealed towering pine trees, only large, inky black forms. As much as I loved windows during the day, they terrified me at night.

"Are you a great poet like your mother?" she asked.

I said, "No."

"But she says you write."

"Yeah. Sometimes. But just, I don't know. Dumb things. Nothing."

"That's not what your mother says." Sommer took another sip of tea.

"Oh. Well, she's just my mother. She doesn't really know. You know."

Sommer set her tea on a cork coaster atop the teak coffee table. "Your mother said you wrote a poem about finding a dried beehive in the woods that was better than many poems by famous writers. That's what she told me. She was serious."

My mother had said the same thing to me. "You will be a famous writer someday. Mark my words." My mother told me this every day.

Our house was filled with books, thousands of them in bookcases that lined the walls. In small skyscrapers set next to beds. On every surface of every table. Books. Sometimes, I would sleep with a book under my pillow because I found them comforting, as artifacts.

"She says that," I told Sommer. "But she's just saying that because she's being nice."

Sommer laughed. "I wouldn't call your mother 'nice.' That's one word I wouldn't use."

And although it sounded like an insult, I knew it wasn't. My mother wasn't nice in the way that many other mothers might be nice. My mother was terrible and true and loud and funny and, somehow, she was superior.

"No, I guess you're right. She's not very nice."

Sommer said, "I didn't mean . . ."

"No, I know what you mean."

"You do?"

"Yeah."

"You're very much like your mother, I think."

"Maybe."

"I think," Sommer said, "you are."

Not long after she met Sommer, my mother had a sharp psychotic break from reality. She began to weep in place, standing still in the room, listening to her dead grandmother, grandfather, her father speak all around her. My mother began to write one large poem, an epic. She stopped sleeping and left the lights on all night.

My mother's psychiatrist stepped in, as he always did, to take her away to a psychiatric hospital in Vermont. She stayed two weeks, I stayed with the doctor and his family.

When she returned, she was drained and even the act of making instant coffee, or standing at the sink with her mug, waiting for the tap water to warm, drained her. She leaned her weight against the edge of the counter where it met the sink and I looked at her hair, pasted to her skull with sweat, with sleep.

She filled her mug, took it with her to the table that once belonged to us as a family and now belonged to my mother, me. She sat. "I'm just so tired," she said. She lit a cigarette. She rested her elbow on the table, rested her chin in her palm, wrapped her lips around her cigarette. Inhaled. Coffee on the table, in front of her, smoking, too.

I sat next to her, trying not to burden. I sat with my back hunched forward and my shoulders pulled in tight toward the midline of my body. To occupy less space. To be smaller.

"Someday, maybe you'll win the Yale Younger Poet's Award," she said.

This is what she always said to me. And whatever it was, it already felt like mine.

"Do you think I will?" I asked.

Here, she did look at me. "I think you will. I think that will be the first thing you win. And then I think you will go on to become one of the most famous writers in the world."

But I knew that's what *she* wanted. So I said, "No, you will."

"We'll see," she said. "I think I'm good enough. But."

"But what?"

"But. It's just . . . It's hard."

"Well then, I won't be, either," I told her.

She smiled at me and reached her free arm across the table to take my wrist in her fist. "No, you're different," she said. "It won't be difficult for you."

Sommer began showing up at our house every afternoon. She wore simple cotton sundresses and brought red nylon sacks of oranges. "Let's clean your office," she would say. Or, "How about if I make something for dinner that will give you leftovers for a week?"

At night, Sommer massaged my mother's feet with Vaseline Intensive Care lotion, while my mother read over one of her own poems, scribbling notes on the page.

Sometimes, Sommer slept on the long down sofa. Sometimes, when I woke up, Sommer was gone.

Over a year passed, and Sommer seemed so much a part of our daily life that I felt she'd been there, always. She felt like a big sister, permanent.

She lived in a nearby town called Granby. In a house meant for a family, but which had been split into units for single people. Apartments. Sommer had one of these, on the top floor. She had a bay window that overlooked the driveway and her car, a rusty Volvo station wagon. A bumper sticker on the rear window of the car was so washed out, all the letters had faded away and only the pale white-blue background was left.

When my mother needed to be alone to write, she would often have Sommer pick me up. "If you could just watch him for an hour or two, I would greatly appreciate it."

So Sommer would come, leave the car running in our driveway and ring the doorbell. "Are you ready?" she'd ask. And I'd say yes. And then I'd get into Sommer's car and she'd take me somewhere.

Many times, we went for long drives: through Conway, Old Deerfield, Buckland. We'd walk across the Bridge of Flowers in Shelburne Falls and then we'd go to the Odyssey Bookstore in South Hadley.

One afternoon, Sommer took me to her apartment to see something she'd just purchased. "I think you'll like it," she told me in the car. "It's really something you just don't usually see. And when you do see it, it makes you sad. Aren't you curious?"

I was insanely curious. I wanted to see her sad thing.

My mother was not writing now, but sleeping. After a major psychotic episode, my mother often required fifteen hours of sleep a day. She said this was so that her brain could rewire itself.

Sommer pulled into her driveway and we got out of the car. We climbed the stairs to her apartment and then she unlocked the door, entering first.

I'd seen Sommer's apartment before: small round oak table in front of the bay window, a hand-me-down loveseat. Lots of books, everywhere. Then, against a wall, a card table and a chair and an electric typewriter. The trash can was filled with crumpled pages.

But now, there was something new: a coffin. It was standing upright in the corner of the room, on the bay window wall. In front of it she'd placed a Victorian armchair and an iron reading lamp.

She set her keys on her card table and we walked over to the coffin.

It was a simple pine box.

Sommer said, "I'm going to have this carpenter I know put some shelves in. And then I can keep my books in there."

I watched her face while she spoke and detected a note of serenity to her features. The coffin somehow soothed her.

"So I'll have this bookcase," she said. "And nobody will think twice about it. But then when I die, I'll already have my coffin. So I won't be any trouble for anyone at all. All somebody will have to do is take out the books and sell them at a yard sale or maybe give them to the Jones Library. And then they can put me in the coffin and that's it!" She smiled at her own efficiency.

I wondered if my mother knew about the coffin bookcase and if so, what she thought of it. I suspected that she did not know. My mother's friends always knew more about my mother than she knew about them.

"But," I said, "don't you think it's a little, I don't know. Depressing? To be living with this?"

Sommer said, "Oh, no! Not at all. I'm really a very practical person and this sort of thing just really makes me happy. Here," she said. "Let me show you something else."

And she led me into her bedroom, which was the only other room in the apartment. It was opposite the tiny bathroom with its small oval sink. She turned on a light and I saw nothing out of the ordinary. No meat grinder that could double as a vase. No backhoe that could become a clothes dryer with just a yard of twine.

Then she opened her closet. "See?" she said. "See how organized everything is?"

Inside Sommer's closet, all her clothes hung from a center pole. The sundresses that she wore most every day were on the left. Then jeans, pressed and on hangers. Next were her shirts. And at the right end of the closet, jackets. Shoes were lined up beneath the clothes, toes pointing outward.

But above the pole was a shelf. And on the shelf, Sommer had arranged hundreds of bottles of prescription medicine. They were lined up in perfectly neat rows, four and five bottles deep.

"What are those?" I asked her. I pointed to the medications.

"Oh, those are my pills. I'm a bit of a hoarder. I save things."

"But what are they for?"

"Oh, you know." She shrugged. "Allergy, anxiety, lung infection, mania."

On the one hand, it looked like a pharmacy. But then because the pills were in a closet, somehow they seemed threatening. Which is saying a lot because there was a coffin in the living room.

Then Sommer closed the door and she turned to me. "Do you know something?" she said. "Do you know that I have my own little boy, just about your age?"

I didn't understand what she meant because I'd never seen her with any boy my age. And she'd never talked about one, either. And besides, she was so young. Much younger than my mother was. So how could she have somebody my age? "What do you mean?"

She sat on the foot of her bed. "I mean just that. I have a little boy, about your age. You're nine, right?"

And I nodded.

And she said, "So is he. His name is Ethan." She was smiling now. And I think it was the first time I'd ever seen her just smile for no reason at all.

"And he lives with his father."

And then she wasn't smiling. Her small features returned, the chin receding.

"Hey, do you want to go for a swim?" she asked, checking her watch. "I told your mother I'd have you back by four. And it's only one. So what do you say?"

"Well, I guess," I said. Although floating around in water was the last thing I wanted. I felt floaty enough as it was. "But I can't because I don't have a bathing suit."

And she stood up and opened her dresser. "I have a pair of Ethan's trunks in here somewhere. I bet you're about the same size." She pulled out a pair of brown striped bathing trunks. They looked my size, exactly.

There was a small pool in the backyard of Sommer's building. A startling luxury, it seemed to me. We entered the water and Sommer immediately went to the far deep end of the pool to tread water. She shouted to me, "You stay down there, at that end. It's too deep for you here." She dipped below the surface of the water, and a moment later appeared just a foot in front of me, sliding the water off her face with her hands as she rose. "Doesn't the water feel great?" she asked.

I was cold. Someone had left an inflatable giraffe in the corner. Moths and dried orange pine needles clung to its printed hide.

A month later, my mother was sitting in the living room, reading over her epic poem. She liked to write in her office, which had been my parents' bedroom when they were married. But she liked to read her work on the sofa, in front of the wood stove. In the winter, the woodstove supplied the heat for the house. My father had added it because the huge fireplace sucked all the hot air up and out. But in the summer, my mother used the wood stove as a surface on which to place wildflowers in large pottery containers. She liked to tuck her legs up beneath her and study her work, gazing at the stove, the flowers, thinking.

The phone rang and she went into the kitchen to answer it. I followed her, as I always did when the phone rang. A ringing phone comprised much of my excitement as a child.

Normally, one of my mother's friends would call her and they would speak for hours. My mother was adept at cooking or smoking or writing or eating, all with the phone tucked between her shoulder and ear. Her range of motion was limited only by the length of the cord.

But today, she didn't shriek a warm welcome into the receiver. Instead, she listened, then sat. Sat slowly, in the chair, listening. Her features creased. Her eyes became very small.

And very quickly, she hung up the phone. She reached for one of her blue Flair felt tip pens and made a note on a piece of paper.

Then she faced me. "Sommer killed herself," she said.

I watched a lot of television. I'd seen a lot of people killed: killed by guns, killed by wild animals, killed in planes, falling from the sky. Crashes and knives and falls from buildings. One man pushing another off a ledge. A woman, thrown from a horse. People were killed on television and the K was always hard. The word itself nearly caused an audible rip. *Killed.* It made me think of knives, of punctures.

I thought of Sommer, killing herself. How? Driving a truck into her own body. Leaping off the roof, the ground smashing her. I thought of Sommer with a knife, arm extended out, then swiftly *in.*

I said, "How?" and my mother looked surprised.

"I mean, how did she kill herself?"

My mother said, "Why do you need to know that?"

I said, "I just want to know."

She said, "Sommer swallowed some pills."

I saw them then: the pills in her closet, lined up like people waiting for movies, like people in the grocery store. Ordinary people, standing, doing nothing, getting there, about to be there, going, going. Gone.

My mother left the kitchen. She walked downstairs to her bedroom and I heard her turn on the shower.

I remained in the kitchen, thinking. Sommer had a son my own age.

That a mother could really go away for good. That a mother like mine who goes away in her head, goes away to a hospital, could also go away and be dead.

I followed my mother downstairs and stood on the other side of the shower curtain. Spittle flew over the height of the curtain rod and landed on my head. The steam smelled sweet.

"Where are you going?" I asked.

"You need to stay here. Can you stay alone? Do you think? I think you can. You're old enough. Just for a few hours."

"Where are you going, though?"

"I need to go," she said, "I need to see some people about Sommer. We have to arrange certain things. Oh my God, this is terrible."

"Don't go," I said.

"I have to go. Sommer's dead. I have to go. Damn it, I'm out of shampoo."

I stared at my mother's closet door, packed with clothing, unorganized, crazy inside. Somehow, the fact that my mother's closet was a mess made me feel secure.

"You have to leave now because I have to get out of the shower," she said.

And I left. I went upstairs into my bedroom.

✧   ✧   ✧

Hours later, my mother returned. And I was nearly surprised. Because I'd spent the hours imagining her car rolling down a hill, glass windshield exploding in her face. I was relieved to see her. But surprised. And oddly mad.

She was carrying a box of books. "Help me with this," she said, offering me a corner of the box. "Help me carry this into the living room."

We set it on the floor, the heavy box of books.

"Where did you get these?" I asked.

My mother said, "These are just some of Sommer's things we needed to get out of the apartment. To make room."

I thought of the coffin, which was her bookcase. I looked at the box of books. Imagined my mother's strong fingers plucking the books from the shelf by their spines, placing them into the box, then I saw her turning the coffin on its back, centering it in the room. I saw her and a friend lift Sommer's body off the bed and lower her into her final resting bookcase.

Try Our New Single Black Mother Menu

These will be fine," I said, fingering a pair of platform ankle boots, which zipped along the sides. They had a big, chunky heel and were made of polished burgundy leather.

"Those will most certainly *not* be fine," my grandmother Carolyn said, puckering her mouth into a frown.

"Yeah, but these are really good," I said, as though I didn't hear the disapproval in her voice.

She gripped me firmly by the arm and leaned down so that she could speak directly into my face. "Those shoes are for blacks," she said. "Those shoes are not for white boys."

"But Tony Orlando wears shoes like this," I argued.

"Sweetie, Tony Orlando is, for all intents and purposes, a black. He wears big, high shoes like this, he dances around on a stage between those two black girls. You are not Tony Orlando." Then she spotted a pair of dreadful blue canvas Keds and reached down and grabbed them. "Here, what about these? These are awfully nice shoes."

"Those are horrible," I said, stepping back away from them as though they were covered in dog shit.

Carolyn looked stricken.

We'd come to Rich's department store for shoes and it was clear we would never agree.

The problem was this. I knew that the platform shoes were for black people and that's why I wanted them. Secretly? I longed to *be* black. Or, to use the term I preferred, Afro-American.

So my grandmother and I had more than a disagreement. We were on the verge of our own little race riot.

Calmly, I placed my hand back on the platform ankle boots and in a confident, low voice I said, "I want these or I don't want any shoes at all."

We left the store empty-handed.

In the car, my grandmother tried to make nice. "Silly, what got into you back there? My word. Even if we had bought you those black person shoes, you'd have been a laughingstock at your school up north." The incident behind her now, she was free to pretend it never happened. "What do you say we go and get ourselves a little something at McDonald's?"

I wanted to hold my grudge against her all night, if not for the remainder of the summer. But I loved McDonald's more and so smiled and said, "Sure, that sounds good."

But racial tension reared up again, later that night.

We were watching *The Tonight Show* with Johnny Carson, and a young black woman was performing some sort of modern dance.

I was entranced. I'd never seen anybody move like that before. Sure, Scooby and Shaggy did a little jig, up and down, then around and around, after they caught a thief. But this was something entirely different. This woman moved as though she had extra joints. She somehow was able to occupy the music, as though it were a chair.

My grandmother stood from the sofa and walked to the television set, a console television cased within a long walnut cabinet. With her mink-topped slipper on her foot, she kicked the television screen gently. "Look at that little colored girl. She thinks she can dance."

Being the only Yankee born in the family, in all generations, I said, "I'd like to see *you* do that."

Which is when my grandmother turned to me as though I were a traitor, her mouth open wide. I was General Paxton, handing over the state of Mississippi along with a bottle of pink champagne. And I was sent to my room.

The rest of the summer, though, passed without incident. And I found myself back in Massachusetts, my hair two inches longer. Long enough, I'd decided, to perm it into an afro.

With my allowance, I bought a red afro pick at Kmart and then stole thirty dollars from my mother's wallet and rode my bike to the Cut Above salon in South Amherst and requested a perm.

The stylist was shocked not only that an eleven-year-old had entered her salon willingly, unaccompanied by a mother making threats, but had then requested a beauty treatment normally reserved for women. In addition, I already had a full head of curly hair, so it just didn't make sense.

"But honey," she said. "What on earth do you need a perm for?"

I explained that I didn't like having loose curls. I wanted tight curls, I wanted my hair to stand straight up. To be frizzy.

"But sweetie, if I perm your hair, you're gonna end up with an afro," she said. Her tone of voice implied there could be no fate worse for a white boy.

"Yes," I said, thrilled. "That's exactly what I want. And I have the money." To prove this, I produced three folded ten-dollar bills from the hip pocket of my Sears Toughskins.

"Well," she said, resigned. "Sit right down in that chair."

An hour and a half later, I emerged from the salon with a mass of frizzy hair that stood straight out from my scalp in all directions. I looked as though I had a halo of light all around my head. I stuck my red afro pick into my hair and was thrilled that it did not slip out, but nested there securely.

I rode home and immediately put on my favorite Odetta album, *Go Tell It on the Mountain*. Then, a few hours later, I begged my mother to drive me to my favorite restaurant, as a treat to celebrate my new hair.

"I'm not going anywhere with you looking like that. Take that damn comb out of your hair."

"It's not a comb, it's a pick. Get with it, sister," I said, moving my hips just so and snapping my fingers.

"What on earth has gotten into you?"

"So will you take me?" I whined.

"Take you where?"

"I told you already," I whined. "McDonald's."

As with most things from childhood, I eventually outgrew my love for McDonald's and my desire to be an Afro-American. I adjusted to my own life as a standard-issue white male alcoholic.

But then something remarkable happened that made me rediscover my childhood passions. A McDonald's opened across from my apartment on Tenth Street and Third Avenue. And once it opened, it never closed. Because this wasn't an ordinary McDonald's. It was a twenty-four-hour McDonald's.

Construction in New York is fast. I hadn't had time to prepare myself psychologically for this. Even though I passed the exact spot every day when I went to the St. Mark's Bookshop, I never saw signs of construction. On the two days I didn't make my typical bookstore pilgrimage, the store must have been created. It's not inconceivable that an entire McDonald's could spring forth within the space of forty-eight hours. Obviously not, because apparently that's exactly what happened.

I walked toward St. Mark's Place and saw the holy yellow arches. The red and white neon sign in the window, NOW OPEN.

It was among the happier moments of my life. Of course, given that my life had been a car sliding across the median and crashing into oncoming traffic, maybe this is not difficult to believe.

When I was in third grade, word spread about the Crocker Farms Elementary School, located in a nearby town. *They,* rumor had it, had a McDonald's located in the cafeteria. It was some sort of *experiment,* is what they said.

So those Crocker Farms brats could have Big Macs and fries every day. While we had perfectly flat pizza that tasted sweet and was still slightly frozen in the center. At the time I had been just sick with grief and envy. I couldn't even entertain the fantasy of what it would be like to have personal, private, constant, exclusive use of a McDonald's during school hours.

Let alone, live right across the street from one.

I told myself, "You're not eleven anymore. You can't eat there."

But didn't I have to at least eat there once? The first night it opened? Of course I did.

So that evening, I consumed my usual bottle of Dewar's while sitting at the computer. I e-mailed Suzanne in California.

"Guess what opened across the street!"

She wrote back, "A crack house!"

I said, "*Exactly.* McDonald's."

She said, "Go there now and order two of everything, and eat the extra set in my honor."

Bleary with alcohol and unable to stand straight without a slight drifting, as though standing on a ship, I walked across the street and stood in line.

Drinking always made me hungry. As though I'd been out in the woods, cutting trees for my log cabin. I ordered a Quarter Pounder with Cheese, a Big Mac, a Double Quarter Pounder with Cheese, and four cheeseburgers. Then I ordered three large fries. And a six-piece Chicken McNuggets, with extra hot mustard sauce.

It took less than a minute. Not only was this McDonald's gloriously new and clean and close to where I slept, but it was the fastest McDonald's ever.

I left the store with my hot, thin paper bag and climbed the stairs to my apartment. Here, I spread everything out on the bed, positioned in front of my television. My *loot*.

While I watched QVC, transfixed by Big Bold Gold, specifically the Greek Key bracelets and matching ear clips, I consumed the slippery, warm food.

As always after eating, I immediately fell asleep. Right there, on the wrappers. And in the morning, I swiped the wrappers onto the floor and showered before work.

This pattern repeated itself the following evening. And the evening following that. And every evening, for three months.

I gained thirty-five pounds. I was the the original *Super Size Me*. My face resembled a boiled egg, swollen with botulism. I ate one meal a day and I ate it at midnight, following the consumption of a liter of hard liquor. Substitute scotch for sake, and my eating habits were not unlike those of a sumo wrestler.

At work, I told my translucent-skinned boss about the McDonald's opening up across the street, and how I ate there every night now.

He recoiled from me slightly as I spoke, as though I were a homeless bum, trying to cuddle. His face registered clear distaste. He said, "McDonald's is for blacks." And he hissed it, *blacks*. Months later, he would viciously whisper the same thing about Cherry Coke, when we worked on the print ad campaign.

I laughed. And I thought, is that true?

So that evening, I paid special attention. And sure enough, I was the only whitey in the place. The people behind the counter, the people in line, everybody had darker skin than I.

I suddenly felt my old childhood shame and longing. I felt as white-pink as the underbelly of a pig and just as unfashionable.

But then I also felt a strange, creepy feeling. It was the same feeling I got when I walked down Eighth Avenue in Chelsea. This was the gay, gay, gay area. It was assumed that if you were gay, you lived right there. It was the one part of town where a man could hold another man's hand and not worry about a rock hitting him in the back of the head.

And while this was good in one way, it alarmed me in another. It was a sign of segregation.

Which was the same feeling I had at McDonald's. Why was I the *only* white person here?

I felt a deep wave of suspicion. And horror. Had McDonald's become the primary food source for a large portion of the population?

Years before, the McDonald's on the way to the Hamptons had signage in the window, announcing a contest. A free vacation. The graphics had an African feel. And read, "Win a Trip Back to the Homeland!"

This struck me as slightly sinister. First, to assume all your customers were of one race. But then, maybe their extensive consumer research showed this to be true. Maybe more African Americans did frequent McDonald's than non-African-Americans.

Okay, fine.

But something about the sign and the contest made me picture fat, white Midwestern brand managers sitting around an expensive polished mahogany conference room table and saying, "Let's ship 'em *all* back!"

And somebody else saying, "Yeah, one by one! We'll have a new contest every day! Billions and billions . . . sent back!"

Laughter all around the table. Anybody got an ashtray?

So if McDonald's is for blacks, what's for whites? I wondered.

Wendy's.

The restaurant featuring a freckled girl with red pigtails as a logo. The fat, white founder himself was the spokesman until he died of a heart attack. And wasn't the pig-girl on the logo his actual daughter? And didn't I hear somewhere that he had *two* daughters? So why just the one girl? And what did the other daughter think of this? Whatever her name was—Karen? Or *Meg*. What did Meg think of her pretty sister, getting to be on the bag?

Maybe it was just this simple: Wendy was the good daughter. And Meg was the daughter that he couldn't stand, because he was an oily Evangelical Christian and she was a dyke.

Maybe Meg moved out of the Ohio house at sixteen and lived with her girlfriend, a bartender at the only lesbian bar within three hundred miles of Columbus.

And then I imagined Meg after college: B.A. in Women's Studies from Smith under her belt, she moves to San Francisco. One block west of Castro Street.

She's active in the local chapter of PETA. She carries a small can of spray paint in her backpack in case she spots a Presidio Heights woman in a sable coat. So she can spray FUR IS MURDER on the back of it.

Meg meets Kate, who is gender neutral. Together, they have four cats, each named after one of the specific parts of the body that only a woman has: Uta, Ova, Falo, Lacta.

Kate would work in public service. She might be a lawyer.

Meg would teach a course in Latina Studies at San Francisco Community College. One or the other would work—they would never be employed at the same time.

And when they saw a Wendy's on the street, they would cross to the opposite side and they would not look at it.

There would be unspoken hatred and loathing for the chain, for Wendy, for big fat Daddy Dave.

The more I thought about this, the more I believed it to be true.

That left Burger King. Who went to Burger King?

If McDonald's was for blacks and Wendy's was for whites, who was Burger King for? Without a definite brand image, and with those grill marks, it seemed Burger King was caught somewhere in limbo. A fallback position. A catchall. For mulattoes?

So then, Subway. That was clearly for single women. Dildo-shaped sandwiches made from more healthful ingredients.

Dairy Queen, with its same-sex undertones, was surely popular with the Evangelical Christians. Especially the bulimic ones, who would stuff their faces with the gay food and then throw it all up and say they hadn't eaten a thing.

Big Boy was a pedophile paradise.

It was fascinating to think about.

And as far-fetched as my conjecturing was, I wouldn't have been surprised to discover there was truth in much of it.

My years in advertising had taught me that categories abound. Long ago, America stopped being a "melting pot" and is, rather, a large land mass filled with tiny boxes, into which groups of people sit, labeled and ready for processing.

The thing is, I come from a family of Southerners. Racism is as much a part of my heritage as grits and incest. In fact, one of my relatives is on record for having purchased a slave from the ship *Amistad*—otherwise known as "The Black Mayflower."

So technically, I should be fine with all of this.

But perhaps my gay gene, the gene responsible for my desire to own platform shoes at an early age, somehow mutated because of my mother's heavy hairspray use. And I became something of a contradiction.

Wearing a striped oxford button-down. But wanting a gold necklace with my name written in diamonds.

The Georgia Thumper

As much as I adored my grandmother on my father's side of the family, I loathed my grandmother on my mother's side, Amah.

After visiting my grandmother Carolyn, I always had to visit Amah, who also lived in Georgia, though in a different part of the state. A dustier part, without peacocks. And she lived not in a mansion like Carolyn, but in a brick house surrounded by bamboo patches and rattlesnakes.

Visiting Amah after visiting Carolyn was like swallowing a handful of broken glass after having a slice of banana cream pie. Why, unless forced, would you do it?

On my final day, Carolyn would pack her silver Cadillac Fleetwood with all the shopping bags, filled with things she'd bought me—shoes, shirts, jeans with built-in creases, travel mirrors, salon-quality hair conditioning products. There was money stuffed in my pockets. And my entire face was covered with lipstick kisses.

"Oh, can't I just fly home? *Please,*" I would whine.

"Oh, baby. I wish you could. I don't like that woman very much, either. But she's your grandmother, too. And you have to see her."

Then she'd drive two hours across the state, meeting Amah halfway. They always exchanged me in the parking lot of a restaurant on the interstate. Like I was a bundle of contraband drugs.

They air-kissed and exchanged pleasantries. Then I climbed into Amah's dusty gray Impala, and was driven to her house in silence. Once there, Amah locked all my Carolyn presents into an unused bedroom. "You can have these when you get back north, but certainly not here."

Where Carolyn was beautiful and always dressed in tailored suits, silk gowns, and sharp, smart outfits of the latest fashion, Amah wore shapeless sacks, in durable, dark fabrics. Things that repelled stains, as well as men.

Carolyn had a high school education and the only job she'd ever had was in the ladies' underwear section of Rich's department store in Atlanta. And she only worked there for the discount on negligees.

Amah, on the other hand, had a deformed arthritic hand, possessed a graduate degree, and taught Latin to high school students.

Amah's husband died just after I was born. He owned pecan orchards, but then lost his wealth, leaving Amah with only a house, a middle-aged son who would never move out, and a grudge larger than Stone Mountain.

In fact, the only time I ever saw Amah take any pleasure out of life was when she stood on her porch and went at the Georgia Thumpers.

Georgia Thumpers were gigantic, three-inch-long grasshoppers. They made a smacking sound when they hopped on her porch. And then the crunching sound of iceberg lettuce tearing in half when she stepped on them. This was her pleasure. "Oh, I love that sound," she'd say, mashing the insect flat, then going inside to get her broom.

I didn't begin life hating my grandmother. Like every child, I adored her. Until I formed a brain and got to know her.

Early in life I would cling to her, only to be slapped away. My pleas for bedtime stories would be met with scorn. And my pre-alcoholic *need* for television was denied.

Each summer, Amah made me do a new awful thing. Anything unfun that would get me out of her hair.

One summer, she sent me to a crafts class down the street from her house, at the public pool.

Here, I was forced to spend the afternoon in direct sunlight and glue clear, round marbles together into animal shapes.

When I tried to make an abstract shape, I was coldly corrected by the instructor. "No, I said poodle. Not blob. *Poodle.* You will go back and you will make a poodle. And you will not rise from this chair until you hand me a pretty glass poodle." All of this said hatefully, and with a bright smile and a sweet tone, as only a Southern woman can truly pull off.

A child unaccustomed to rules and obedience, I loathed the mandatory poodle manufacturing. And when Amah finally picked me up, I complained. "Why did you make me go to that dumb class? You made me miss my two o'clock show. And I had to sit in the sun and get a rash. And they made me make a poodle and I *didn't* give it a penis, like she said. It was a belt buckle. I'm supposed to be on *vacation.*"

Amah turned to me and said, "Sometimes, we have to do things we don't want to do." She was smiling, thrilled at my misery.

The only thing I liked about visiting Amah was that right next door lived her sister, Curtis. And I adored Curtis.

Curtis was a retired computer programmer, who programmed the first satellite that AT&T's Bell Labs sent into the sky. Even before I knew what a satellite was, I knew that she had programmed it. Whatever that meant.

Curtis had a master's degree in mathematics from Princeton and had lived for a number of years "back East." Which made Amah treat her as though she gave blowjobs to truckers at rest stops for five dollars. *"Five-fifty if I swallow."*

She looked just like Katharine Hepburn. Her husband, who died years before I was born, dated Amelia Earhart before he left her for Curtis. Curtis had Amelia's compass and one of her gloves. And everything about her made it perfectly clear why a man would dump Amelia Earhart for her.

So I spent most of my time there, in Curtis's house, thumbing through endless copies of *The New Yorker* and reading the cartoons.

"Aunt Curtis?" I would ask.

"Yes?"

"Why can't you be my grandmother, instead of Amah? I hate awful Amah."

"I know, Augusten. I know you do. You just think of me as your *real* grandmother, okay? Even though she's technically your grandmother, she's not your grandmother in here." She pressed her hand to my heart.

Curtis and Amah didn't seem to care much for each other, either. I picked this up because one was always saying something hateful about the other.

"Don't you listen to everything Curtis tells you," Amah would say. "She's quite liable to make up lies and disappoint you in the end."

And Curtis would tell me, "Your grandmother—and I am pained to admit this—is the biggest stick in the mud. What a shame. A waste of a woman."

So I spent my days with Curtis, going to the Piggly Wiggly to shop for peculiar Southern foods in cans: boiled peanuts, frog's legs, okra. Taking long rides in her yellow Mercury Grand Marquis. Or in her garden, learning that rose petals were edible. But at night, I had to sleep at Amah's house.

And Amah didn't believe in air conditioners. Or fans. "Your mother slept in this very room all her life without a fan. And so will you." At night, she changed into some sort of heavy-cotton slumber smock in a sweet-dreams shade of beige.

Amah had dreadfully thin hair. Although she took great pains to style it—rolling it at night, then combing it out into a tall bush atop her head—her skull was clearly visible, a light bulb glowing through some fuzz.

As the days passed, I grew bolder and more resentful. I made it a point to remark on her round, visible head at every possible opportunity.

"So, Amah, would you like me to close this window? It's become a little chilly in here this evening and I wouldn't want your skull to be cold."

She would gasp and excuse herself from the room. Later she might say to me, "I had no idea your mother had raised such a hateful boy."

And I would say, "Now I know why she always calls you a bitch."

I would wield my Curtis weapon. "Curtis is my real grandmother," I would say. "Not you."

This stung her, I knew. But she tried to hide it. She would say, "No, she's not. She's *my* sister. That makes her your great-aunt. Not even your aunt. But your *great*-aunt. Hardly a relation at all. *Certainly* not a grandmother. Sorry, dear."

Each year, I begged my parents to let me see Carolyn and then fly straight home. But every year, they made me see Amah, too. Although I only had to spend half as much time with Amah, it felt like twice as long.

One July 4, Amah told me we were not going to see the local

fireworks. "You have such a vivid imagination," she said snidely. "Why don't you make up your own fireworks?" And she gave me two sticks. "Here, pretend these are sparklers."

Then she locked me outside where it was hot and awful.

I walked along the dusty, red clay street and carved "hag, hag, hag" into the dirt.

Then I walked over to the side of the house where I found the garden hose, coiled up like a snake.

Wonderfully, the water was already on. All I had to do was push the trigger handle and a long, powerful line of water sprayed out.

I took the hose and aimed it up into the open window at the top of the house. This would be Amah's bedroom.

For twenty minutes, I sprayed, transfixed by the rainbow that appeared in the mist.

Then I stopped and dropped the hose on the grass, bored.

A moment later, the front door slammed and the car was started.

Amah came around to the side of the house and clasped my upper arm in her talons. She yanked me across the yard and shoved me in the car.

Without saying a word, she drove me to the Eastern Airlines gate at the airport.

"You are a terrible, ugly child," she said.

"And you are a cunt," I said.

This caused her to gasp, and her eyes to water. And I felt fairly certain she'd never been called that name before. As an overly polite, mindful boy, I was fully aware of how atrocious and rude and unspeakable that word was, especially when directed at one's grandmother. I was also certain that it fit, absolutely.

When I arrived in Massachusetts, my parents already knew I'd misbehaved and filled Amah's bedroom with water, soaking her walls and furniture.

What they could not understand was how deeply the bitch had deserved it.

I was punished with the task of sending her "a card."

Silently, I sat poring over all our photo albums and neatly removing Amah's head from every photograph.

I saved the heads in an envelope, which I then mailed to Amah along with a note.

"Here. You keep your bald bitch heads."

I never received a reply from that card. And in fact, never had to fly south to see her again.

When she died, I felt nothing. Immediately followed by devastating sadness. And all I could think about was every terrible, awful, horrendous thing I had ever said to her.

How spoiled and ungrateful I was. How rude and selfish.

Surely, had I tried harder I could have forged a deeper, closer relationship with my own grandmother.

And then I remembered her eyes. The way she looked at me with such distaste. From long before I'd behaved in such a way as to warrant it.

I thought of my own mother, how she'd spent her life "trying to get out from under the spell of that terrible woman."

And I had to admit, there really had been something terrible in her. Something that hated children, even her own.

I realized I was sad. But only because I wasn't *more* sad.

Little Crucifixions

Okay, people, form a circle." This was the first instruction of the day in my third grade homeroom class. The two long, rectangular activity tables in the center of the room were to be carried away by us, the children, and moved against the wall beneath the row of windows, out of the way. Chairs were to be gathered and stacked, freeing a large area of carpet-covered floor space below the chalkboard. We were addressed as "people" because our teachers saw this as respectful. As opposed to "kids," which would make us little goats.

After moving the tables we were to sit cross-legged in a circle. Mrs. Macaluso sat, too. She made a distinctive sound when she did this, as she was festooned with silver bracelets, some beaded, gathered on both arms. She had kinky black hair that reached the middle of her back and she wore some sort of handmade vest, itself decorated with bells. Her face was moon-shaped and she wore no makeup. She wore earth shoes and tied an additional small bell to each lace. So because of all these clinking things attached to her, she made a tinkle sound whenever she moved. Ordinarily, this gave nice advance warning of her approach. As did the patchouli oil she wore.

As she spoke about the day, what would be expected of us, what activities were planned, who might be visiting the class, I extended my cracked, bleeding fingers and rubbed them quickly back and forth on the carpet beside me. This not only wiped away the blood on my fingertips, but the friction warmed my fingers, quickly making them hot. And when I then looked at them, the tips appeared to me to be polished, somewhat glossy. The sheen, I hoped, might help keep the blood inside my fingers and not leaking all over the place.

Of course, within moments, the blood would begin to seep from the cracks in the skin again. And I would, once more, spend the day leaving streaks of blood on everything I touched.

I simply cannot remember a period in my life when my fingers were not cracked open and bleeding and vile. The tips of my fingers, the sides, the knuckles of both thumbs. The skin would become dry in a patch, red. Then it would split and bleed. And even though I often wore twenty Band-Aids on each hand, two per finger, the cracks never healed. Or they would trick-heal. Heal long enough for me to think they were okay and then split apart after the first hand-washing.

When I was ten, my mother finally took me to a dermatologist. But of all the dermatologists my mother could have selected, she somehow selected the only one in town who had been in a car accident and suffered third-degree burns on her face, rendering her features into a scarred approximation. Her blue eyes were startling as they looked out from beneath thick, dry lids that blinked with great effort. Her nose was little more than a surgically constructed tent, providing an opening for two black holes. And her lips, painted red with lipstick, were not made out of lip skin, but out of scar skin, like the rest of her face.

Her name was Dr. Ledford and she terrified me.

"But that's ridiculous," my mother said. "There is nothing in the world to be terrified of. Dr. Ledford is a perfectly wonderful woman. And I think she's remarkably courageous," my mother said.

"But I don't like her," I whined. "She creeps me out."

"I'm sorry you feel that way," my mother said. "But you're going to see Dr. Ledford, and you will be very polite to her. And she will heal your fingers. Because I cannot have you leaving blood on every single thing in the house. Do you know I found blood on all my good bras? Would you care to explain *that* to me?"

That was another problem my fingers caused me. Because I left behind blood on everything I touched, I could touch nothing undetected. It was as though my every move through the house was studied.

And so, deciding it would be better to face Dr. Ledford than leave a constant trail of evidence, I agreed to see her again.

On my first, shocking visit, I had hardly been able to say a word. I simply raised my hands up for her to inspect. I was too terrified to speak. But also, I didn't want to see *her* speak. Because when she did, the skin on her face looked as though it would crack and fall away, exposing her bones.

She'd told me to use a thick hand cream, available at the local pharmacy. She'd instructed me to slather the cream on my hands before bed. And then see her again in a week.

And now, on my return visit, Dr. Ledford noted the improvement. "They're looking better already," she said.

When I nodded and then took my hands away and sat on them,

Dr. Ledford looked at me, tipping her head sideways. She asked, "Does my face scare you?"

I froze, shifting in place on the examination table and causing the stiff white paper beneath me to make a loud crinkling noise.

"Because it scares a lot of kids. It can be hard to look at a face like mine, I understand that," she said. "Would you like to know what happened to me?"

I could only nod.

"Well, I was in a terrible, terrible car accident a long time ago. When I was not that much older than you. And there was a fire in the car. And I was burned very, very bad. And it hurt a lot. It hurt so much. And I had to have many, many operations. And you can see for yourself how the operations turned out." She smiled, showing me her white, real teeth.

"I became a skin doctor because one of the things I understand is what it feels like not to have nice, pretty skin. I have very ugly skin. And my face is spooky. But do you know what? Underneath this face? I am exactly like you, but much older and without such pretty jewelry," she said, touching my gold chain link bracelet.

I swallowed. "Can I touch your cheek?" I asked.

She smiled and leaned down so her face was at my level. "Of course," she said. And she seemed happy to do this, to let me touch her. And so I did. And it felt like skin, but like extra thick skin. Like the skin on the heel of your foot. Except smoother.

"So your hands look a lot better. You just continue to use the cream. And we'll make another appointment for you to come back here in a couple of weeks, so I can check your hands again."

I walked out of Dr. Ledford's office and into the reception area, finding my mother sitting in one of the chairs, writing in her notebook. She looked up. "So?" she asked. "What did the doctor say?"

The doctor was standing behind the reception desk speaking to the receptionist. My mother stood and I followed her to the desk.

"We'll see him again in two weeks," the receptionist said. And she handed my mother a small card, with the date of the appointment written on the back.

In the car my mother asked again, "Well? What did the doctor say?"

I said, "She told me my skin looked very bad. And she would see me again in two weeks. But that probably I would have to see her a lot. Maybe even once a week for a year. Because my hands might not heal."

My mother had started the ignition and put the car into reverse, but now she stopped and looked at me. "She said what?"

I repeated the lie. And my mother said, "Well, that doesn't make any sense at all." She grabbed my hand and inspected it herself. "I mean, I can see myself your hands are better. You couldn't have understood her correctly. She couldn't have said your hands aren't healing and you'll have to see her *every week? For a year?*"

"Well," I said. "That's what she said. She said maybe they look okay *today*. But they might not keep looking so okay *tomorrow*."

My mother looked at me now with deep suspicion. I'd been known to place the thermometer against a hot light bulb, just to fake a fever of 110 so I could stay home from school. My mother didn't know *what*, but she knew *something* was going on. "Mmm hmm, well, we'll see," she said. And we left the parking lot and headed for home.

As I sat beside my mother on the seat, I turned slightly away from her, so that she would not see me picking at my fingers. Tearing at the newly healed skin with my fingernails. Opening the cracks, inviting the blood.

I had decided that I loved Dr. Ledford and that I wanted to see her constantly. For reasons I did not understand, I felt related to her.

When she described her accident and the fire and her ugly face, I felt she was describing me. Even though I wasn't burned. For some reason, I felt like I was the same. And suddenly, I liked her face very much. And I almost wished I had the same face. Because then I would have a reason for feeling the way that I always felt: defective. So if I looked ruined on the outside, at least I would know why I felt ruined.

My nightly routine changed. Instead of using globs of the lanolin-based hand cream and rubbing it into my skin, polishing my knuckles and the dry areas of my fingertips, I picked. I washed my hands a dozen times a day in the hottest water I could stand. And then I sprayed Windex on them.

Within just a few days, I was leaving my bloody fingerprints everywhere again. My father walked into my bedroom one night and opened his wallet. "Do you care to talk about this?" He removed the bills, each of which was bloody.

"I didn't take any," I said. "I just wanted to smell them."

"You just wanted to *smell* them?"

"Yeah," I told him. "It's neat how money smells like nothing else in the world except money. Just like cardboard always smells only like cardboard and carpet only smells like carpet."

My father walked out of my room. He was not charmed or amused, but inexplicably heavier. As though he'd instantly gained twenty pounds. He became leaden. I'd always known he hadn't wanted me. And it seemed I continued to make him want me less and less, without even trying. My father was logical, this was his specialty. And I was something that defied logical explanation.

But my mother was concerned with all the blood, with the fact that my fingers had, for one short week, begun to heal. But were now worse than before she took me to Dr. Ledford in the first place.

I was careful to remove large scoops of the hand cream from the tub and flush these gobs down the toilet, in case she checked the container to see if I was still using it.

In two weeks, I was back at Dr. Ledford's office, sitting on the stiff white paper, thrilled and biting my lips while I waited for her to enter the room.

"Hello there," she said, after I'd waited for what felt like an entire year. "Let's see those hands. How are they doing? Much better?"

But when I showed her my hands, picked at, dry, etched with deep cracks that almost looked like rivers of lava, she was alarmed. "What in the world?" she said.

I told her, "I don't know what's going on. I use the creams and everything but . . ."

She said, "Are you picking at your fingers?"

I knew the right answer was "no." I knew I had to lie. But I could not lie to her. I could lie to my parents because I felt they were only temporary. I constantly felt on loan to them and overdue to be returned. But I could not lie to this person. She would see clean through me into my core because she had alive eyes. So I said, "Well. I have been picking at them some, I guess."

And she said, "Why, though?"

And I said, "Because."

And she said, "But because why?" and then she climbed right up on the examination table and sat right next to me so that her doctor legs were touching my own legs and she put her hand right on my back. I'd never seen a doctor do this before because all the doctors I'd ever been to weren't like people you could touch, but only people you could look at. And maybe not even real people at all but experts or something. So when she did this and when she said "why" again, I told her. "Because I don't want them to get better because then if they do, then I won't be able to come back here anymore because you're the skin doctor and I won't have any more skin problems."

And she laughed out loud, like I'd told a joke, but then her voice fell right onto the floor and it wasn't a laugh voice at all, but almost a cry voice, or a dog voice, one you would use to talk to a puppy. And she said, "Oh. No, no, no. You mustn't think that at all. No. You need to get your hands better. Precious hands," she said, and she reached right over and took my hands in her hands. "You need to use your cream every single day, just like I told you, right before you go to bed. And then whenever you get sick or you have a checkup or you need a shot or anything at all, whenever you come here to the doctor's office, you can see me. You just have to tell the nurse you're here and wherever I am, I will come and say hi to you."

And it was awful that I cried, but I did. Not a lot. But enough so that she could see that I cried.

"I think you're very pretty," I said.

And she didn't say anything at all. She just looked at me and she smiled. And then after a long time of just looking at me, she said, "Thank you."

I would see her many times over the following years. If I went to the doctor's office for a sore throat, I made sure to walk by Dr. Ledford's office and wave or just smile.

I also used the cream every night and my fingers healed. The little crucifixions on each fingertip closed up. But unless I applied the cream, and so much of it, every single night, and then more throughout the day, and then didn't wash my hands, they would open up again.

And when I was a teenager, I became busy. And I also didn't have any money for hand cream. So I would sometimes use Wesson vegetable oil or hair conditioner, which I could afford.

All through my twenties, my hands were like extremely high maintenance pets that required excessive grooming. If I skipped just one day of applying hand lotion, my fingers would seemingly split apart at the seams.

Always, I had plenty of Band-Aids in my apartment. I would use three per finger. And when I peeled them away after two days, the open gash would be closed. But fragile. They could split at any moment.

I noticed another thing. When I was under stress, my fingers could not be sealed. It was as though there was simply too much of something inside my body, that my skin was simply not strong enough and would split.

And then, no amount of hand cream would soothe it.

Over time, my fingers scarred.

The tips, the sides, the knuckles—all my dangerous areas from childhood—became something other than skin. A fragile covering, easily shattered like the skin of an onion.

My fingers became scarred like the face of Dr. Ledford.

But fate or the Finger Gods decided that it was not enough for me to have these cracked, bleeding fingertips. Oh, no. Fate said, "Now let's give him a career to match."

And so I became a writer who publishes books, then goes on book tours, meeting people and shaking their hands. Signing their books. Posing for photographs with them while I hold up a copy of my book. It's rather like being a porn star with two festering, open wounds—one on each breast. And then wearing a low-cut swimsuit top to show them off.

My career—if not much of my life—is all about my fingers. I type with them. And then I go on the road and tour with them. The only possible career I could have that would be more finger-intensive would be as a hand model. And I've thought of this. I could be the "before" model in lotion ads.

Many times I have worn a long-sleeve sweatshirt at a book signing, even though the bookstore is hot. A long-sleeve sweatshirt that covers my hands, with a cuff that I can grip, while I also hold the pen. So that my fingers can bleed into the sweatshirt and not onto the person's book. And then, because I am aware of this small ruse, I sweat profusely and look guilty, as though I am hiding something from people, which I am: bloody stumps.

Let me tell you. There is little in life as mortifying as signing a copy of your very own book for somebody and then sliding it across the table for them and seeing you have left behind a long stream of blood across the title. And then seeing their horrified face. And then having to take the book away and say, "Oops, I'm sorry. Let me get you another book." And then seeing the face of the next person in line and knowing they want to step out of line. What should be a proud experience is rendered a mortifying spiral of shame.

I also hate shaking hands when I have on a dozen Band-Aids, which is always the case. But better this than leaving somebody with a red, glistening hand.

I do everything now, but they never heal. I sleep with cotton gloves. I slop moisturizer on constantly. I even cover the open wounds with a Super Glue-like liquid bandage that breaks apart and pulls away more skin with it. Once, I forgot I was holding the Super Glue tube while I was waiting for my finger to dry and the tube became attached to my finger, like a little tumor. I flapped my hand around, hard, and the tube remained.

I could not have more ghoulish and desecrated hands if I stuck them into the mouth of a seething and slobbering Rottweiler.

Somehow, I lack the grace that my burned dermatologist from childhood possessed.

She became my hero, on contact. First, she terrified me with her plastic face and her black nose holes and her shiny eyes. And then, as soon as the contents of her interior were placed before me on the paper-wrapped examination table, she became luminous. Somebody I looked up to, wanted to be like.

I do not come across like this. People sometimes ask me, "What have you been *doing* with those hands?" And that's exactly what they say, "those" hands. Not "your" hands, because the hands now have their own identity, a mangled personality all their own. I joke in reply, "Oh, I got them caught in the lawn mower," or "You know, just playing around with barbed wire." But you can't joke about hands like this. Because people, they really want to *know*. Because they want to make sure it doesn't happen to *them*.

And in the morning when I wake up, my fingers are stiff. At first, I thought this was arthritis settling in. But then I caught myself with my hands clenched into tight fists. So this is how I sleep. With angst hands. Chewed raw in the night by my own mind. Another part of me that will never heal, no matter what I do.

What's in a Name?

My older brother had a supernaturally low voice at the age of seventeen. This fact, combined with his undiagnosed Asperger's Syndrome, resulted in a boy who sounded like a machine, speaking from the center of a deep cave.

"Varmint!" he would call from his bedroom. "Get in here, Varmint."

And I would drop whatever I was doing—which usually involved a hairbrush for one reason or another—and walk into his room, feigning an air of disinterest, but secretly thrilled.

"Yeah, what do *you* want?" I would say, in as superior a tone as I could muster.

My brother never called me by my actual name. He was seven when I was born, and from this moment on he called me Varmint. Because I idolized him in the fashion that younger brothers will idolize older brothers, no matter how freakish and defective they might be, I loved the name. When I asked him once, "What is Varmint?" he said, "A varmint is a small, furry animal."

Standing at his door, my brother said, "Varmint, I need you to do something. I need you to go next door and attract the Halles' dog over here. Use scraps of meat or hot dogs. Whatever's in the refrigerator. Just lure it inside and then bring it into the basement. Go now. Hurry!"

My brother was always in the midst of an experiment.

If he wasn't connected to the mainframe computer at the University of Massachusetts and reprogramming it to obey only him, he was making all our telephones ring when somebody pushed the doorbell. Although my parents became very upset, and sometimes potential defendants, they were proud that he was clever enough to create problems that they, themselves, couldn't even quite understand.

I was happy to be part of any sort of plan he had in his head. I may not have understood much about my brother, but I always felt he had a large plan, and if the plan was allowed to unfold, it would be entertaining.

"Okay," I mumbled. I always had to watch my tone around him because high-pitched, girlish screams of delight would irritate him and I might find myself locked inside of something.

Luring the Halles' dog into the house would be easy. It was a stupid-friendly Irish Setter with a smooth bubblehead and a tendency to follow.

I went to the refrigerator and opened the sliding drawer marked *Salad Crisper*. Why my mother kept the meats in the salad crisper drawer, instead of the drawer marked specifically *Meats*, was a mystery to me. One of many about her.

I pulled a hot dog from the greasy Oscar Mayer package. And then removed another, for an emergency situation.

Next, I walked outside and cut through the woods that separated our house from the Halles'.

It would have been much easier to simply shout, call their dog over to our front door. But then, this might have attracted attention. People would think nothing of little Augusten calling their dog. But this is not what they would have thought. They would have thought, with some distress, *Why is John's little brother calling for our dog?*

My brother had infected me.

With hot dogs crammed into my pockets, I stalked through the woods, avoiding the pit. The pit was an area of excavation roughly three feet wide by five feet deep. It was covered with branches and then a top layer of brown leaves and pine boughs, to blend into the floor of the forest. I dug the pit myself with the intention of creating an in-ground swimming pool. As it turned out, it was far more difficult to dig a swimming pool than I expected. So I'd covered the pit with branches, creating the next best thing: a trap.

The Halles' home came into view. It was a three-story contemporary saltbox, tall and flat in the front, tapering down at the rear. It was exactly the house I wished we lived in. A much nicer house than ours, with three fieldstone fireplaces and shag carpeting in every room and central vacuuming. Instead of central vacuuming, all I had was a mother who pushed the Electrolux around while she smoked and dropped ashes behind her.

When I got to the edge of the Halles' property I stopped because I saw Rusty curled up in the sun on the top step. I needed to get his attention, but not startle him and cause him to bark.

I removed the hot dog from my pocket and held it up in the air, hoping that the scent would drift past his nose, carried on air currents.

When nothing happened, I stuck it back in my pocket and used my psychic abilities to call him over. I silently repeated his name, even mouthing the words.

When this failed, I picked up a stick and cracked it across my thigh.

This caused Rusty to raise his head up and look in my direction.

So I immediately threw both arms up above my head and waved them. Then I did a little dance in place.

Having recognized me, Rusty stood, stretching and arching his back. Then his tail began to wag and he clopped down the steps, skipping every other one.

He came right up to me and I grabbed an ear in each hand. "Good boy," I said. "Good, good boy." I shook his ears, something he liked.

Then I said, "Come on, Rusty. Follow me."

Rusty remained in place.

"Come on, Rusty," I said. As friendly as possible. No threat. No *basement* in my voice at all.

Still, Rusty refused to follow me. Instead, he glanced back at his house and the look on his face told me he was unsure.

To make him sure, I pulled out the hot dog.

Now, he followed me.

Along the way, I broke off small, motivational pieces to feed him.

When I got Rusty up to the front step of my own house, I couldn't get him to follow me inside. I tossed the last piece inside on the area rug and I could tell Rusty wanted it, but he wouldn't go.

So I removed the emergency hot dog and showed it to him. "*Look*," I said, turning it slowly. "A big, whole, fresh hot doggy."

I tossed it inside and Rusty chased after it.

Then I followed him in and closed the door, calling out for my brother. "Okay, I got him!"

My brother appeared, a smile on his face. "Huh," he grunted with a smile, clearly pleased. "You really did get him. That's good work, Varmint."

My brother's compliments were extremely valuable, because he rarely doled them out.

"Yes, very good work. Now we've got him. But we need to get him downstairs. Here, I'll just carry him down."

My brother moved in and hoisted Rusty in his arms.

Rusty looked alarmed.

I followed my brother downstairs and into the basement. "Close that," he said, and I shut the basement door behind us.

To my surprise, the basement had been transformed. A clean, white sheet was spread out on the floor. Along with two cans of paint. And some brushes.

"Okay," he said. "Now. You have to hold the dog while I equip him."

"What do you mean, *equip* him?" I asked, holding Rusty in place where he stood, stroking his belly from below.

"We're going to equip him for the track," my brother said.

I had no idea what he was talking about. Even as be began painting a thick, black line down the length of Rusty's back, I had no clue what he was doing.

Only when he added the number "57" in orange paint did I get it.

My brother said, "There. Racing stripes."

I was thrilled.

I let go of Rusty and he did a mad sniffing dance around the basement. He bent forward on his front feet and wanted to play.

Then he caught a whiff of himself and started sniffing the air, then his tail, trying to touch his nose to his back.

My brother laughed. "Isn't that great!"

It *was* great. "Do our dog," I said. "Paint her!"

My brother said, "No. We can't paint our dog because then people will know who painted this one."

I threw a balled up sock for Rusty and he bolted for it. He didn't seem damaged by the customization. He seemed perfectly happy.

"Will the paint hurt him?" I asked, suddenly worried.

"Nah. It's paint for kids. Kids can eat this paint and be okay. Even if he's able to lick it all off he might throw up, but that's it." Then he added, "I would have preferred to use car paint. But that might have had an adverse effect on the animal. So we had to use kid paint."

Then I said, "Paint me!"

And my brother said, "No, it's time for a new activity now. Here, go let the dog out." He walked across the basement to the door that led to the backyard.

Now Rusty didn't want to leave. Quickly, he'd become ours.

"Come on Fifty-Seven," my brother said. "It's time for you to be released into the wild and race among the other animals."

The dog for some reason listened to my brother, seeming to understand him. He stepped over the doorjamb and trotted across the yard, looking back once. My brother reassured him, "Go on. You're free to run now." And the dog took off for his house.

That evening, the phone rang. As always, my mother picked it up expecting it to be one of her many poet friends. But a moment later she called out, "John Elder, come here."

My brother was back in his room, and I was in there with him. I was sorting through the debris on his floor—copper wires, transistors, small electronic components—in search of pennies, which I was gathering into a pile. So far I had thirty-two. My brother was attached to the university computer, using a modem.

My mother came into the room. "John Elder. Did you paint racing stripes on the Halles' dog?" she demanded.

Without looking up from his screen, my brother said, "I'm busy now, Slave. Go away."

My mother gathered authority. "*Answer my question.* Did you paint racing stripes on the neighbors' dog?"

Again, my brother failed to look at her. "No, I did not paint racing stripes on any local animal. And I'm extremely busy. Go away."

She exhaled in frustration and turned to leave.

"Slave?" my brother said.

She turned back. "What is it?" she asked, angry and abrupt.

"Bring me a glass of ice water."

My mother closed his door, nearly a slam. But returned a moment later with a glass of ice water, resting it on the only clear spot on the table next to him.

I was astonished by my brother's ability to get our parents to do things for him. Especially considering the names he called them. Our mother had been answering to "Slave" for years. Our father he called, "Stupid."

He didn't reserve these names for private use, in our own home. These were the names he called our parents at all times, even in front of company.

Inspired by him, I began calling our parents by other names than Mom and Dad myself.

I called my mother "Hey," and my father "Fucker."

My mother would occasionally comment, "I wish you'd call me by my name and not by 'Hey.'"

But my father remained aloof. It was clear to me that he'd somehow been suckered into having kids in the first place. And would have been much happier had he been allowed to remain the intellectual academic that he was, instead of having to come home from the university at night and step over my latest aluminum foil project.

The only relationship we had was that of occupying the same volume of physical space at the same time.

As a result, I found him more of an abstract concept than an actual living, breathing human being.

Many times, I brought neighborhood kids to my house and impressed them with my ability to swear at my father, without punishment.

"Watch this," I would say, leading them into the living room where my father would be sitting in a Shaker rocker and smoking a Benson & Hedges.

"Hey, Dad?" I would say, causing my father to turn and face me with disinterest.

"Fuck you."

My father would turn away, back to his thoughts.

Then I would turn to my friend. "See!"

"Wow," they would say. "I could never get away with that."

Had my brother not already broken them down, I'm not sure I could have gotten away with calling my parents foul names, either. But he'd been more than they'd expected in a first child. He'd reduced them to their most rudimentary components.

For the remainder of the summer, my brother called Rusty "Fifty-Seven." Long after the Halles had washed the paint off his coat, the dog responded to his new name. And even though my brother never admitted to what he had done, the Halles knew. And made every effort to keep Fifty-Seven indoors.

But the same year, the principal of the high school gave my brother a name of his own: Suspended.

By his account, the principal suspended him "because I'm too smart and they don't know what to do with me."

But when my parents inquired further, phoning a number of my brother's friends, they got another side to the story. A story that included a motorcycle and a hallway near the gym.

"Now, you tell me the truth. Did you ride your motorcycle inside the school building?" my mother wanted to know.

My brother shrugged. "Yeah, I guess." As always, his monotone veiled his emotions.

"Well, that's, I . . ." my mother stammered.

"Yup. That's exactly what the principal said," my brother replied.

"But you're expelled!" my mother cried. "What are you going to do now that you're expelled?"

My brother shrugged. "I don't know. Maybe I'll collect garbage for the town of Springfield. Or, who knows? Maybe I'll take that little Shelby girl and reconfigure her as a boy."

My mother was horrified. "Don't you even joke about something like that. You need to apologize to the school so they take you back. And then graduate."

But really, what was the point? My brother had read all the textbooks for the entire four years within the first five weeks of his freshman year. And the only reason he hadn't been suspended was because he programmed the high school's computers for them, as a favor.

"Well, Slave. Why don't you make yourself useful? Go get me an iced tea. And maybe then I'll think about returning to school."

My mother sighed. "Well, I'll get you this one iced tea. But then I need you to think about what you're going to say to the school."

She remained in the doorway, watching him. But my brother had already turned away and was focused intently on his new project: he was going to build an electric guitar that could spit fire and shoot a rocket.

The Wonder Boy

My mother *tried* to buy healthy foods but I would have none of it. She'd slip a carton of fresh beans or a head of broccoli into the cart, and the moment she turned her back to grab a bunch of organic scallions, I shoved the offending vegetables onto the nearest shelf and then tucked a tub of Betty Crocker vanilla frosting deep into the cart, under the other items.

My mother would choose brown or wild rice. And I would whine and snivel until I got my way. "I can't eat that," I'd say. "It's brown and dirty and touched by poor people in foreign countries."

"It's not dirty," she'd say. "It's healthy."

"It's filthy," I'd argue, my face contorted into a mask of disgust, as though she were suggesting a box of freeze-dried rat feet. I was horribly spoiled, like mayonnaise left out in the summer sun. I was festering with ideas about what food should be. If a green bodybuilder with acromegaly or a geriatric dwarf who lived in a hollow tree didn't sing, dance, or otherwise celebrate the product, I didn't want it on my plate.

Eventually, my mother would crumble. "Every time we go to the supermarket it's a damn production with you," she'd say. "Fine, fine, fine. I give up. Which rice would you prefer?"

I'd grin and run to another aisle to get a box of Lucky Charms.

As a rule, I would consume most anything that came from a can. Canned *meat* particularly thrilled me. I loved Underwood Deviled Ham with its stylish white paper wrapper, and Vienna Sausages, my little meat finger treasures. And if given the opportunity, I would eat Spam every day of my life. The exception to my love of canned food was tuna, which had to be baked in a casserole dish with cream of mushroom soup and topped with crushed Lay's potato chips.

My mother's dinner consisted of tofu slices, which she fried in tap water in a cast iron skillet that once belonged to her great-great grandmother. To this she added chopped scallions and the smallest dash of La Choy soy sauce.

I was fascinated by her austere dinner and would sometimes poke at it with the nearest instrument. *"Look at that! Look how slippery it is. And you're eating it!"*

She would slap my hand. "Do not stick that radio antenna into my dinner."

Another item we could never agree on was bread. My mother preferred the whole grain goodness of Roman Meal. While I would eat one bread and one bread only: Wonder.

What I loved about Wonder Bread was that if you peeled off the crusts and fed them to the dog, you could compress the remaining bread into a dense mass, then roll it in your palm to create a perfect sphere.

Then you could watch television and take bites from the dense bread ball, as though it were a jumbo-sized apple.

In this way, I could go through a loaf of bread a day. Which is why my mother always bought three or four loaves at a time.

One terrible autumn, however, my routine was broken when a power outage hit the East Coast and knocked us back to the Stone Age for nearly a week. The color television sat on the kitchen counter like a taxidermy puppy. I could only look at it and remember how much fun it *used* to be.

My father was horrified because if the power remained out, we'd have to empty the refrigerator and throw everything away. "This is just a terrible, terrible waste. A catastrophe." A pathological worrier, he sealed the door closed with wide packing tape to preserve what cool air remained inside. "If it comes back on tonight, *maybe* everything will be okay. But don't open this door for anything." Fat chance I would. For what? The nasty headcheese my mother kept in there?

But the power didn't come on the next day. So everything in the refrigerator had to be placed into green plastic trash bags and brought downstairs to the hot basement, to rot with the rest of the garbage bags from previous weeks. My father's bad habit was letting the garbage collect.

I didn't care about losing all the food in the refrigerator; there was nothing in there I wanted anyway. I was perfectly happy to open a can of Chef Boyardee ravioli and eat it straight from the can with a fork.

The problem was, no television. And unlike my brother, I wasn't about to read a book unless I was paid three dollars to do it.

This left me with only two things in the world to do: clamp the dog's front and hind feet together using rubber bands or read all the text on the various boxes of cereal, cake frosting, and egg noodles.

And this is how I learned about the magic trick, printed on the back of a bag of Wonder Bread.

"Amaze your friends and family!" read the headline. "Impress everyone with your *psychic abilities!*"

The trick required three people: two to conspire and one to be shocked and amazed.

It worked like this. One person sat in a room with the innocent trick victim. The trick victim then thought of a number—any number from one to a hundred. And whispered the figure into the ear of the conspirator.

Then the third person entered the room. Next, he placed his fingers on the temple of the conspirator.

The conspirator now had to bite down, grinding his teeth. This activated the muscles in the jaw, and a small bump could be felt at the temples. Felt, but not seen.

These bumps were very distinct. So the conspirator could simply bite however many times was needed to communicate the figure. It seemed like an ingenious little ruse, but would it really work?

My father and I decided to play the trick on my mother.

I left the room while they sat in the kitchen. A moment later my father called, "Okay, we're ready!"

I ran back into the kitchen and grabbed my father's head. I was appalled to glance down at my fingers and see that pearly scales from his psoriasis-covered scalp were already stuck to my fingers. But I swallowed my nausea and placed my fingers at his temples. After a few seconds, I felt the bump.

My mother watched us with a low level of interest.

My father bit down very slowly, and stopped biting at seventeen.

I said, "The number you guessed is seventeen."

This got her attention. "How did you do that?" she shrieked. Then, suspicious of me and my ways, she said, "You must have listened. You do that again, but go outside the house this time."

So now I left the house, closing the front door behind me.

I returned a few moments later and we performed the trick again. The number was ninety-nine.

My mother was astonished.

But she was something else: she was impressed. And here, the trick turned right around and slapped my father and me in the face.

She jumped up from her chair and she clapped. "I knew I'd raised a psychic son! I just knew it!"

She threw her head back in maniacal laughter. "Oh my God! Oh, what a treasure!"

My father laughed, but in shock. He was stunned by my mother's reaction.

"I can't wait to call Mother. Can you do this with her? Do you think it'll work over the long distance lines?"

I said, "No, I don't think it will work. I need to touch the person's head."

Now she was curious. "So what is it like? How can you read the number? How can you tell?" Then she said, "Do it again."

So I left the room and a moment later, she called me back. "Okay, come here and do it again."

Once more, I placed my hands on my father's head. He bit down once, and not again. I let my hands remain in place in case he bit again, but he didn't. "Your number is one."

She screamed, choking with joy. She was red-faced and wild with excitement. She lit a cigarette, coughed out the smoke, and then immediately lit another. She smoked them both at the same time, inhaling deeply. As she exhaled she burst into crazy laughter, her eyes wide and unfocused.

Then she dropped her cigarettes in the ashtray, leaned forward and grabbed me by the waist, pulling me close to her. "I am so happy you have this ability. You just can't know how happy I am!"

I couldn't possibly tell her.

And my father was now annoyed. "I'm going downstairs to take a nap." My parents used to share a bedroom upstairs. Near all the other bedrooms. But now they occupied the carpeted half of the basement. It was dark down there and damp, because water leached up through the cement foundation and stained the carpet. He would drink, and then retire to the cellar. My mother would write until late in the evening, then join him downstairs.

The next day, the power went on and I was able to watch television again. Except I wasn't able to watch television because my mother wouldn't leave me alone.

"Do it again! With just me!" She'd say, throwing herself into the nearest chair.

"No, I can't. It takes two other people. We need my father, too."

"No, we don't! I'll tell you if you guess it right, I won't lie. I want to see it again."

Eventually, I had to tell her the truth. But when I did, when I revealed the trick had come from the back of a bag of Wonder Bread, this information didn't seem to penetrate.

"Nonsense," she said. "That magic trick only got you in touch with your inner psychic abilities."

For years after this, I was able to get my way with my mother by making simple threats. "Look, Mom," I'd say. "If you don't buy me that belt, I'm going to make it rain on Saturday and your plans with Claudia will be ruined."

"Oh, all *right*," she would say, frustrated and powerless. "But I advise you, use your powers well."

Never once did she believe anything other than that her son controlled the world.

After my parents divorced, my mother's fascination and belief in the paranormal increased.

She became convinced that she could visit with her dead relatives in her sleep. "I dreamed my father was standing right next to me smoking one of his Camels," she'd say.

Sometimes, she would take a nap in the afternoon so she could go looking for her long-dead sister. "I need to see how she is. I hope I can find her."

It was not uncommon to come downstairs from my bedroom in the morning to find her sitting at the kitchen table, staring at a fork.

"What are you doing?"

"Shhhhh," she'd say. "I'm concentrating. Don't say a word."

My mother was trying to bend the fork, or at the very least make it move.

She believed that it was only a matter of time before she could cause cutlery to scatter across the table with the mere blink of an eye.

"I can't stand that yellow," she said one summer, standing in the living room, looking at the walls.

The next day, I found her in the same position, only now she had her eyes closed, both fingers at her temple.

"What do you think you're doing?"

Without opening her eyes or moving her hands, she said, "I'm trying to darken the hue. I hate yellow, but I love warm brown."

My mother's disturbing psychiatrist only encouraged her. "I think it's entirely possible," he would say, "that you have enormous reserves of untapped mental abilities. I think every one of us has powers we are not in touch with. This is one of the Great Flaws of humanity." One hour with the shrink and my mother would be home, trying to levitate the sofa.

But nothing encouraged my mother more than the telephone. Every time it rang she would shout, "It's Claudia!" before answering. And more often than not, it was Claudia. Because my mother and Claudia spoke dozens of times each day.

If it turned out to be somebody else, my mother would say, "I must have been receiving a future call from her. You just watch. Claudia's going to call any moment."

And sure enough.

One summer my mother sank into a deep depression. First, she'd had a psychotic break and been committed to a psychiatric hospital. Then a month after being released, she was fighting this depression and struggling with her daily routine. The manic enthusiasm for her poetry writing was gone. It was as though a valve had opened and all of her had been drained.

She slept fifteen hours a night, remembering none of her dreams.

Her stereo, which was always playing opera, was silent.

The shrink had placed her on a regime of powerful antipsychotic medications. These left her lethargic and reeking of chemicals. When I hugged her, she smelled like metal.

It crushed me to see her so deflated. As horrifying as it was when she was manic, writing a hundred pages a day and furiously drawing portrait after portrait at the dining room table, believing that each had been channeled by a dead relative, she was worse like this. Flat.

So I decided I would elevate her mood by once again displaying my astonishing psychic abilities, still intact from childhood.

Early one morning while she was in her coma-sleep, I took a length of fishing line and nailed it to the end of a broom. Then I screwed a series of hooks into the kitchen ceiling, stringing the fishing line through. I carried the line to the opposite side of the room and then I waited.

That morning when my mother came downstairs, she padded into the kitchen in slow motion. Her eyes were puffy and she said, "I need some Sanka."

But I said, "Wait. Look at this. Look what I've learned to do."

Standing near the window, I pointed to the broom on the opposite side of the room. "See that? Watch."

She stared at the broom without expectation or even interest. Her gaze was blank. She might have been simply staring at a wall, lost in thought.

With my right hand, I pulled on the fishing line. The broom jerked in place. And then I raised it a foot off the floor.

My mother turned to me. "Are you doing that right now with your mind?"

I said, "It's been very hard, but yes, I finally broke through."

She walked over to the cabinet and pulled out her blue and white mug. Then she grabbed the Sanka and unscrewed the lid. She dumped some brown crystals into the mug and placed it under the faucet, filling it with tap water. "I'm very impressed," she said, flat. "That's a wonderful thing that you're able to do. I've tried my whole life to do something like that. I guess the gene skipped me and went right to you."

Then she blew on her coffee and took a sip. Realizing she'd used cold tap water, not hot, she shrugged and took a deep swallow.

"I think I need to talk to the doctor about my medication. Even though I'm sleeping so many hours, I'm not having any dreams. And it's just making me very depressed. I miss my family," she said. "I really need to have a talk with Daddy."

She took her lukewarm coffee and left. I stood in the kitchen, grinding my teeth, counting silently with my jaw.

Fetch

My parents' house was on a dirt road that turned to thick mud in the spring. For thrills, there was a pond just next door. A larger body of water was across the street from the pond, but this was the Atkins Reservoir, and was marked with warning signs. "Private Property: Public Water Supply, Town of Amherst. NO TRESSPASSING." The signs were white with black type and they frightened me. As a boy who was terrified to remove the tags on his pillows for fear of "penalty of the law," I wasn't fond of playing in the woods near the reservoir, because in my mind it was a heavily patrolled area. I saw myself being plucked from the banks of the water by a uniformed officer and taken in for aggressive questioning and possibly torture.

But the pond was different. The pond, I felt, was mine. It was swampy and thick with pollywogs. Cattails sprouted from the edges of the water. This was the public water supply for nowhere.

Occasionally, a car would pull into the dirt patch in front of the pond, before then turning around. Nobody actually pulled into this area and then got out of the car. Nobody intentionally visited the pond. It was not the sort of place where a person would willingly spend time. After all, if the mosquitoes didn't get you, the snakes would. And if you were foolish enough to take a swim, the snapping turtles would take you down. There were a few kids on my street and all were aware of the unfortunate Packer girl who, according to neighborhood legend, took her inner tube out on the water and found her death at the hands of a beaver.

So I was quite stunned one day after school to see two men at the pond, throwing small white canvas logs into the water. Next to them on the shore, two black Labrador retrievers tracked the white logs with their focused gaze and trembled with anticipation.

The men blew whistles at the same time, and the dogs leapt off the shore and crashed into the water, spraying the banks and causing the cattails at the edge of the water to sway.

I watched from across the street, invisible behind a bush.

Over and over, the men sent the dogs into the water. And after a couple of hours, they got into their pickup truck and left.

It was the most exciting and unusual thing that had ever happened to me.

Who were the men? One, rugged with blond hair and a mustache. The other tall and lean, with dark hair and sunglasses.

And the dogs. Two black labs, each the size of me.

Where had the men come from? What was the white canvas log? Why were they throwing it into the water? And most importantly, how could I manipulate the situation for personal gain?

That night, I was so discombobulated from the events of the day that my comforting routines failed me.

As a matter of habit, before bed I enjoyed listening to a record of hymns by Mahalia Jackson, waiting for the place where the record always skipped. "Over the hills and everywhere," she sang, then the needle replayed the phrase over and over. Once the record reached the skip, I was able to take a piece of Scotch tape and press it to my nose. I pressed the tape firmly, and then peeled it away to reveal tiny pine trees of dirt and oil. I repeated the Scotch tape trick all over my face, removing dried skin and gunk.

I had to be careful, because if I kept the volume as loud as I liked, my mother or father would come into my room and demand I turn off the stereo. "That skipping is making me just crazy," my mother would say.

But if I kept the volume low, my parents couldn't hear it over the din of their own fighting.

Another of my bedtime routines involved sitting on the floor and pouring pennies out onto the carpet. While listening to the skip in my record, I sorted through the pennies, looking for a 1972 "double print." I'd seen something on television about them. These pennies had the words "In God We Trust" double printed on the face, and searching for one occupied much of my life. They were extremely rare and valuable and I was determined to find at least one, and thus never have to have an actual career when I grew up, but sell the penny and live well off the handsome profits.

But tonight, even these acts could not stop me from replaying the events of the afternoon over and over in my head.

The men. The truck. The dogs. My pond.

The pond was where I went every day after school. I knew exactly where to find the beaver dam, and I knew which stones to step on to reach the cattails. I knew where the frogs lived. And only I knew under which rock lay a small pile of *Playgirl* magazines from the Brook's Pharmacy in South Amherst.

That night, it was clear to me that I was in danger of losing my pond to these perfect strangers and their animals. I had to do something. Somehow, I had to drive them away.

But first, I had to study them.

So the following afternoon, I dressed not in my regular outdoor outfit of brown Levi's corduroy slacks and white turtleneck, but in a pair of dress slacks, the only green slacks I owned. With this, I wore a matching green sweater, despite the sweltering heat and humidity of June.

It was important to be in full camouflage. And thank God I'd paid attention when we learned how to walk through the woods silently, like Indians, in Cub Scouts. Toe first, then heel. You could track an animal this way, bending twigs and dried leaves instead of snapping them. At the time it had seemed like a pointless exercise, an excuse to keep us kids in nature and away from the television. Now, I was grateful for my outdoor survival skills.

I dumped the contents of my school bag on the bed and went through the house filling it with items I might need in my surveillance: my brother's binoculars, the big kitchen knife my mother used for everything, a can of hairspray to use as a weapon, four chocolate Space Food Sticks, and a handful of pennies.

Thus prepared, I walked to the pond, avoiding the road and instead making my way through the woods. And through the trees, I saw the glint of chrome—a bumper. I crept forward, now on my hands and knees.

"Mark position . . . *back!*" one of the men shouted. And then there was a splash.

I edged up nearly to the road and tucked my backpack under a bush. I covered it with leaves. If the men found and killed me, police would certainly discover the bag when they combed the area. This would show that I had been onto something.

Safely shielded by a low bush, I watched as the men sent the dogs into the water. They used whistles as well as voice commands. The dogs didn't bark or exhibit any frivolous dog behavior. They were like robot dogs, perfectly trained and flawless. They were eerie.

Then after an hour, the men left with their dogs, and after I was sure it wasn't a trick and that they wouldn't return a moment later with gaffer's tape and a stun gun, I grabbed my backpack and crossed the street to search for evidence.

I found: butt of cigarette, new. Boot prints in the muck. Nothing else.

My parents smoked, so this was a positive coincidence. Certainly a smoker wouldn't harm the child of another smoker?

The following day I returned to my surveillance spot and the men were back. This had become their routine. And it seemed as though they had always been there. Clearly, ownership of the pond was in a state of transference.

Although I didn't have a plan per se, I had begun using my mother's knife to carve sharp points into the ends of long sticks. So far, I had seven of them, lined up next to my backpack on the ground. I didn't know what I was going to do with the sticks. Or even if I'd need them at all. The only thing I did know was that it was better to have seven spear-ended sticks than to have none.

You just never knew.

"Hey, kid!" one of them shouted.

I was crouching low, peeling back the foil wrapper from a Space Stick snack. The shock of being personally addressed made me freeze and hold my breath. Could they be yelling for another, unseen kid?

"You, behind the bush. Come over here."

And now one of the men was walking toward me. The rugged man, with the mustache.

He was smiling, holding his hand out, as if to shake.

"What are you doing in there, kid? Come on out here and say hi."

I stood up and felt suddenly ridiculous in my dirty dress slacks and sweater. My long blond hair was plastered to my face.

"Holy cow, look at you," he said, when he finally got to my side of the street. "What happened? Did you fall out of some birthday party in the sky? Huh?"

I knew he was making a jab at my clothing, something the kids at school did, too. I said, "In case you didn't notice, I'm dressed in camouflage."

He said, "Oh yeah? Isn't that the same outfit you've worn all week?"

I didn't say anything to that. I was humiliated that he'd seen me all along.

He grabbed my hand and shook it. "I'm Larry. That's Bill over there and those are our dogs. Do you wanna help us out?

It was too much to absorb, too soon. An information dump. I wanted to sit on the ground, close my eyes and rock back and forth, banging my head on a tree trunk. How could he have seen me?

"Come on, kid. Get out of the woods and come help us."

My mother had never warned me about talking to strangers, but on television, kids got that warning all the time, so I knew the dangers. Still, I followed him across the street. The danger made the back of my neck tingle.

"Bill, this is the kid. Kid, what's your name?"

I told him my name and then Bill shook my hand, but he gripped it extra hard to let me know who was in charge. The dogs sat in perfect obedience, side by side, watching me and waiting for me to pull long sausages out of my pockets.

"If you're not busy, and it doesn't appear that you are, we could use your help," Larry said. He winked.

I have always responded to people who winked. My Uncle Mercer winked at me constantly and I loved him for it. It wasn't until I was an adult that I learned he was schizophrenic and his wink was really a twitch, caused by neurological damage.

"What do you mean, help?" I asked. I was wary of the word "help." I was a lazy child, and the word conjured up images of hoisting dead weight and sweating, moving and dragging, the possibility of damaged clothing fibers, a splinter.

"We train dogs," he said. "We train labs for competition. I also breed them. In fact, my bitch just had a litter and we have four brand-new pups."

I suddenly imagined my mother, whom my father called "bitch," curled up next to a rock and giving birth to four black puppies. Somehow, I could very well imagine it happening.

"What are you going to do with them?" I asked.

"Well, eventually we'll train them, too. Three of them show good signs for competition work."

Then he winked again and said, "In the meantime, we could use some help here with these dogs. What do you say?"

"Well, what kind of help?"

He told me that all I had to do was stand on the opposite side of the pond with one of the white canvas logs, which he called dummies. Then when he gave the signal, I was to throw the dummy into the water. And that was it. I didn't have to go into the water myself or lift anything or get dirty. And he'd give me three dollars.

"Here, why don't we try it?" he said, tossing a dummy at me. I didn't catch it and it fell at my feet.

"You play outfield, right?" he said.

I said I didn't play football at all.

He smiled and said, "No problem. Pick it up and head over there, across from us. When I raise my arm up into the air like this"— he raised his arm straight up into the air—"that's your sign to throw the dummy into the water."

"Then what?" I said.

"Then you run back here and get another dummy and do it again."

I shrugged. "Okay, I guess."

"Okay, then. So let's give it a shot."

I took the dummy and walked to the opposite side of the pond. This was the side closest to the street, the most public side of the pond. Thus, I was less familiar with this area. I didn't know every rock, every rotting log. There was the possibility of stepping on a nest of water moccasins or maybe a nest of baby beavers. Plus, I was wearing loafers and already the mud was creeping over the edges and soaking my socks.

But I found a place that felt free from threat and I stood, watching. Larry and Bill were talking and then Bill lit a cigarette. Bugs pestered my head and I wished I'd worn some Off.

Then I saw his arm shoot straight up into the air. Even from across the length of the pond, Larry's blue eyes excited me. My parents both had dark eyes. And seeing somebody with light eyes made me realize how much I was missing.

I raised the dummy above my head and threw it as far and as high as I could. It smacked into the weeds by the side of the pond.

I saw Larry kick the mud.

I shouted, "Sorry!"

He shouted back, "It's okay." Then he blew his whistle and his dog crashed into the water, swimming toward the dummy. The weeds at the edge of the pond were thick and the dog had a difficult time seeing the dummy, so he had to resort to sniffing it out. After he gripped it in his mouth, he turned around and got back in the water, swimming in a line directly back. I was impressed that he didn't just climb out of the pond and take the easier route: running on dry land around the pond. This is the route I took when I went back for the dummy.

"Try next time to hit the water," Larry said. "Don't throw it so high, just toss it straight out."

Throwing things horrified me. I suffered extreme, paralyzing anxiety when it came to anything remotely athletic. I wouldn't even run to catch the school bus because I knew I'd trip and then get teased for a year.

I took the dummy and returned to my spot. This time, I tossed it underhand. And while it veered dangerously close to the shore, at least it landed in the water. Larry sent his dog in after it, and then motioned for me to come over.

"You'll do great. So what do you say? Three bucks a day, doing what you're doing."

I said, "Okay."

And he said, "Great. We're finished for the day, so show up here tomorrow. Same time. But don't hide in the woods. And wear something like jeans."

I told him I'd see him tomorrow, then I walked home.

My mother was on the phone and I grabbed her arm. "I got a job," I said. "Three dollars a day. That's twenty-one dollars a week, which is more than three times my allowance."

She waved me away, mumbling, "That's wonderful, I'm so happy for you," and then returned her attention to the phone. "But what about the third line? Does it feel emotionally honest? Does it ring true? I worry about the Christ imagery."

I went to my room and turned my desk lamp on. Then off. Then on again. I did this until the itch in my brain was soothed. I thought of all the things I could buy for twenty-one dollars a week. I had my eye on a pair of men's clogs that I knew cost seventeen dollars. I could get these and *still* have enough left over to get four hundred pennies from the bank.

I lit a stick of incense and stuck it into the soil of the only potted plant in my room. It was a spider plant that hung in the window and sprouted satellite spider plants, which dangled from green shoots. The shape of the spider plant reminded me of a potted palm; something rich people had, usually two of them at the foot of the driveway.

Not a day passed that I didn't beg my parents to move to a mansion or the next best thing, a slum. If I couldn't live in a mansion, I reasoned that I could be happy in a slum because the slums of the nearby city, Holyoke, most resembled New York City. Sidewalks, streets, multistory cement and brick buildings. Living in the country hadn't been my choice. I'd have taken an elevator over a tree any damn day.

Still, since I was stuck where I was, at least now I would make cash. I could throw a dummy all day, if I got three dollars. And I could practice, so I didn't toss it in the weeds again. And maybe eventually, I would go to them and request a raise to five dollars.

Then I thought of the puppies. Four glossy black puppies, fresh and untrained. And suddenly, I understood that I had to have one of these puppies. Because a puppy would provide me with the one thing I truly lacked: friendship.

The next day at the pond, my aim was better and I only screwed up twice. Both times the dogs were able to pluck the dummy from the muck. And at the end of the day I asked Larry, "So what about the puppies? Can I see them?

He said, "You want to?" And I said I did.

He said, "Well, they're at my house and we'd have to drive there. So you'd need to ask your parents if it's okay."

I said, "It's okay, they don't care."

And he said, "I'm sure they care. You better go ask them. I can drive you up the street to your driveway and you can run in. Or better yet, I can introduce myself."

I agreed and climbed into his truck. I'd never been in a pickup truck before and this one smelled exotic: like wet dog and aftershave. And cigarette smoke.

He pulled into my driveway and we both got out. I ran up the stairs and opened the door, "Mom," I shouted.

My mother walked over, and when she saw Larry her face tensed. She looked between us, then her eyes landed on me. *What have you done,* she was thinking.

"This is Larry. He trains dogs and he's gonna take me to his house to see his puppies," I said.

My mother said, "Hi, Larry." And shook his hand. "Would you like something to drink? Iced tea?"

I said, "No, he doesn't want anything. We have to go. 'Bye."

Larry glanced at me like, *Wait a minute, kid.*

But my mother said, "Okay then. Well, have fun." As I knew she would say.

If she was worried about a strange man driving me away in his truck, she didn't show it. And I was rather excited that a strange man was driving me away in his truck.

Larry lived in a log cabin just up the street from our house. Although I'd walked past his house countless times in my explorations, I'd never noticed the narrow dirt driveway or the house that was set back into the woods. I wondered what else I was missing. Here I prided myself on my knowledge of my immediate area and there was an entire log cabin within walking distance that had escaped my attention.

He unlocked the door and there, in the main room right in front of the fieldstone fireplace, was a red and blue plaid dog bed, filled with four puppies and one big mother.

The puppies were sleeping when we walked in, but then the mother climbed out of the bed and padded across to us, wagging her tail. The foyer was narrow and her tail thumped against the wall. The puppies then climbed out of the bed, following.

The largest puppy came directly to me. And this is when he became mine.

The other three puppies went directly to Larry. But this one was now in my lap. And I was so captivated by him that I was unaware I'd even sat on the floor in the first place.

He head was much too large for the rest of his body. Something that seemed suddenly essential in a dog. And one of his ears was lopsided. This was also now a prerequisite.

I stroked his back and he extended, little arms and legs sticking out straight. Even like this, he still fit between my legs, with his head pointing toward my feet.

"Looks like that one belongs to you," Larry said.

I said, "Yeah, I wish he did. He's sweet."

Larry said, "I'm serious. He never acts that way around us. He's the lazy one, won't get up for anybody. Not even the can opener. All these dogs will do cartwheels for the can opener, except him."

Now, I tapped him on the butt a number of times and he sat up. Perky and activated: ready for games and activities.

I needed him. I thought, maybe if I look pitiful enough, Larry will give me the dog. Or just adopt me himself and let me live here with him and the dogs.

So for the next half an hour, I remained with the puppy and pretended to be happy for the first time in my life. I imagined myself as a boy with cancer, getting his wish.

But then Larry said, "Well, I got to get you back."

And just like that we were back in his pickup truck.

"Maybe you should ask your parents if you can have a dog," he said, pulling into my driveway.

"I can," I said.

"How do you know that for sure?" he said, looking at me. "Just how can you be so sure?" He was smiling a crooked smile.

"Because I can do anything I want. They let me."

"They do, huh?" he said. But he didn't seem impressed.

✧   ✧   ✧

That night I asked my mother if I could have a puppy. She said, "No, I couldn't deal with that."

I pressed her. "Why couldn't you deal with a puppy? Why?"

"Because," she said. "I am just at the end of my emotional rope."

Like any child, I'd studied my mother and knew her better than she would like. I liked to think of her as my sock puppet. "Well, your emotional rope is around my physical neck."

"We are not getting a dog," she stated again.

So I said, "Then I'll kill myself."

My mother said, "Fine. You kill yourself. And then this dog issue will be closed forever."

I hated her.

"Now. Since we're not getting a dog because you're going to kill yourself, I need you to leave me alone for a while. I'm working on a poem about my sister and it's very emotionally draining."

I left her at her typewriter.

I went into the kitchen.

I smiled.

A number of hours later, I heard my mother call my name. She was down the hall, at her office door. She called and I held my breath. She called again, "Augusten!"

I heard her open the door to my room. "Are you in here taking a nap? Wake up, now. I have to ask you something."

Then she walked down the hall, past the bathroom door. I heard her call me again, "Augusten. Can you hear me? Come here. I need you."

I took the shallowest breaths possible. I imagined myself breathing the smallest amount necessary to remain alive. I imagined my chest making not one movement.

I heard her on the stairs, then calling from within the basement.

Then, back up the stairs. She opened the front door, called my name. "Augusten!"

Finally, she opened the bathroom door.

By her silence, I knew she saw me. Was looking at me.

There was a scream.

It was the direct, wordless communication of instant terror.

I opened my eyes. And laughed.

My mother's shock caused her voice to break. A sob. "Oh, then fine. Okay, get the damn dog. Get whatever damn dog you want. Take the whole litter," she said. And slammed the bathroom door.

I was thrilled! I could get the dog!

I looked at myself in the tub—clothes stained with catsup. Catsup on the tile walls, smeared. On the white of the tub, my fingerprints, red. Razor blades dropped on the floor beside the tub.

That afternoon, she drove me up the street to Larry's house. He was surprised to see me with my now emotionally flat, deflated mother in tow. "Hi, Larry," I said brightly when he opened the door. "You said I could have him?"

My dog looked at me.

I scooped him up into my arms.

My mother said, "I have my checkbook, is that okay?"

And it was okay.

Mrs. Chang

Music class was loathsome. We had to sit cross-legged in a large circle on the itchy carpeted floor of the library and sing Indian folk songs like *"Land of the Silver Birch."* We had to make the motion of paddling a canoe up river. Any of us would happily have licked the inside of a toilet rather than attend music class. So in music class, we were fidgety. We made jokes and noises and tied our shoelaces together. We made armpit farts and chewed bits of paper, then spit them at each other.

But there was another time the third-graders were rounded up in the library, and we were silent in a way that was almost holy. Because this was "Reading Aloud" with Mrs. Chang.

Mrs. Chang was the lady who came to our school once a week and read children's books to us. *The Three Rabbits, The Ugly Duckling,* and during the holidays, books about Santa Claus and Frosty the Snowman, complete with colorful illustrations, which she always allowed us to see by turning the book around to face us.

Mrs. Chang was a tiny snow pea of a woman who sat quite comfortably in the small wooden ladder-back chairs meant for us children. Her thick black hair was cut to her shoulders and her skin was the color of tea. She sat at the keystone of the circle and we argued over who got to sit next to her.

Mrs. Chang was the only Chinese person I'd ever seen in real life, not just on television. And I was fascinated by her. Because like many children, I had entertained the idea of digging a hole in my backyard, straight through the earth to China. Where I expected to find people like Mrs. Chang walking upside down.

I liked to look at Mrs. Chang's fingers as they held the book on her lap. They were strong fingers, bony yet powerful. When I touched them, I was shocked at their coolness.

Because she spoke so softly, we had to take extraordinary measures to hear her—the girls all tucked their gum behind their ears and the boys stopped snorting and then swallowing. We leaned forward and closed our eyes so that the only thing in the room was the sound of Mrs. Chang reading. Even Steve McLester stopped trying to smell his sour toes and sat perfectly still.

She scanned our faces slowly, with intent. Which had the effect of hypnotizing us and making the library disappear. She then picked up the book from her lap and began reading from *Little Red Riding Hood*.

"Once upon a time there lived in a certain village a little country girl, the prettiest creature who was ever seen."

Except because Mrs. Chang was Chinese and spoke no English beyond Children's Book English, the story came out sounding like, "Wun upun a tye they rive in a suhtain virrage a reee-tle cuntahry girh . . ."

I couldn't understand a word she said, but I was entirely fascinated by her nonetheless. After all, this was Western Massachusetts, in the 1970s. Everybody around these parts was paper white and had facial hair, even the women.

Mrs. Chang was the most exotic creature I had ever seen. She had tiny slits for eyes and I was sure she could only see half of everything. And she had no facial expressions. Or, rather, one facial expression for everything. I saw her not as a woman or a human, but as something magical and special. Like a unicorn that could tap-dance and spit fire.

Because Mrs. Chang was the only person who read to me, and because she read with such a thick Chinese accent, I subconsciously merged her accent with every story she read. As a result, I believed that every character in all the books she read was Oriental.

When I imagined Little Red Riding Hood walking through the forest, I saw a little Chinese girl—Mrs. Chang in miniature—in a beige smock dress with a red circle stitched onto the front.

And it was because of Mrs. Chang that I spent my childhood secure in the knowledge that Santa Claus was Chinese.

In fact, it was always a shock to see Santa in the local department store, fat and white, with a definite Holyoke, Massachusetts, accent.

"That's not Santa," I would say to my mother as I walked past, nose in the air.

"How do you know that?" my mother would ask.

And I would say, *"Because I know."*

My mother was proud of me. She assumed me to have penetrating wisdom at a very early age. She hadn't raised a gullible child, after all. She had raised a boy who saw clean through the red Santa outfit to the ordinary white man underneath. A boy who understood that Christmas wasn't just about merchandise.

That is, of course, until one day in March when we were sitting in my allergist's office.

I was there for my usual: nine shots in each arm. To protect me against mold, mildew, dogs, cats, milk, and all other forms of nature. I was waiting for the nurse to fetch me when I saw a Chinese man sitting quietly across from me and reading a magazine.

My heart began to race at the thrill. I watched him, to see if he would glance over at me and maybe wink. When he didn't so much as blink, I could no longer contain myself. TO BE IN THE SAME EXACT ROOM AS SANTA CLAUS! AND TO BE NOT EVEN TEN WHOLE FEET AWAY FROM HIM!

I ran to him and jumped up in his lap, causing the magazine he was reading to fly out of his hands.

"Santa!" I shrieked, absolutely thrilled. "I love you, Santa! And I want a bike with a banana seat!"

My mother was horrified. "Stop that!" she screamed. And ran across the room in her clogs. "I'm sorry, I am so terribly sorry. I have no idea why he did that." Then she grabbed me by each arm and hoisted me off the startled man's lap, muttering apologies while she dragged me away.

Back in our seats she asked in an angry whisper, "Why? Why did you do that?"

"Because it's *Santa*," I said. "That's the real Santa," I said.

My mother looked at me as though I were saying dirty words in Latin: she was both disgusted and somehow fascinated.

The man glanced up from his magazine, cautiously making sure I was still seated. Only to find me already looking at him and smiling. I mouthed the words, "Hi, Santa! I love you!" and he looked away.

My mother pinched me on the arm, hard. "What is the matter with you? That *isn't* Santa. I thought you understood perfectly well that there is no Santa Claus. Santa is myth, told to young children. Santa isn't real. And Augusten, if Santa were real—and he most certainly is *not*—what on earth makes you think he'd be at your allergist's office in March?"

But it wasn't only Santa. I believed all the characters that populated the books Mrs. Chang read to us were Chinese. The Three Rabbits? Chinese. Snow White? Chinese. And Humpty Dumpty? Why, he fell off the Great Wall of China, of course.

This wasn't something I consciously considered. It was just a fact, like air. Over time, after years of weekly readings by Mrs. Chang, I came to accept that the world of make-believe and fairy tales was the same world that created my father's AM radio: MADE IN CHINA.

Mrs. Chang never yelled at us. She never punished us. And because none of us ever misbehaved around her, she never sent any of us to the principal's office. Once a week, all of us had an hour of perfect comfort and fairy tale wonder.

So it's no wonder that when I grew up and became a sad, isolated alcoholic I would often find comfort in the CBS Evening News, starring Connie Chung.

Many nights I would sit on my filthy bed, propped up against a mound of old deformed pillows and dirty laundry, clutching my bottle of scotch. I would take sips and watch as Connie spoke of airline crashes, kidnapped children, and floods. Forty-seven toddlers maimed by a circus clown wielding a machete? *Tell it to me again, Connie!*

This half hour became the single period of the day where I found solace. The flat, clean face of Connie Chung more than resembled that of Mrs. Chang's—if I squinted, they became the same person. It was no matter that Connie spoke in media-coached, accent-free English. To me, she might as well have been saying, "Ana then a klazy man wita gun, he kirra arra chirrehn."

After the news I spent hours online at night drinking and visiting Web sites created by other fans of Connie Chung.

"Connie Chung is one of a very small group of women who have achieved prominence in American network news," read one such site. But I wasn't interested in Connie's accomplishments as a woman in television, let alone as an Asian-American woman in television. I just wanted her to read me *The Little Engine That Could.*

Looking back, I can only imagine that Mrs. Chang was the grandmother of some Chinese American who came to live in Massachusetts, probably attracted by one of the five colleges. I imagine a young professor and his wife raising their daughters in Pelham, and maybe the wife decides she wants her mother to come to America. "She's old. She's alone. I think we should bring her over."

And so Mrs. Chang was packed onto a jet and sent to Bradley Field International Airport, in Hartford, where she was met by her daughter and son-in-law.

Of course she would live with them. But what would she do? First, she would have to learn to speak English. And what better way to learn English than the way *we* Americans learn English: children's books. And why not do this and help children at the same time? Why not read children's books at a local elementary school?

It makes sense.

Mrs. Chang used us to learn English.

And in return, I learned that there really and truly is a Santa Claus and he is a shy Chinese man who has allergies, just like me.

Julia's Child

My mother put her creative talents to use in a number of different forms over the years. The word for this is probably "dilettante" but I thought of it as "artist." In the 1950s, she painted. I wasn't alive then but I saw the results, because they hung around our house: runny, unsure watercolors of wildflowers or baskets of fruit sitting on a table. But then she gave birth to my brother, and later me. And she gave up painting, moving to writing instead. She wrote poetry every day, then went through long periods of submitting her work to journals and waiting anxiously for the likely rejection slips, which she then used to decoupage the wastebasket in her office. "I won't let rejection get *me* down," she'd say. Over time, she was able to collect enough rejection letters to decoupage the kitchen table, a file cabinet, and a medium-sized tray.

During this period, my mother's moods fell to extremes. She was manic with excitement or she was crushed flat by depression. I worried about her constantly, often sitting up in my bed at night praying to God. "Please make her normal." She'd gone away once to a mental hospital because she'd had a "nervous breakdown." I didn't know exactly what this was, but I pictured her like a broken-down car: stranded on the highway, all her tires flat, possibly unfixable. My mother wrote, she said, "because if I don't write, I will die." So part of me was comforted when I heard her typewriter clacking long into the night.

But then in the mid-seventies, after finishing her M.F.A. in creative writing, she picked up her brushes again. And by this time, she'd discovered mixed media. She started painting with acrylics and sand. She added fragments of dried leaves or twigs. Sometimes, she painted the occasional blooming vagina, which she would call "my O'Keefe." These paintings would often have flower petals mixed into the pigment, forming a texture. "Feel the labia," she would say. "Isn't it nice when you can experience a painting with more than just your eyes?"

But mostly, my mother painted religious icons and portraits of her dead grandparents. She would listen to opera while she worked, the sliding glass doors of the living room wide open. The weighty aroma of turpentine clung to everything and made my mouth water. Sometimes, I slept with a turpentine-soaked rag on the desk in my bedroom because I loved the pungent and distinctive smell so much. Next to jet fuel, turpentine was my favorite scent.

Beside her metal tubes of paint and her brushes, my mother kept a clay bowl filled with sand. She would dip her brush into one of the pigments and smear this on her palette. Then she would use the point of her spatula to blend in another color. Finally, she added a few pinches of sand to give the paint its unique texture.

The sand clumped in certain areas, making everybody in her portraits appear as though they had nuclear acne or perhaps had survived a disfiguring jet ski accident. Even as a child, physical de-

formity and personal misfortune appealed greatly to me and I loved
her paintings. I begged her to paint me.

"I won't fuss, I won't. I'll sit perfectly still," I promised.

But my mother always refused. "I have to paint what I am moved
to paint. Someday, I will paint you. But right now, I have to finish
St. Francis."

Of course, the real reason I wanted my mother to paint me was
because I wanted her to stare at me for long periods of time. Not yet
ten, I still craved my mother in the way a person craves water or
certain fashion accessories.

But my mother was unreachable when she was working. I was a
distraction and I knew it. And it made me mad.

Fortunately, my mother had the sense to put me in the care of
another woman who would spend hours staring at me. Every day,
as a matter of fact.

My mother engaged Julia Child as my babysitter. In the form of
a public television cooking series on WGBH, our local PBS station.

Each Saturday morning, I sat in front of the television, eating
raw cake mix batter and watching Julia prepare fascinating and
complicated entrees from things I didn't know you could eat.
"Duck" had been simply the illustrated visual representation of the
letter "D" on an alphabet chart for most of my childhood. And now
I was watching my babysitter stick her hand up one's ass and stuff it
with raisins.

Julia took snails like those we had crawling around our backyard
and yanked them out of their shells, filled the shells with butter,
and then stuck the snails back in the shells after steaming them only
briefly.

And it was Julia Child who taught me that a can was not a natural anatomical part of a tuna fish.

I was inspired.

My parents slept late on Saturdays, so I had the entire house to myself. It would be hours after noon before my mother came upstairs to the kitchen. And my father was likely to remain in the dark basement master bedroom and drink on his day off.

So when Julia's show ended, I picked up where she left off.

I went into the kitchen and spoke to the picture window above the sink, as though it was my television camera. "Hi, and thank you very much for joining me," I said. "Today we're going to bake a cake." I moved through the kitchen with utter confidence, opening drawers and pulling out spoons, long forks, the garlic press, as though I knew exactly where everything was and how to use it.

I removed Gold Medal flour from the cabinet and then took my mother's sifter down from the high shelf above. Julia didn't measure, so I didn't either. I simply dumped the flour into the sifter and pressed the trigger handle, watching while a fine dusting of flour covered the counter. "I'd like you viewers at home to notice how fluffy this thing makes the flour," I said. As an afterthought, I reached for a mixing bowl to catch the remainder of the flour. Then I tossed the sifter on the table behind me.

And this was the fun, really. Because after Julia used a pan or a spatula she would toss it to the side or behind her. In the next scene, the pan or the spatula would be gone. As if by magic! When I did the same trick in my mother's kitchen, the sifter did not entirely vanish, but at least it was out of "camera" range.

I used an entire stick of butter to grease the pan, mashing the stick back and forth until all that was left in my hand was a greasy wax paper wrapper. Clumps and thick streaks of butter stuck to the bottom, sides, and rim of the pan.

"I believe in butter," I told my viewers. "No matter what they say, Parkay just doesn't have the same taste or richness. Sometimes, a simple butter sandwich in the afternoon is the zenith of my day."

My vocabulary was impressive for a nine-year-old. Television had a lot to offer a smart, attentive child. People generally scoffed at children like me who spent all their time in front of the tube. But what these people failed to consider was that the answers on game shows had been fact-checked for accuracy.

I removed a dark bottle from the cabinet. "Add vanilla to taste," I said, dumping all of it into the mixture, then tossing the bottle on the rug in front of the dishwasher.

Sometimes, I would forget a step and this would make me mad. "Cut," I said out loud, then turned on the oven. Back in character, I returned to my show, smiling. "By now your preheated oven should be ready to accept the cake."

My recipes involved no actual knowledge, but rather a collection of ingredients I'd seen Julia use in various recipes. So there would just as likely be bacon in one of my cakes as vinegar in a batch of my muffins.

After pouring the batter into a pan and setting my cake into the oven, I quickly swiped the counter clean of debris, like I'd seen Julia do, before moving onto the next recipe.

"But what is cake without rack of lamb?" I asked my viewers. And here, I once again announced, "Cut," before going downstairs to the basement, where we kept the frozen meats.

We weren't a lamb-level family. We were a ground beef-level family. But years before, my father had purchased half a cow at an incredible bargain. And the pieces of it sat wrapped in wax paper in this freezer. The beef was far too old to eat now, discolored and frosted with ice crystals. But it was certainly not too old to prepare, live on my cooking show. I selected a large parcel and brought this back upstairs with me.

"Ask your butcher for a generous cut," I instructed my viewers, unwrapping the frozen block of animal and letting the paper fall to my feet, where I kicked it away.

But here, I experienced failure. Because Julia was always doing something to meat: hacking chunks out of it, ripping away bones, making holes and then stuffing them with things. But my meat was solid. A frozen brick. So I again had to yell "Cut" and then go soak the meat in the bathtub, in the hottest water.

After an hour of television viewing and waiting, I carried the warm, partially thawed meat back into the kitchen. I removed my mother's Dutch oven roaster from below the sink and set the meat into the pan. "Olives," I said, "make everything better." I opened a can and dumped them into the roaster. I chopped onions, skin on, and added these. Next came some potatoes I found in the dark rear of the pantry closet. The potatoes were soft, but I just plucked off the long green stems that had sprouted and added them whole.

Next, I filled the roasting pan with a liter of Tab, one of my mother's favorite beverages. It resembled the color of broth, I reasoned. And because this was television, a few corners had to be cut here and there.

I set the meat in the oven next to the cake and then went into the living room to watch television.

But I lost interest in my cooking show after my cake batter-fueled sugar rush wore off. After a while, I walked sluggishly back into the kitchen and turned off the oven, leaving everything inside for my mother to find.

Hours later, my mother climbed the stairs, groggy and hungover from her own festering mental illness. "Oh my God," she moaned upon stepping into the kitchen. "What on earth have you done?"

"I had a show," I hollered from my seat in front of the television. Next to me was a half empty bag of corn chips, along with the last of my maple sugar candy.

Then I heard the flap of plastic as she shook out a fresh green plastic garbage bag. My mother shuffling around the kitchen. The sound of an empty jar being tossed into the bag on top of another empty jar. The faucet went on, the dishwasher door was opened.

Eventually, I lost interest in cooking entirely. It was, after all, so much work. And at heart, I was a lethargic, pleasure-seeking child, constantly in search of the easiest route.

And it was far easier to sit in my room and stare at the wall, watching the movies that played endlessly in my head.

My mother was thrilled with this activity and sewed pillows for my bed.

Then she bought me a tape recorder, a blue one. "You can tell it stories," she said.

I said, "Okay! What a great idea!" And I began locking myself in my room at night, speaking to my tape recorder.

"What do you talk about?" she asked after the third week. Suddenly, it was the only thing I was interested in.

"Oh, stuff. I talk about my life, just what's going on."

"What is going on?" she asked. "You never leave your room anymore. What could possibly be going on?"

I said, "Well, I talk about you and my father."

"Oh," she said, smirking, and blowing a plume of smoke into the air. "Well, don't say anything hateful about me."

"Don't worry," I said, smiling. "I would never do that."